Food in the Ancient World

Food in the
Ancient World

John M. Wilkins and Shaun Hill

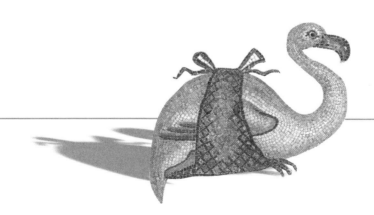

Blackwell
Publishing

© 2006 by John M. Wilkins and Shaun Hill

BLACKWELL PUBLISHING
350 Main Street, Malden, MA 02148-5020, USA
9600 Garsington Road, Oxford OX4 2DQ, UK
550 Swanston Street, Carlton, Victoria 3053, Australia

First published 2006 by Blackwell Publishing Ltd

1   2006

Library of Congress Cataloging-in-Publication Data

Wilkins, John, 1954–
    Food in the ancient world / John M. Wilkins and Shaun Hill.
      p. cm. — (Ancient cultures)
    Includes bibliographical references and index.
    ISBN-13: 978-0-631-23550-7 (hardcover : alk. paper)
    ISBN-10: 0-631-23550-7 (hardcover : alk. paper)
    ISBN-13: 978-0-631-23551-4 (pbk. : alk. paper)
    ISBN-10: 0-631-23551-5 (pbk. : alk. paper)
    1. Food habits—History—To 1500. 2. Food—History. 3. Civilization,
  Ancient. I. Hill, Shaun, 1947– II. Title. III. Series: Ancient
  cultures (Malden, Mass.)
    TX353.W535 2006
    394.1′2093—dc22

                                                                  2005013069

A catalogue record for this title is available from the British Library.

Set in 10/12.5pt Rotation
by Graphicraft Limited, Hong Kong
Printed and bound in the UK
by TJ International Ltd, Padstow, Cornwall

The publisher's policy is to use permanent paper from mills that operate a sustainable
forestry policy, and which has been manufactured from pulp processed using acid-free
and elementary chlorine-free practices. Furthermore, the publisher ensures that the
text paper and cover board used have met acceptable environmental accreditation
standards.

For further information on
Blackwell Publishing, visit our website:
www.blackwellpublishing.com

Contents

John Wilkins is responsible for the chapters and Shaun Hill
for the Introductions and recipes

Figures

Figures 1.1, 1.2, 1.3, 2.2, 4.3, 4.4, 5.4, 7.2, 8.1 and 8.3 are taken from A Matthioli's edition of *Dioscorides*, which was produced in an expanded form in 1598 to take advantage of the plants recently discovered by Europeans in the Americas. Matthioli was thus able to put American peppers beside the Asian peppers long known to the Greeks and Romans. Matthioli's updating of the record continues a long Classical tradition of botanical and medical works that strove to keep up with the latest introductions to the Mediterranean world from Asia and Africa.

Preface

The modern world has inherited many images of food and eating in antiquity. Among them might be the orgies of the Roman emperors, the plants distributed throughout the empire, the cookery book of Apicius, and the colourful use of foods in satirical and comic texts. In other respects, the food the ancient Greeks and Romans took for granted is often obscure to us. This book will try to restore the food itself and the contexts in which it was eaten: the dining rooms built beside Greek temples, for example; and the altars where animals were slaughtered.

This book will attempt to review the diet of the millions of ancient Greeks and Romans who did not belong to the pampered Roman elite of the pages of Suetonius. Comparisons will show a surprising degree of similarity between Greek and Roman practices.

In addition, this study will also deal with particular types of foods. Take meat, the food with the highest status. Meat is a natural product. Raising animals for meat is a comparatively inefficient form of farming since the plant energy in fodder (such as barley) can be only partially transferred to the human eater. Animals, therefore, were widely acknowledged as indicators of wealth. Rich citizens, not to mention the gods, expected to benefit from the flesh of animals. The Greeks marvelled at the wealthy Persians who cooked huge animals, such as camels and oxen, whole. The Homeric heroes feasted on beef. Large-scale sacrifice was a feature of life in the ancient city state as it continues to be at the Hajj at Mecca. The major role played by animals is reflected in myth and religion where they contribute to a sense of identity and of belonging to a group. We might compare some native American peoples who believed the buffalo herd was provided by the gods. Buffalo belonged to the plains and not to the corral, deep in excrement, that European immigrants brought to America. The social structure of the ancient world was patriarchal and for this reason men were likely to eat more meat than women, a situation paralleled to some extent in Judaism, Christianity and Islam.

For the Greeks and Romans, like the modern anthropologist, civilization was linked with agriculture and technology. In addition to meat, farming brought the cultivation of cereals. We are often told that the Greeks ate *maza* or barley porridge rather than bread. Porridge might seem an unattractive dietary staple, but this book will try to imagine what could be done with cereal products. Consider the variety of uses for rice (sweet and savoury dishes), wheat (bread, bulgar and pasta) and maize in the modern world. Cereals are hard seeds whose husk must normally be removed before they can be processed by the human digestive system. Such preparation and the grinding of the grain are hard and time consuming. In antiquity, owing to the patriarchal nature of the social structure, women were more likely to do this work than men, unless the family could afford to keep slaves or buy commercial bread products.

Cereals and many other animals and plants eaten by human beings were gradually introduced into the Mediterranean world over a period of millennia, if they were not native to the region. Wheat and barley arrived early; chickens before the fifth century BC; peaches and apricots later still; rice in the period of Arabic influence (after AD 700); maize after Columbus. In the ancient world, new arrivals made a continuing impact.

The Greeks and Romans had extensive contact with Asian and African peoples at all periods, and inherited much from their eastern neighbours in particular. Along with these borrowings from the Persians and Egyptians, for example, came unease. Plutarch makes this clear in his *Life of Alexander*. The young Macedonian warrior king whose campaign as far as India brought greater contact with lands that produced unusual animals, plants and spices also had, according to Plutarch, reservations about 'luxury'. This is a complex matter, as we discuss later. Plutarch tells us (22) that Alexander was a very temperate eater and avoided pressures from his mother to eat more cakes and to enjoy food prepared by bakers and cooks. The best cooks, declared Alexander, are a night march and a light breakfast. Alexander's moderation of his appetite fits the favourable presentation of the world conqueror that Plutarch tried hard to create out of a historical tradition bulging with stories of Alexander's excessive drinking and bodily passions. A word is needed on cakes, cooks and the control of the appetite.

Cakes in the ancient world might be small offerings of wheat and honey to the gods, homely products recommended by the austere Roman politician Cato the Elder, or the most significant part of the meal, according to the Persians in Herodotus 1.133. Cakes had many forms and, as in the modern world, a variety of cultural significances. (Compare, for example, cattle cake, Christmas cake and the contents of a French patisserie.) In ancient kitchens, bakers and cooks were often humble personnel, but they were linked with high-level eating. Livy links them with new luxuries arriving in Rome in the second century BC, Plato with imported luxuries into fourth-century Athens. Cooks were also used by generals on campaign, most notably the Persians in 480 BC (Herodotus 9.82). These practical artisans of the kitchen were at the same time hired hands working in a hot, smoky environment, and purveyors of luxury.

Ancient sources are frequently dominated by the dangers of luxury which expand uncontrollably out of the basic human needs for housing, clothing and food. Plato has been a particularly powerful influence on this aspect of western thought. One of his legacies to later philosophy and to Christianity is a dualist rather than holistic approach to the individual. For the dualist, the body must be strictly controlled so that the mind and spirit may concentrate on matters of great importance rather than on the fleeting excitement of food and sexual pleasure. Plato himself recognized the role of food and wine in social and religious practice – witness his *Symposium* and *Laws*. In the *Timaeus* he presented a model of the body and of the cosmos that was a landmark for later medical scientists such as Galen.

Medicine has an important role to play in this book, both ancient theories of nutrition and theories about the impact of medicine on culture. Medical thought will contribute to the claim that food had a cultural importance for the ancients comparable perhaps to its role in Chinese culture. This large claim is distinct from claims to gastronomy and a 'cuisine', such as that seen in France during the past two centuries. The main ancient authors we use for the study of food across Greek and Roman cultures are Galen, Pliny and Athenaeus. Each might in a sense be termed 'encyclopaedic' in range and approach. We have frequently consulted a rather different form of modern encyclopaedia, in particular Harold McGee *On Food and Cooking*, *Larousse gastronomique* and *The Oxford Companion to Food*.

Timeline

Periods

Bronze Age	3500–1100
Archaic Period	600–480
Classical Period	480–323
Hellenistic Period	323–31 BC
Roman Empire	27 BC–AD 330

Dates

BC

753	Traditional date for foundation of Rome
750–700	Traditional date for the final stages of composition of the Homeric poems
Late 7th century	Ashurbanipal king of Assyrians
550	Cyrus defeats Medes and establishes Persian power
490–480	Persian invasions of Greece; battles of Marathon, Thermopylae and Salamis
454–404	Athenian Empire
?429–347	Lifetime of Plato
384–322	Lifetime of Aristotle
336	Alexander becomes king of Macedon
334–323	Alexander's campaign against Persia
167	Roman defeat of Macedon
146	Destruction of Corinth and Carthage by the Romans

133	Pergamum bequeathed to Romans
31	Octavian defeats Mark Anthony and Egyptian forces
27	Octavian named Augustus (first Roman Emperor)

AD

23–79	Lifetime of Pliny the Elder
?50–?120	Lifetime of Plutarch
129–?216	Lifetime of Galen
161–80	Marcus Aurelius emperor
?200	Athenaeus composes *Deipnosophistae*

Atlantic Ocean

Emporion•

•Rome
CAMPANIA
Naples•
Pompeii•

Cadiz•

Mediterranean Sea

Adriatic

SICILY
Syracuse•

Carthage•

Emporia•

MAP 1   Map of the Mediterranean

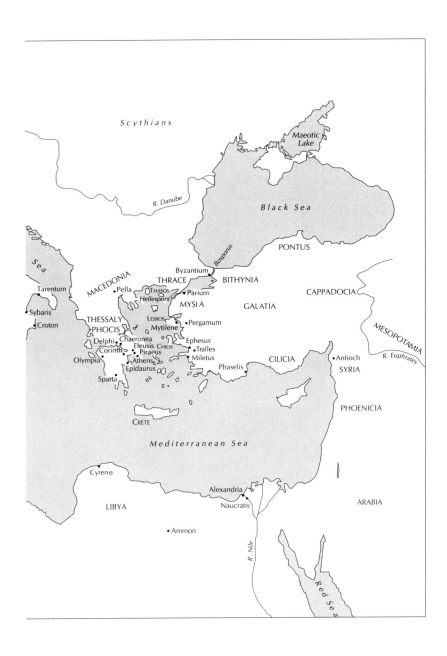

Scythians

R. Danube

Maeotic
Lake

Black Sea

Bosporus

PONTUS

Byzantium

BITHYNIA

CAPPADOCIA

MACEDONIA

THRACE

Pella

Parium

Thasos

Hellespont

MYSIA

GALATIA

MESOPOTAMIA

Sea

Tarentum

LESBOS

Pergamum

THESSALY

Mytilene

R. Euphrates

Sybaris

PHOCIS

Croton

Delphi

Chaeronea

Ephesus

Antioch

Eleusis

CHIOS

Tralles

SYRIA

Corinth

Piraeus

Miletus

Olympia

Athens

Phaselis

CILICIA

Epidaurus

Sparta

PHOENICIA

CRETE

Mediterranean Sea

Cyrene

Alexandria

ARABIA

LIBYA

Naucratis

Ammon

R. Nile

Red Sea

1
Introduction

The food of previous eras is intriguing. The experience of eating and smelling the same dishes and aromas which would have been part of life at another stage of history may be the nearest one can come to understanding the pattern and texture of everyday life, the reality of being there rather than an academic exercise in recalling the ups and downs of political and battleground life.

This is not a matter of cooking up possible recipes and re-creating dishes from well-documented feasts. Rather it is a question of exploring the tastes and preferences of the time, the preconceptions and mis-conceptions held about food and eating, and their impact then, as now, on what was served both to the wealthy and to the poor, for grand occasions and for everyday eating.

There is little advantage to be gained in exploring the diets of people who lived near the brink of famine. They ate what they could and used whatever was edible and grew or lived around them. More interesting are the choices made by those with the ability to pander to preferences.

In theory these preferences should be fairly straightforward and unchanging through the centuries. In practice they are complex and respond to many social and perceived medical pressures, and these do change. Contemporary ideas regarding the dangers of a fatty diet and the desire to be thin are in stark contrast to post-war notions when a well-fed baby would be regarded as bonny, a cause for joy rather than a worry concerning future obesity.

We choose from what is available to us, so a brief scan of what may have been obtainable will throw up major differences between now and then. Not least because seasonality was a much greater influence on meat as well as fruit and vegetables, storage techniques were more restrictive and more likely to alter the nature of whatever was being stored through salting and curing, and of course a deep hole in the ground was the nearest cooling device to the chiller cabinet.

The greatest barriers to understanding what may have been on offer are preconceptions regarding the 'Mediterranean diet' which have firmly lodged in the consciousness. Fish and cereals are fine but much of what we think of as part of the term is post-Columbus. So of course, amongst other things, no tomatoes, peppers, maize for polenta, or chillies. Wheat came in various guises, all of which were too expensive for the poorer classes who had millet and barley as staples. Lesser strains of wheat like emmer and spelt could be made into flat unleavened sheets like pasta, and finer strains like durum, which makes the best bread, were at a premium and, during Roman times, grown and imported in quantity from across the Empire.

The time span of our work is large, Homeric times until Early Christian, so some account must be taken of changes not just in availability but in religious sentiments, relative prosperity and even fashion during this period. The sources for our work have also to be considered and evaluated for reliability in this context. Writers like second-century AD Athenaeus, who gave great insight into food-writing now completely lost to us, were products of their time, with all the prejudices and preconceptions then current. Any analysis and comment on food and eating before then will have filtered through these. References, for example, to the gastronome and writer Archestratus, who wrote and lived in the fourth century BC, are touched with ridicule as his stern views on food and cooking, along with the metre in which he wrote, were no longer smart to hold. Think of a book on Elizabethan or Jacobean food and attitudes written from today's perspectives and the time gap becomes clear.

Actual recipes can be conjured out of some texts but not many. Cooks were unlikely to be avid readers and collectors of cookbooks, if they could read at all. There are some usable recipes, of course, a good explanation of the pastry 'tracta' by Pliny, for example, and some interesting recipes from Cato in his 'de agricultura', a treatise on farming written around 160 BC, one for a pudding made with flour, cheese, egg and honey. Mostly though, we have to work on descriptions of the food by those who ate it rather than anyone who expected us to cook it.

A dilemma arises. If we prepare the dish exactly as it was made over two thousand years ago, the unfamiliarity of the tastes and textures may overpower our ability to judge nuances of flavour that would have been apparent to anyone of the period, like giving a curry to somebody who had never experienced Indian food and expecting them to notice subtle variations in the spicing rather than just be hit by the chilli. If we re-create the dishes exactly we will have to re-create the palate and expectations of the time also.

Alternatively, if we lower the intensity of the spicing and flavouring so that the general character of the food comes across, have we weakened the authenticity of our efforts? We are now fairly familiar with Thai and Vietnamese cookery and many of the ingredients used are comparable to those in the Mediterranean in the period we address. The universal dipping sauce, garum, was made in much the same way as Nam Pla, by fermenting small fish, and it's interesting to note that the results are quite delicate, not the stinker that the idea of rotting fish conjures up at all.

What emerges is the fondness for rank flavours in foods like garum or cheese combined and contrasted with sweet flavours such as honey and dried fruit. Not significantly different, in fact, from the use of fruit sauces with game, or sweet biscuits and port with blue cheese. Stronger spices like asafoetida and more astringent herbs like hyssop that would seem medicinal now were in use, presumably to sharpen up the cereal porridges which would have otherwise made for a dull eating experience.

Restaurants did not exist as such. There were inns to feed and lodge travellers, of course, but serious dining was the preserve of private houses with cooks and servants, staff meals the mainstay of agricultural labourers and street food the preserve of the urban poor.

Within these diverse groups, there were similarities of flavour objectives and shared cultural ideas on food and diet. Snobbery and pretension went with wealthy dining then as now, and the ignorance and superstition on food matters that seem laughable now point uncomfortably towards the amusement that our current ideas may hold for future diners.

An Overview of Food in Antiquity

This introductory chapter is in four parts. First we set out the broad historical framework. Next we present the evidence and how we propose to interpret it. We then summarize the main elements of the diet. A final section shows how food and eating were incorporated into Greco-Roman culture to a striking degree.

The Historical Framework

This book covers a broad period, roughly from 750 BC to AD 200, and focuses on the cultures of Greece and Rome. In that period Greece developed into a large number of city states ruled by oligarchic governments and sent out colonial settlements throughout the Mediterranean. The city states had varied constitutions, including a few democracies, and remained largely independent until the rise of Macedon in the fourth century BC. Alexander the Great and his successors then dominated the Greek world (now including Asia Minor, Syria and Egypt, along with southern Italy) in a series of dynasties, all of them eventually taken over by the end of the first century BC by the Romans. In the same period, the Romans had been developing their strength as an Italic people, coming to terms with the Greek cities of Sicily and southern Italy, with the Carthaginians, and with all the influences these neighbours exerted on them. By the time of the first Emperor, Augustus, the Romans had a world empire many of whose inhabitants in the East spoke Greek and Latin. There was much cultural exchange between these two systems. This book draws in particular on three authors who tried to make sense of this cultural fusion as far as food was concerned.

These are Plutarch of Chaeronea (in particular his *Sympotica* or *Table-Talk*), Athenaeus of Naucratis (his *Deipnosophistae*) and Galen of Pergamum (in particular his treatise *On the Powers of Foods*). All three were Greek authors writing under the power of Rome in the second or early third centuries AD. Their commentary on food, eating, medicine, religion and regional diversity is rich and stimulating.

This book does not confine itself to the homelands of 'the Greeks' and 'the Romans'. It takes into account a vast area, from the Black Sea and Syria to Spain, from the steppes of Russia to the sea and deserts of North Africa. The seaboard will be the main focus, but many people in the region did not live by the sea. There were mountain dwellers, farmers and many who did not travel. The Romans, indeed, constructed themselves as originally a people of small farmers who had nothing to do with influences from outside. Thus Ovid in his *Fasti*, for example, describes the goddess Carna as one who dislikes travel by sea, and exotic birds and fish, preferring instead traditional Roman beans, bacon and emmer wheat (6.169–86). But in many ways, trade and travel were vital to the history of eating in antiquity. Foods and perhaps technologies tended to move westwards. Furthermore, the Greeks and Romans were influenced by other cultures. A particularly striking example was the Assyrian practice of reclining at a meal, which the Greeks, Etruscans and Romans seem to have imported from the seventh and sixth centuries BC onwards. This major development is discussed further in Chapter 2.

The movement of people, too, was crucial. Foods and other goods were traded extensively, to meet local shortages, to meet the demands of local elites for distinctive goods, and for other purposes. Travel came to have a close relation with food. We can see this first in Homer, where Homer's Odysseus travels round the Mediterranean meeting people who do not eat the grain and olives and drink the wine that he does. Later, in the 'sympotic' literature attached to the symposium or drinking session, wines and other products imported from many different places were listed and celebrated. In Rome, the impact of expansion produced strong political and literary reaction, from the time of Cato the Elder onwards (late third/early second century BC). Cato and others voiced concern over the influence of imports, the richness and attractiveness of foreign foods and goods, and the perceived neglect of Roman traditions. We shall explore the latter in particular in Chapters 7 and 9. This Roman tradition, however, only serves to highlight the impact and importance of foreign foods. Cato's fears in

I

V. MEDICA MALVS.

rentia, facilè te
tentia ego quoqi
Quippe cùm acc
rum, alioquin v
peritißimum, n
tatum, & voca
dem, vt apertißt
arbor eft arbuto
mnes ferè Græci
herba, & andra
rùm adrachne e
milis vnedoni, f
Hinc ergo facilè
perpetuò virefcit
raße Theophraft
perpetuò virefcit
que ſpinoſos. Flor
pillamentis quib.
pomifera eft: alia
alia verò ſubnaſt
tas, cum magnit
in tantam excre
quent, cuiuſmoc
que pelagi inſuli
limonum magni
à Lacu Benaco ce
locum. Nam etj
quis ab ore ineun
cioſa magnitudi
multum placean
verùm quòd pulj
charo vel melle a
ga, vt limonum, ſed denſiore corticis pulpa: cortex illis rugoſus, flauus, odore
medullam, ſucco plenam, in qua ſemen latitat hordei figura, grandius tan
Matureſcunt integro anno, decerpunturque cum aureo colore fulueſcunt: na

FIGURE 1.1   An Indian plant, the citron was the member of the citrus family that was certainly known to the Greeks and Romans. At first glance less appetising than the lemon, this huge and pithy fruit has a fragrant juice. Galen says people ate it with vinegar and fish sauce. He also noted its complex pharmacological properties. It was also believed to be an antidote to certain poisons. See Dalby (2003). Reproduced by permission of the Dean and Chapter of Exeter Cathedral

the second century may have reflected new pressures, but the interest in foreign imports, both material and intellectual, as his own writings display, was substantial and had been so for decades.

Evidence and Interpretation

Archaeology is able to make a large contribution to our understanding of these developments. Analysis of plant, animal and fish remains has revealed much about the distribution and kinds of animals and plants that were eaten, and some idea of the distribution by trade of plants and cereals, fish and all the equipment of the table (Renfrew 1973, Luce 2000). Much too is revealed of food technology (Curtis 2001) and means of preparing and storing a wide range of foods (Sparkes 1962, Forbes & Foxhall 1995). So too vessels for dining, in particular silver-ware and painted pottery (Vickers & Gill 1994); and the architecture of the dining room, including buildings, wall-coverings and flooring. Mosaics are particularly well preserved (Dunbabin 1999 and 2003).

A further class of evidence is provided by the analysis of human bones and of residues in cooking and eating vessels (Garnsey 1999). An example may be found in recent studies on evidence from Minoan Crete which reveal the diet in the late Minoan III period (fourteenth century BC) of a population of over 350 adults and children buried in the cemetery at Armenoi, south of Rethymnon (Tzedakis and Martlew 2002). There is no evidence for seafood (even though contemporary pottery has plentiful marine imagery), though the remains do suggest a 'fair amount of animal protein' (whether milk or meat) and plant protein. Furthermore, the researchers found little differentiation between the diets of the rich and the poor, as expressed in chemical deposits in the bones; but there is evidence that men ate more animal protein than women. Infectious diseases found include osteomyelitis, brucellosis (transferred to humans from infected goat's milk), tuberculosis (transferred from infected cow's milk), and nutritional diseases such as osteoporosis, scurvy, rickets and iron-deficiency anaemia. A smaller sample of bone tissues from Grave Circle A at Mycenae revealed some eating of seafood, with men eating more than women. However, there was little or no marine protein in the chemical analysis of bones from Grave Circle B at Mycenae. As far as alcoholic beverages were concerned, both wine and beer appear to have been drunk. These findings confirm some evidence already considered by Garnsey (1999), and are also suggestive in other areas. It was possible, it seems, for Greeks to drink milk and beer, even though many texts link such beverages with foreign peoples. I shall return to this evidence.

Archaeological evidence is supplemented in abundance by literary and technical sources. The written text is a feature of Greek and Roman culture which is not found in many other food cultures until the modern period, if then. Food plays a major role in many different kinds of text, from Homer and Herodotus onwards. The Greeks were the first people in Europe to produce cookery books (in the fourth century BC). And Greeks and Romans produced texts which had a particular focus on eating and drinking. Comedy and satire are the best examples (Gowers 1993 for Rome, Wilkins 2000 for Greece).

There is a considerable mismatch between many of the literary sources and the vast majority of the population. The nature of the literary sources is explored further in Chapter 9. Even where literature does turn its attention to poorer members of society, they are likely to be idealized in a discourse that reflects more on criticism of the city than on the poor for their own sake. Simylus in the poem *The Moretum* (*The Ploughman's Lunch* in Kenney's 1984 translation) and the poor huntsmen in the Euboean Oration (7) of Dio Chrysostom exemplify the idealized literary peasant.

A more accurate picture of food in the rural economy (though not of peasants) is given by the agricultural writers. Cato writes for rich investors, but sets much practical detail beside this focus. Varro writes for his wife, with apparently a broader focus than Cato. Columella combines much practical detail with standard moral concerns of the period. All of these writers have a broad geographical overview. Cato focuses on Campania but has much Greek material in mind; Varro and Columella are concerned with much of Italy and beyond. All this contrasts with the *Works and Days* of Hesiod, an early Greek hexameter poet, who wrote within a tradition of wisdom literature on the agricultural year. For all its detail, the moral framework of thrift, hard work and focus on the locality, in contrast to foreign trade, is at the heart of the poem. Varro and Columella also reflect the moral tradition, but to a smaller extent. Thus 'on imported birds for fattening, Varro says of the peacock (3.6.6), 'Quintus Hortensius is said to have been the first to serve these at his inaugural dinner as aedile. The fact was praised more by men given to luxury than by the severe and upright.'

There were also technical texts in many other areas related to food, on medicine from the fifth century BC, and from Aristotle and

Theophrastus in the fourth century BC onwards, on zoology and botany. These helped to place the human animal in its context in the natural world. There were texts on the different cities of the Greco-Roman world; there were works on agriculture; there were travel books and geographical surveys; and in the 'Hellenistic' period (the last three centuries BC) and Roman period encyclopaedic works were written that reviewed and summarized all this information. The *Natural History* of Pliny is an important example, as are the works of Plutarch, Galen and Athenaeus already mentioned. All these encyclopaedias came with ideological perspectives both on the history of food and on contemporary eating practices.

Of particular interest to this book are the two Greek authors of the Roman Empire in the second and third centuries AD, Galen and Athenaeus. The first was a medical writer with enormous philosophical and cultural interests, the second is hard to define but is a food encyclopaedist of a kind. Athenaeus does not always follow an alphabetical order like *Larousse gastronomique* or the *Oxford Companion to Food*. His decision to follow the order of the meal and to encourage as much quotation of evidence as possible makes him difficult for the modern reader to follow. The reasons for his decision, however, are revealing.

Both Athenaeus and Galen were writing about a millennium later than Homer. They each provided a cultural overview of this thousand-year period and at the same time offered an impressive summary of how Greek and Roman culture had interacted over a period of four centuries and more. They reveal, too, how local diversity might have survived within an empire-wide system, and also where the major influences for change arose. With their assistance we will thus be able to trace differences and influences between and within the two cultures.

We do not go on to explore the gradual development of these cultures into Christian cultures. There is much valuable material available from such authors as Clement of Alexandria, Philo of Alexandria and the church fathers such as Tertullian. Veronika Grimm has used such material to reveal different approaches to fasting in the pagan, Jewish and Christian traditions of late antiquity. For this book, our latest author is the NeoPlatonist Porphyry, whose *On Abstinence*, written in the third century AD, reviews arguments for and against abstaining from meat. This is a fundamental text for the history of vegetarianism, but also, like Athenaeus, a repository of earlier thought on eating in Greek culture.

It is Galen and Athenaeus, however, who make the greatest contribution to this study. They each wrote extensive works on aspects of food and nutrition around the end of the second century AD. They wrote during a period in which writers reflected more than ever on the past, on the vast cultural heritage of Greece, and how it might be deployed and negotiated. The great overviews of food and eating that they provide help us to chart how the world looked in their time and in earlier times. They reveal how much technical literature was written on food: treatises on botany, vegetables, salt fish, drinking cups, symposia, garlands, diet, pharmacology and many other areas. Furthermore, these authors help us to define what we might mean by 'food' in Greco-Roman culture. Athenaeus' inclusion of riddles and music, for example, shows what is relevant to such a study. They are also particularly strong on regions outside Athens and Rome. This is important, for these two great cities both contributed much to food and culture and at the same time were exceptional because of their size and influence.

Naturally, Galen and Athenaeus have different objectives. Galen, the doctor, identifies (in *On the Powers of Foods*) the standard foods in the diet, many of which are surprising to the modern eye. Along with the expected cereals and fruits there are many unpleasant grasses, wild plants and strange animals. Athenaeus, meanwhile, bases *The Deipnosophistae, or Philosophers at Dinner* on the symposium and sympotic literature produced for the leisured Greek elites. He too lists many different and surprising foods and quotes from many authors who had written on the subject. Athenaeus focuses in particular on Homer, Plato, the comic poets and the accounts of the Hellenistic kings who succeeded Alexander. But Galen too sometimes draws on Homer, Plato and comedy – these authors were part of the mental world of an educated person of the period and Galen considered their references to foods important. Conversely, Athenaeus has Galen as one of his semi-fictional 'Deipnosophistae' or philosophers at dinner, and quotes extensively from Hellenistic treatises on diet and nutrition by such authors as Diocles of Carystus, Mnesitheus of Athens and Diphilus of Siphnos. Nutrition is discussed in detail in Chapter 8. We should add to these literary riches the dining practices that Athenaeus' diners follow. Although they are mainly Greek, and quote mainly Greek authors, they drink wine from the beginning of the meal, in Roman style. They appear to have synthesized Greek and Roman dining customs. The implications of this for the structure of both Greek and Roman meals are discussed in Chapter 2.

Between them these two authors name hundreds of foods, from hundreds of cities and regions. They bring home the diversity of eating

in the Roman Empire of the second and third centuries AD. They also
have a focus which is not solely Rome or Athens, as was mentioned
above. Athenaeus reports on the cities of the Greek mainland, the Celts,
the Egyptians, the cities of Asia Minor and Syria; Galen on Macedonia,
Bithynia, Asia Minor, Alexandria and Italy. Galen too offers the best
evidence available to us in a literary text of what poorer people and
countrymen ate. His diet is the human diet, not merely the diet of the
leisured classes. In this respect his testimony is priceless. It is discussed
in Chapter 4.

Galen and Athenaeus reflect also general cultural features in their
discussions of foods. There was a demand for more foods and new
foods from outside; there were new ways to prepare these and well-
known foods. Both areas, along with pleasure and refinement, were a
focus for competition within the city elites. In contrast with these
pressures for innovation, a desire for simple foods based on local agriculture was also frequently expressed, as noted in Ovid above. A
'technical' author is not immune from these cultural assumptions. To
take an example, Galen distinguishes himself from cooks at *On the
Powers of Foods* 2.51: 'For we physicians aim at benefits from foods,
not at pleasure. But since the unpleasantness of some foods contributes
largely to poor concoction, in this regard it is better that they are
moderately tasty. But for cooks, tastiness for the most part makes
use of harmful seasonings, so that poor rather than good concoction
accompanies them' (trans. Powell). We shall see in Chapter 7 that
Galen's words closely echo Plato's influential distinction six hundred
years earlier between the useful doctor and the meretricious cook. But
the doctor and the cook are not complete opposites. The cook aims
mainly at pleasing the palate. However, the doctor cannot ignore pleasing tastes, since unpleasant food is generally bad for the digestive
system.

The interests of the two authors intersect, further, in their desire
to identify, define and classify. This applies to terms: Which plant does
the term X identify? What is the Latin equivalent? Has the name changed
over the centuries? When was it introduced? Both authors were at
pains to discover what earlier experts had written about a particular
food, only to find that there were confusions in identification and
terminology. We may take as an example Athenaeus' entry on the cherry
(*kerasia* 2.50b). He quotes several Greek authorities, among them
Theophrastus, and the Bithynian grammarian Asclepiades of Myrlea.
Larensis, the host, counters with the claim that Lucullus the Roman

general was the first to import this tree to Italy from Cerasus in the Pontus. A further speaker recalls that the medical author Diphilus of Siphnos mentioned cherries in a work of the third century BC.

At first this appears to be a pedantic argument in which Greek and Roman claims take precedence over historical priority. Athenaeus quotes his sources, enabling us to put dates on the information. In the late fourth century, Theophrastus described in some detail a plant, which Athenaeus identifies as a cherry. Athenaeus' editor, Charles Gulick, identifies the plant described by Theophrastus as the berry of the hawthorn. The next authority quoted by Athenaeus, Asclepiades of Myrlea in Bithynia, is, in Athenaeus' view, describing an arbutus. He was writing in the first century BC, roughly in the same period as the campaigns of the Roman general Lucullus in the Pontic region (the Black Sea). Diphilus of Siphnos, the final authority, was writing at the court of Lysimachus in western Asia Minor in the third century BC. We thus have dates on the evidence. We also have location. Theophrastus describes a bush – perhaps in Attica and perhaps not a cherry. By the time of Diphilus, there is a variety of the proper Pontic cherry in Miletus. But is it a cherry? Asclepiades explicitly describes a different variety, in Bithynia. Lucullus brings about the major move from the Pontic region to Italy and Rome. This passages bears witness to an interest in cherries and to discussion of cherries over several centuries. But in itself it raises as many problems as it solves. It is unclear which species precisely is described in each text and also which plant(s) the term *kerasos* and its relatives accurately describes. Furthermore, the term may change from city to city. Then, the identification of foods may be subject to regional variation, ideological claims and pressures such as Larensis reveals. These do nothing to aid scientific precision. This example brings home the vastness of the ancient world; the thousands of cities over many centuries. How are we to capture any of its essence? Only a broad treatment with specific examples is possible. But Athenaeus' approach, bringing together a number of texts, is instructive for us as a general principle. When does a food become established? What counts as evidence? Who is asking the questions?

So Larensis and Daphnus slug it out. What can we do in our turn, if we consider, for example, the domestic fowl – the hen or chicken? We can resort to archaeology and faunal remains. We can look in texts. But the texts give very ambiguous evidence. Safest for us is not to pronounce on the quantity of chicken consumed in the Athens of Aristophanes – where it is still attested as the 'Persian bird' – or in the

GALLINAE ET GALLI.

FIGURE 1.2   Like the citron, the chicken or domestic fowl was an immigrant from Asia. It (and its eggs) was eaten as a bird among others, and, although common, it never had the prominence in the diet that it now enjoys. Reproduced by permission of the Dean and Chapter of Exeter Cathedral

Italy of Augustus. Rather, we may note the increase in consumption and familiarity over time, its use as a sacrificial animal, and its normal inclusion as one bird among others. Galen suggests it was *the* bird for human consumption, but not on the scale it now is.

Terminology is a problem that will not go away. There are many other examples in Athenaeus and Galen where which plant or animal is in question is unclear to them, let alone to us. Galen tries to establish a general principle in his discussion of small Italian mammals (*On the Powers of Foods* 3.1, trans. Powell). Galen says that when an unusual animal is eaten, the doctor is best advised to compare it with a similar animal known to him. 'At any rate I shall no longer need lengthy statements to discuss all indigenous animals in all countries, such as the small animal in Spain which resembles the hare, that they also call "rabbit"; and the one in Lucania in Italy that lies somewhere between bear and pig; as also the one eaten in the same part of Italy and in many other places, that is halfway between the so-called *eleion* and field-mice or dormice.' Galen identifies a new arrival (the rabbit) and indigenous species. A doctor newly arrived in an area needs a broad framework for identifying animals and an analogous species for comparison, in order to prescribe food with confidence.

Clearly terminology was a problem for Galen and Athenaeus and continues to trouble us now. The classification of fish and certain plants is still far from agreed. At the same time, the massive body of reference to so many foods in Galen and Athenaeus, along with the lists in Pliny's *Natural History*, is a tremendous resource. They attest a great curiosity in the foods indigenous to Italy and Greece as well as noting new introductions, such as the rabbit from Spain. We should view new introductions as a continuous process, moving normally, unlike the rabbit, from east to west. Cultivated plants arrived early (if the technology was imported from the Near East and was not developed indigenously on many sites). These include the olive, the vine and cereals. The domestic fowl arrived considerably later, migrating slowly from the forests of Thailand to the Mediterranean. The pheasant was introduced. The peach and the apricot reached Rome apparently by the time of Augustus. It is not clear when the lemon arrived in the Mediterranean. The citron was certainly present in antiquity, the lemon possibly not. It is certain that the lemon, the orange, the aubergine and rice all came to the Mediterranean under Arabic influence after 700, possibly earlier. The main centres of power and commerce drew new foods to them, just as the European courts of the sixteenth century became interested in the foods of the Americas such as chocolate, tomatoes and potatoes (see e.g. Coe and Coe 1996). Courts, as we shall see, were important generators of innovation. They competed in display; they also sought to acquire the best antidotes in order to deflect poisons. A special ingredient for an antidote might go on to prove a pleasing addition to the diet.

Comparisons of this kind between the ancient world and later historical periods and indeed the twenty-first century will be an important feature of this book.

Food plays a number of major roles in modern western culture. Agriculture, global corporations, advertising and our social structure, together with a long history, all contribute towards embedding food and ideas about food in our culture. In contemporary Britain and the United States, the separation of the consumer from agricultural supply is more pronounced than in countries such as France and Italy. Similarly, in Britain and the United States, industrial production and distribution through supermarkets are particularly strong, as are foreign influences, for example from India, China and Italy.

In many ways, the societies of the Greeks and Romans resembled pre-modern societies in experiencing recurring food shortages (particularly in the spring) and disease. For example, shortages were frequent in Britain until the twentieth century; and France, for all its modern sophistication and the richness of its markets paraded weekly throughout the country from the smallest villages to the streets of Paris, also struggled to feed itself until the nineteenth century. 'Seventeenth- and early eighteenth-century France was wracked by spasmodic "mortality crises" which saw the number of deaths in a locality spiral upwards three-, six-, even ten-fold, under the impact of hunger and famine. In the "pays de grande culture" [in North and North-eastern France] in particular, the price of grain acted as a kind of demographic barometer, high prices caused by bad harvests sending the number of deaths spiralling upwards in so-called "steeples" of mortality . . . Peasants starved in their droves in the final years of the "Grand Siècle" of Louis XIV' (Jones 2002: 151). We shall see reports from Galen on food shortages in the countryside, particularly during the spring.

In a book of this kind it is imperative to introduce the small farmer and the poorer citizens at the earliest stage, for it is they that form the vast majority of the population and produce the majority of the food. At the same time, it is the political elites that 'develop' 'culture', demand the best food and drive forward innovation and gastronomy. Consequently, histories of food frequently focus on small and privileged groups – in Hollywood terms, those who participated in the orgies of the Roman imperial court. In Chapter 2, we shall see analogues in antiquity for Colin Jones' account of eighteenth-century France. While the court was developing fine foods, and to some extent sharing the benefits with the troublesome citizens of Paris, the provincial peasantry starved. Even when food was plentiful, the peasants sent the best food to market: 'vast cornfields growing rye (for local consumption), oats (for local livestock) and wheat (for the towns and the rich) stretched away as far as the eye could see' (Jones 2002: 149–50).

The food supply is a vital concern for all states, ancient and modern. But it is not the only concern. Food did not only keep people alive; it also helped them to shape their identity. Colin Jones again gives an early modern analogy: 'just as the conventional wisdom had it that the king should "live off his own", so the ideal of rural living was the household, which was at once a unit of production and consumption, and which had the wherewithal to look after most of its own needs. Most peasant family heads spent most of their time producing enough food for themselves and their families to live on. The staff of life was bread, and home-produced tasted sweetest . . . In the peasantry's lexicon, *gagner son pain* ("to earn one's bread") was synonymous with *gagner sa vie* ("to earn one's livelihood, living or life") and people had as many names for bread as the Eskimos for snow and the Bedouin for sand, each richly encrusted with connotations of nutritional quality, geographical provenance, economic status and social aspiration. Thus the rich might afford white, wheat-based loaves; the hard-up a black unleavened loaf of rye and barley or a maize-based porridge; and the very poorest – like the disinherited paupers of the Vivarais – a practically indigestible chestnut bread which comprised, one village proudly boasted, "our aid, our principal foodstuff, the wherewithal on which we nourish our families, our servants, our pets, our livestock, our poultry and our pigs"' (Jones 2002: 148–9). With the exception of maize, which came from the Americas post-Columbus, we shall find Galen and literary authors making very similar statements about patterns of food consumption in the Roman Empire.

In addition to comparative approaches to the ancient evidence, we shall also draw on the work of anthropologists. Food is an important feature of all cultures. As mortals, human beings must eat, and to do so they must harness the natural and cultivated products of their local and wider environment. In doing so, human beings establish a relationship with the natural world, with the plants and animals that they consume, and with the natural forces of which they are part and to which they are subject. These relationships generate powerful religious, social and intellectual constructions, which lie behind the economic activity of the production and distribution of food. The consumption of food is often ordered to reflect essential aspects of the social structure of a society, such as the relationship between the genders and the structure of power. These relationships are a concern for anthropology, but anthropological studies have not always focused on food as much as on other aspects of life, such as social hierarchy, the life cycle and death ritual. Over the past half century, however, Claude Lévi-Strauss, Mary Douglas and Jack Goody, for example, have made a major anthropological contribution to the study of food. Douglas (1966) tackled the Jewish food laws and issues of identity; Douglas and Nicod (1974) decoded the structure of the British meal, while Douglas (1984) explored the interaction of native and immigrant food cultures in the United States, again touching on cultural codes and identity. Goody (1982) explored the determinants of 'development' in food practices between different cultures: how does France come to have a 'cuisine' and other countries not? Of these studies, the work of Lévi-Strauss has provoked most comment (see Buxton 1994, Goody 1982, Garnsey 1999). His system is based on methods of cooking and the place they are considered to have within the thought and linguistic systems of the cultural order, in particular expressing the relationship between nature and culture in that order. While some of the categories of Lévi-Strauss can be shown to be too culturally specific and arbitrary to allow for general application, Greek culture has proved to be a very fruitful area for its application, since the Greeks integrated religious, mythical and cultural thought in particularly instructive ways. The work of Jean-Pierre Vernant and Marcel Detienne, for example, will inform this work, for example in the discussion in Chapter 3 of the festivals of the Thesmophoria and of Adonis.

Much of the evidence about food in the ancient world, as we have said, derives from written texts complemented with archaeological finds. Many important aspects of eating, however, are simply not attested and many questions can only be answered partially. One such area is the division of eating according to gender in Greek culture. If Greek men of status dined apart from women of status, where and how did women of status dine (if at all)? Did they not dine with friends? Did the genders dine together when only in a family group without strangers present? If they did so, did males and females eat the same food? Where textual or archaeological evidence is lacking, anthropological and comparative studies have a vital role to play in helping us to suggest answers.

The Foods and Drinks of the Ancient Diet

This section sets out an indicative picture of the ancient diet and then suggests how that might have been modified over time, and in particular according to place, since regional influences were strong.

The Hippocratic treatise *Regimen II*, which was written around 400 BC, offers a convenient and focused summary of the Greek diet at a comparatively early date. The main cereals were barley and wheat, the former normally made into 'cakes' and porridges, the latter, much rarer on the Greek mainland and islands, made into bread and other cereal products. Primitive wheats were also widespread, in particular emmer, einkorn and spelt. Oats too are mentioned, and millet. To supplement cereals, there were beans and pulses (in particular fava and other beans), peas, chickpeas, lentils, vetches, linseed, sage, lupin seeds, hedge-mustard, cucumber seeds, sesame, safflower, beef, goats, pork, lamb, donkeys, dogs, wild boar, deer, hare, fox, hedgehog, doves, partridge, pigeon, cocks, turtledoves, geese, ducks and other waterfowl. Fish are mentioned from over twenty species, including cuttlefish, shellfish and crabs. There are eggs, cheese, water and wine, vinegar and honey. Vegetables and herbs listed are garlic, onion, leek, radish, cress, mustard, rocket, coriander, lettuce, anise, celery, basil, rue, asparagus, sage, night-shade, purslane, nettles, mint, sorrel, wild spinach, cabbage, beet, gourds, turnip, pennyroyal, marjoram, savoury, thyme, hyssop, wild vegetables. Fruits mentioned are: mulberries, pears (wild and cultivated), apples, quinces, service berries, cornel berries, pomegranate, gourds, grapes, figs, almonds, other nuts and acorns.

This summary is intended to be a working guide. It is distorted by the medical objectives of its author, particularly in the number of herbs mentioned. On the other hand, it is not a list drawn from myriad authors with no uniform indication of purpose. Such a list of foods drawn from a wide range of texts is available in Dalby (1996) and in particular in Dalby (2003), *Food in the Ancient World from A to Z*. Dalby indicates all known foods, at least those for which terms were written down. It is not always possible to give an indication of date, location and context. Thus, for example, pepper is mentioned in a fragment (274) of the comic poet Antiphanes. The quotation comes from a lost play written in the fourth century BC, and concerns hostility towards someone seen taking pepper home. We do not know how often pepper was used or in which cities, only that the name was mentioned. It would be reasonable to conclude that pepper was reasonably well known in Athens, if a comic poet mentioned it in front of an audience of 15,000 fellow citizens. This source might indicate wider use than mention by a Hippocratic doctor alone. The term 'pepper', at the very least, had registered in the Greek mind. As Dalby makes clear, many foods arrived in Greece and Rome at different times over a period of some millennia, and were slowly assimilated into the diet. It is often not possible to be certain when any particular food became widespread. To return to pepper, however, we may note that in the 'de re coquinaria', the cookery book of Apicius, which was probably compiled in the fourth century AD, it is to be found in a majority of the recipes.

What are the important foods omitted from this summary list? We might have expected silphium, a powerful and characteristic flavour (see below) and a drug at the same time. We might have expected more birds and fish. But, herbs apart, the list appears to give a reasonable summary as it stands. Galen's list, in *On the Powers of Foods*, includes more items but none radically new, other than such items as peaches and apricots, which may have been brought from the East in the first century BC. In other words, new foods in the Roman period were not all that numerous. It is, however, likely that foods imported from Asia became more plentiful – such as pepper and other strong flavours with pharmacological applications – during the Hellenistic and Roman period.

Medicine was often the spur for the import of new products, rather than their pleasure-inducing tastes. When the tomato and chocolate were introduced into early modern Europe, they did not immediately appeal to the palate, but had desirable medical applications, including use as aphrodisiacs. Silphium was thus both medicine and essential flavour. So too the indigenous garlic and onion. Pepper, possibly an essential taste later in the Roman empire, was first and foremost a medicine, and one of a class particularly sought after in Hellenistic courts, namely as antidote to poison. This quality in pepper was noted as early as Theophrastus, who says that there are two kinds of pepper, both of which are heating and counteract hemlock (9.20.1 and Athenaeus 2.66e). Athenaeus' discussion seems to embrace both flavour and medicine. The court of Mithridates in the kingdom of Pontus perhaps contributed to the luxury of Rome; but it also promoted the use of antidotes against poison. Mushrooms, on the other hand, are as often cited as a poison as a food.

This brief review of foods aims to be indicative rather than comprehensive. The important question to ask is what are the status and position of the person classifying the food? Doctors were likely to find pharmacological uses for many foods that were not otherwise palatable, such as bitter vetch (normally a cattle food), puppy or camel. Hippocratic authors mention all of these. Vegetables played a large part in the diet of the poor. Wealthy people often scorned them, unless they were aiming at the simple life. But for the ascetic philosopher and the doctor, vegetables had many virtues, as Galen shows in the second book of his *On the Powers of Foods*.

Above all, certain criteria are crucial. First, location. A camel is a frequent sight in Egypt or Mesopotamia but not in Greece. Then geography and climate. Then season. Some people had to live or chose to live by season, others could ignore season, certainly as far as food shortages were concerned. Few could obliterate seasonality outside paradises such as that of the Homeric Phaeacians and Cyclopes and of literary utopias (for which see Chapter 9). The closest to achieving this seems to be the Ptolemaic festival in the Nile valley, for which see Chapter 3.

Greek culture and Roman culture

This book surveys a millennium of food consumption in Greek culture and some six hundred years of Roman culture, together with brief consideration of certain other cultures, including Persian, Egyptian and Celtic. A word is needed on the composite structure of 'Greco-Roman' culture. Greek culture was highly distinctive and cooking played a central, defining role within it that may allow the Greeks to claim a place among the great food cultures of the world (see below). This book begins with the poems of Homer which are conventionally dated to the eighth century BC. The Romans, with whom we engage from the third century BC onwards, conceived of themselves as in some ways very different from the Greeks. We consider in Chapter 7 their self-characterization as originally simple farming folk untainted by foreign influence and the luxury trade. There is plentiful evidence, however, that the Romans engaged with the Greeks and with Greek-influenced Italic peoples from the sixth century and even earlier. Furthermore, the Greeks had established cities on the Italian peninsula from the eighth century BC onwards. This helps to collapse the distinction between Greek and Roman, and the distinction is further blurred after Roman expansion annexed Greece in the second century BC and ruled Italy and Greece as a vast Mediterranean empire for the next four centuries of our period. Greeks, then, were not confined to Greece – the greatest culinary advances normally did not come from the Greek mainland at all – nor the Romans to Italy. Once Roman imperialism had transformed itself from Republican to autocratic government by an emperor, it was the Roman – in effect the Greco-Roman – Empire which had become in Andrew Dalby's phrase the 'empire of pleasures'. To help bring all this together, this book draws on the four encyclopaedic works of synthesis by Pliny, Plutarch, Galen and Athenaeus.

What is distinctive about food in Greco-Roman culture?

While a study of Greek and Roman food as a distinctive cultural system is desirable in its own right, a stronger claim for this system can perhaps be made. Greek culture, together with its close Roman relative, is a cultural system into which food is built to an unusual extent, which bears comparison with the great food cultures of China and India. As well as reflecting the patterns of production, distribution and social structure, food also lay at the heart of the medical system developed by the Hippocratic doctors of the fifth and fourth centuries BC. The liquids of life (the humours) of the plant and animal world were closely related to those that governed the human body and were as subject to seasonal and climatic factors. One Hippocratic treatise, *Regimen I*, even placed human beings within a cosmic order based on fire and water. A further Hippocratic theory imagined the process of digestion as the cooking of nutriment with bodily heat. Cooking the food before eating was simply part of the civilized way to assimilate food for human absorption. For many ancient authors, human beings were animals, but a race of animals apart. A different rationale governed the religious system, but here too food – both animal and non-animal – remained at the heart of exchanges between gods and mortals. The lesser being, the human, offered the higher being, the god, the life of the animal or plant that was being sacrificed. The religious order combined mythical thought with the ritual activities of festival and worship, and it also integrated the individual into the community.

A further distinctive feature of Greco-Roman culture is an extensive literary production – both oral and written – which reflects food and its multiple associations in many of its genres. This production even includes cookery books, which many cultures do not produce. These were produced by 400 BC, within half a century of the earliest medical treatises. As far as other literature is concerned, food plays a powerful role in Homer, the earliest literary text known to us. Later, some literary genres, such as tragedy and comedy, were linked with festivals, where sacrifice and consumption on stage reflected in coded forms appropriate to each genre what actors and audience had been doing in the ceremonies preceding the drama. Other genres were linked to ceremonial drinking (or symposia), including much early poetry and, in a paradoxical way, quite a lot of philosophy. Roman satire, too, found food and dining a particularly vivid medium for its invective against all the social evils it claimed to detect. Then there was the technical literature, of farming manuals, medical treatises on nutrition and pharmacology, the cookery books already mentioned, zoological and botanical works, and strange mixed works such as the cookery poem of Archestratus (fourth century BC) and the fishing poem of Oppian (second century AD).

Regional foods

Regional considerations are of particular importance for this study. Many examples will be found in Chapters 4 and 5. First of all, such differences highlight the diversity in time and space of the area under investigation. There was the greatest difference between major centres – the large cities of Rome, Alexandria and (on a smaller scale) Athens – and all other places. There were also differences between east and west, between mountain and plain, as we shall see in ancient and modern accounts of Italy (p. 122). There was diversity too between places very close together: the microclimates of Greece favoured different cereals and other crops in different places. The medical botanist Dioscorides insists the doctor inspect each plant in its place, because location is decisive. The comic poet Eubulus lists special plants from special cities (fragment 18): 'Cypriot mustard and scammony sap, Milesian cress, Samothracian garlic, silphium stem and silphium from Carthage and Hymettian thyme, oregano from Tenedos' (trans. Dalby). At sea, *The Life of Luxury* of Archestratus guides readers to the best fish to be found in particular cities. For example, fragment 35.5–7 advises, 'it is good in Byzantion and in Karystos, but Kephaloidis on the famous island of the Sikels raises tuna that are much better than these' (trans. Olson and Sens). Dalby's *Empire of Pleasures* (2000) studies just these regional connections with food and drink, which pervade ancient texts.

Regional considerations also help us to see the ancient Mediterranean in terms similar to those of the modern world. Just as modern Italy is intensely regional, so was its ancient counterpart. No sources bring out these differences better than our encyclopaedic sources Pliny, Galen and Athenaeus. Pliny reveals the excellence of regions of Italy; Galen distinguishes cereals in regions of Asia Minor; Athenaeus distinguishes Greek cities in Greece and Asia Minor. Particular claims are made for Sparta, Crete, Thessaly, Boeotia and many other regions. Social systems influence agricultural produce and consumption: see Chapter 2 on Sparta and Athens.

Athens is our first location – a city state with some fertile plains, such as the grain-producing area of Eleusis, many rocky hillsides, and much land suitable for vines, olives and woodland products such as charcoal. With a large urban centre, the city state did not find it easy to be self-sufficient and so imported heavily. This gave access, particularly during the Athenian imperial period of the fifth and to a lesser extent the fourth centuries BC, to all sorts of imports which are celebrated by comic authors, and also by Xenophon (*Poroi* 1) and Pericles in Thucydides' account (2.38). Accounts of eating set a certain pattern to Athenian eating. There were possibilities of over-indulgent eating, especially of fish (Davidson 1997, Wilkins 2000). There were pressures too for simplicity and restraint, as discussed above. Athenaeus (4.131f–132f) brings out an Athenian style of eating, with many small dishes like a modern Indian meal. (His sources are comic and so may be misleading.) Festivals reflected in religious ritual certain ideological attitudes. These festivals, of which Athens had a great many, possibly allowed the Athenians to eat more beef and other meats than some other Greeks. Festivals, too, celebrated her imperial strength and caused goods to be brought to Athens, which could be reflected in the comedies put on at the festivals of Dionysus. To judge from the comic evidence, Athenian audiences appear to have revelled in the portrait of their war-torn neighbours the Megarians as starving and now in need of what they normally exported, namely salt and garlic. By the same account, Boeotians were dim witted and prepared to sell rich agricultural produce and eels at a loss (Aristophanes, *Acharnians*). Athens emphasized her simplicity in particular at the central hearth of the polis, in the prytaneion, where, again according to a comic source, Chionides fragment 7, barley pastry and olives reminded everyone of the simple foods of early Athens. This self-presentation shares much with Rome in a later period. An instructive comparison could be made with a polis that was far from the sea and in a mountainous area. In the latter, there would be a possibility of milk-drinking, even beer-drinking, and less likelihood of fish-eating and of foods imported from abroad. It is important to consider these, if only as theoretical possibilities. We hear less about them, because, of course, the major cities were centres not only of more diverse eating but also of the production and dissemination of texts. See further Chapters 4 and 5.

Consideration of the mountainous areas of Greece and Italy (let alone Asia Minor in the Roman period) can lead us to ask whether the inhabitants of these less populated areas shared certain foods with non-Greek peoples. Herodotus vividly brings out different eating practices in descriptions of the Persians, Egyptians, and the pastoral Scythians and Libyans in books 1, 2 and 4. This focus on contrast masks similarities, which a regional perspective helps to bring out. Consumption of wheat or olive oil, for example, is as much determined by geographical considerations in the Mediterranean as by cultural practices. Those who lived away from the classical centres of the world may have been more likely to drink milk, eat butter, grow different cereals and even sacrifice slightly differently from city people. In other words, to lead a life that was not based on olive oil and wine to supplement the cereal staple. If there were similarities between pastoralists in Italy and Greece and those on the fringes of the Greco-Roman world, there were also two further similarities with 'barbarian' peoples. The first is the diversity of Greek and Roman cities as they came into contact in their hundreds with other peoples and other ways of life. Thus, even though the Greeks did not sacrifice fish, Athenaeus was able to find some surprising cases of such a practice. And many surprising practices are brought to light in his vast survey of Greco-Roman culture, as Greeks and Romans came into contact with native peoples around the Mediterranean. The second feature, present on a vast scale in imperial Rome as in many Greek cities, was a taste for luxury and excess. This pleasure-seeking often appears in Classical texts as a vice of the barbarians which all too often found its way into Greco-Roman culture. See the discussion in Chapter 7 of Rome's early image of herself as a culture which knew nothing of maritime trade and fish, and of Pliny's recoiling in horror from a discussion of shellfish which he found to be wickedly sensual. Such luxury seems to have flourished in certain Greek settlements, deriving in particular from good agricultural production. It flourished in Rome because the centre of a world empire could draw wealth to itself. Some of this supposed luxurious living, such as in the cities of the Ionian coast of Asia Minor, was influenced by Persian and other eastern cultures. Other examples, particularly in Sicily and southern Italy as far north as the Bay of Naples, seem to have grown within Greek culture. The cities of Sybaris and Croton are early examples.

Within the Greek world and Roman world, therefore, we should expect, and will find, much variation, which is brought out in many different ways.

Other cultures

We have referred on a number of occasions to particular practices or ingredients that are linked with specific places. But we have also seen that influence of one place on another and the movement of foods and technology from one place to another are also important. There was much movement for trade and military and political purposes around the Mediterranean, which brought extensive dissemination of goods and techniques. Thus it is very difficult to speak of the Greeks and Romans as being confined in the Greek mainland and in Rome and Latium respectively. From a very early period, southern Italy was colonized by Greeks, and by the time of Augustus, Roman influence on Asia Minor was considerable. Consequently, comments on whether 'barbarian' drinks were consumed in Asia Minor at the time of Aeschylus in the early 5th century BC would have to be posed in a rather different form in the first century AD. Greeks and Romans had a notion of the Mediterranean as their sea, with their spheres of influence surrounded by peoples who were different, the meat-eating Celts of northern Europe, and the nomadic peoples of the north Sahara and the Russian steppes. But there were also cultures which controlled parts of the Eastern Mediterranean before they did; the Persians and Egyptians, among others. These were people who were not Greek, but presented a different form of non-Greekness from the Celts. It was possible to describe the Persians and Egyptians as luxurious and decadent, topics which I explore in Chapter 7, but a stereotypical description of that kind fails to do full justice to these complex neighbours, with whom many Greek communities were on very close terms.

Egypt was always a special case in the Mediterranean because of the unique contribution of the Nile to agriculture, and the unusual wealth that the Nile brought. Egypt was thus an important case study for Herodotus in the fifth century BC, and the site for the Greco-Egyptian culture of the Ptolemies in the Hellenistic period. It was also an important point of reference for our summarizing authors, Galen and Athenaeus (the latter an Egyptian Greek himself, from Naucratis), in the second and third centuries AD.

Persia too was the subject of much comment on food and culture. The Great King sat at the apex of an elaborate hierarchy that distributed food and other resources from the centre. Some Greek authors described this system as 'luxury'. But it also reflects a different religious system, and attempts were made to describe it in terms that were not prejudicial. The Great King expressed his pre-eminence through the distribution and consumption of meat, through hierarchical mealtimes, and by stimulating innovation. Heraclides of Cumae, author of *ta Persika*, or *An Account of Persia*, which he wrote in the fourth century BC, describes royal meals:

> Of those who are invited to dine with the king, some dine outdoors, in full sight of anyone who wishes to look on; others dine indoors in the king's company. Yet even these do not eat in his presence, for there are

two rooms opposite each other, in one of which the king has his meal, in the other the invited guests. The king can see them through the curtain at the door, but they cannot see him. Sometimes, however, on the occasion of a public holiday, all dine in a single room with the king, in the great hall. And whenever the king commands a symposium (which he does often), he has about a dozen companions at his drinking. When they have finished dinner, that is the king by himself, the guests in the other room, these fellow-drinkers are summoned by one of the eunuchs; and entering they drink with him, though even they do not have the same wine; moreover, they sit on the floor, while he reclines on a couch supported by feet of gold; and they depart after having drunk to excess. In most cases the king breakfasts and dines alone, but sometimes his wife and some of his sons dine with him. And throughout the dinner his concubines sing and play the lyre; one of them is the soloist, the others sing in chorus. (trans. Gulick)

Heraclides proceeds next to describe the meal itself, the king's *deipnon*.

The 'king's dinner,' as it is called, will appear prodigal to one who merely hears about it, but when one examines it carefully it will be found to have been got up with economy and even with parsimony; and the same is true of the dinners among other Persians in high station. For one thousand animals are slaughtered daily for the king; these comprise horses, camels, oxen, asses, deer, and most of the smaller animals; many birds also are consumed, including Arabian ostriches – and the creature is large – geese, and cocks. And of all these only moderate portions are served to each of the king's guests, and each of them may carry home whatever he leaves untouched at the meal. But the greater part of these meats and other foods are taken out into the courtyard for the bodyguard and the light-armed troopers maintained by the king; there they divide all the half-eaten remnants of meat and bread and share them in equal portions. Just as hired soldiers in Greece receive their wages in money, so these men receive food from the king in requital for services. Similarly among other Persians of high rank, all the food is served on the table at one and the same time; but when their guests have done eating, whatever is left from the table, consisting chiefly of meat and bread, is given by the officer in charge of the table to each of the slaves; this they take and so obtain their daily food. Hence the most highly honoured of the king's guests go to court only for breakfast; for they beg to be excused in order that they may not be required to go twice; but may be able to return to their own guests. (trans. Gulick)

These extracts from Heraclides are preserved by Athenaeus (Deipnosophistae 4.145a–146a), who tries to calculate the comparative cost of this system against the expenses of Alexander the Great – an important but unsuccessful attempt. Athenaeus also considers Herodotus' comparison between the Greeks and Persians, and Xenophon's valuable comparison with Greek tyrants and the discourse of pleasure, which we consider in Chapters 2 and 7. Athenaeus also adds innovation in recipes and the broader influence on Antony and Cleopatra. This is a very valuable consideration – it is too fragmentary to be called a study – of the transfer of royal dining from Persia to Rome, by way of the Greek tyrants and Hellenistic kings. For a discussion of dining and distribution in Persia see Briant 1996: 297–309.

Cultural development?

The magnificence of the Persian court predates much of the period we are considering in this study. By the end of our study, the imperial court of Rome had access to even more wealth than the Persian king. Can we talk of the 'development' of 'gastronomy' in the Greco-Roman world in this period?

  Broadly speaking, regional products and social rituals were tied to agriculture and climate and were not subject to rapid innovation, though there might be changes over time in products grown or political and social systems. Change in styles of eating and products available more often came from outside. Thus consumers in Rome benefited from new fruits such as cherries, peaches and apricots that came to the city as the empire extended its influence in Asia Minor. New birds and fish seem to have become available. At an earlier period, as we shall see in Chapter 2, the practice of reclining rather than sitting at meals was introduced into the Greek and Italic worlds from the Near East. There were other developments in food and eating that we will explore. Is it possible to declare therefore, that at the end of the period covered by this book, people ate in a more advanced way than they had at the beginning? As we shall see below, the Greeks certainly believed in cultural developments of this kind, at least as expressed through the medium of ideology and myth. We can be reasonably sure that the majority of the population in general did not enjoy any such development, and that for the rural poor, food shortages were as endemic in the second century AD as in earlier centuries. Galen attests eloquently to this truth. Among the privileged elites, there were developments, but they do not appear to have been sustained throughout the period. Here I review briefly two cultural phenomena, the cook and the cookery book – and their implications for cultural development.

Cooks, by their nature, are ambiguous figures. The Greek word for 'cook', *mageiros*, covers roughly the modern trades of cook and butcher, and in addition the role of cutting the animal's throat in sacrifice. They were artisans who on the one hand performed arduous and dirty work, the slaughter and butchering of animals, the cooking of meat and other foods in smoky and greasy conditions, and on the other were linked with meat which carried status and high religious regard. In the ancient world, they might be camp followers or slaves, or skilled artisans for hire. In contemporary Britain, they might stand at the barbeque; they might also be one of our great restaurant chefs. Because of this ambiguity, they are to be found in a number of different settings. Inscriptions record them making sacrifices at certain religious gatherings (Berthiaume 1982). They are also found in the retinues of powerful rulers. The King of Persia and his generals had cooks on their staff. Herodotus makes a telling contrast between Persian and Spartan practice (9.82):

> when Pausanias saw [the tent of Xerxes], with its embroidered hangings and gorgeous decorations in silver and gold, he summoned Mardonius' bakers and cooks and told them to prepare a meal of the same sort as they were accustomed to prepare for their former master. The order was obeyed; and when Pausanias saw gold and silver couches all beautifully draped, and gold and silver tables, and everything prepared for the feast with great magnificence, he could hardly believe his eyes for the good things set before him, and just for a joke, ordered his own servants to get ready an ordinary Spartan dinner. (trans. de Selincourt)

In parallel with this, according to Xenophon, novelties were offered to the Persian king: 'for the Persian <king>, they travel round the whole country seeking out what he might drink with pleasure, and myriad people devise dishes that he might eat with pleasure' (*Agesilaus* 9.3). The king is thus attended by cooks in his royal palace, and when he was on the move, whether with his army or not. The Persians had meals that were distinctive from the Greeks, as Herodotus makes clear (see above).

Whether this constitutes a 'cuisine' is difficult to say, but the retinue of cooks certainly helped to express the supreme power of the king. When the Greeks discovered the possibilities of cooks, did they eat more 'royally' or use more of them? There is no clear evidence that they did, though there is much comic comment on cooks introducing 'luxury' into private households.

A stronger case for a court cuisine can probably be made for the Greeks of Sicily. Cooks from the courts of tyrants there are attested in Xenophon, Plato and a Hippocratic text (see Chapter 2). Cooks begin to appear in Athenian comic texts of the fourth century BC. Does this reflect significant competition among the Athenian elite to display the latest and the best in modern cooking? The evidence does not really allow us to go that far.

A speaker in Athenaeus claims (14.659a) that cooks were normally free men before the Macedonian period, after which they were slaves. The Macedonians certainly used cooks at court, and in their turn exported them to Rome in the second century BC, along with all the other luxuries that Cato and Polybius complained about in the wake of the conquest of Macedonia and Greece. Cooks and bakers were these alien influences, as they had been in the tent of Mardonius. In Rome, cooks appear to be slaves. They certainly are in Athenaeus' *Deipnosophistae* and in Petronius' dinner of Trimalchio, where they appear to be skilled slaves attached to the household.

The connection between cooks and cookery books is interesting. The books instruct, and assume the requisite skills are in place. Mithaecus, Archestratus and Apicius concern themselves with cooking skills, but also have other interests, as we shall see. But when considering the development of cooking in the Greco-Roman world it is difficult to see the development of a cuisine in a systematic way. Too little of Mithaecus survives to allow us to judge his style of cooking. Archestratus rejects complex flavours and promotes the cooking of the freshest fish with simplicity and sophistication. Nothing could be further from the heavy spicing of Apicius who uses multiple flavours that derive from both imported and local plants. What survives of these works and such writers as Paxamus is too scarce and too diverse to allow us to describe developments in gastronomy. The Greeks do not clearly inherit significant features from Persia and Egypt, which they then pass on to the Romans. Rather, Rome seems to adapt Greek ways with enthusiasm in this area as in so many others, and then adapts it to its own political system. Meals in Rome are expected to be lavish and to reflect produce from all over the empire, as it had for the Persian king. Food was also important for display. It should be on a lavish scale, or should perform, as a shield of Minerva (Suetonius, *Vitellius*) or a hunted boar (Petronius,

Dinnes of Trimalchio). But there is no apparent interest in essences or delicacy of flavour, as there had been for Archestratus. The imperial court at Rome would appear to have everything necessary for a great cuisine – apart from the interest in discernment in food. Grandeur and display seem to have taken the place of sophistication and refinement – as far as we can tell.

Mythical Accounts of Cultural Development

We have considered ambiguous evidence for the development of cooking in Greece during the period. Whatever the actual practice, the Greeks and Romans certainly believed that cooking was closely linked with culture and the development of civilization. Food in this system seems to bear comparison with the other great food systems of the world, for example those of India and China which build ideas about food and a medical system around man's place in the universe.

Greek culture, and (with modifications) Roman culture, built food into its view of the world. At a comparatively early stage, accounts of cultural development showed how mankind had declined from a golden age where food was automatically available; an alternative model showed how mankind had progressed from a primitive, bestial, base to a sophisticated cultural life. I give some examples below. At an early stage too, myths were developed which accounted for the arrival of certain important foods in Greece and Italy. These foods arrived with the help of gods and culture-heroes. These, too, I explore below. Particularly important were the myths which defined the relationship between human beings and animals, the myths of Heracles the bringer of cattle to the classical world and of Prometheus, who established the complex system of animal sacrifice to the gods. Cooking was at the heart of these myths of development. It was at the heart of the medical system, too. As a theory of digestion was developed by Hippocrates and others, the model adopted seems to have been a process of cooking of the food within the body, which was tied to the body's own heat and was a way of breaking down food into nourishment of the blood and other tissues. So too in philosophy, Plato in his *Timaeus* builds the nourishment of the body into his account of the creation of the cosmos and the human form (see Chapter 7).

The Greeks and Romans gave a number of different accounts of human progress, from primitivism or the Garden of Eden to divine intervention. Examples to be given here are Hesiod's version of the myth of Prometheus, the early *Hymn to Demeter*, and a later mythical account of the arrival of the wine god Dionysus in Greece. Beside these mythical accounts of how gods brought civilization we will place a scientific account from a Hippocratic author and a moralizing account from Ovid. Moralizing reflections on eating and drinking were ubiquitous in antiquity and need to be identified for what they are.

First, Hesiod's version of the myth of Prometheus, which is a Greek version of the Garden of Eden story in Genesis. Men had hitherto eaten with the gods and had no concerns about heat or food provision. Then a dispute arose between the Titan Prometheus and the Olympian Zeus. Prometheus divided up an ox into different, unequal portions. Zeus chose the portion of thigh bones wrapped up in fat, leaving for the human beings the meat wrapped inside the great stomach of the ox, like a giant haggis. Zeus was angry and in retaliation removed fire from man. Prometheus, concerned for fragile man with no fire, stole back Zeus' fire and gave it to man in a fennel stalk. Zeus retaliated by instructing the gods to create the first woman, Pandora. Furthermore, both man and woman have to work in the fields because Zeus has concealed the means of life in the soil. Humanity now has to farm the land. There are various complicated details, but the great interpretation of Jean-Pierre Vernant (1989) emphasizes certain elements. This is a negative myth in Hesiod's telling (farming is hard and women are extremely suspect), and there is clearly established bad feeling between gods and humans, based on the concealment of vital things, in particular the means of life. Food can now only be wrested from a reluctant earth through agricultural production. Zeus was angry with the Titan Prometheus, but human beings were punished in the dispute between these gods. Human beings remember their subservience to gods by performing animal sacrifice whenever they eat meat.

But it is also a rich cultural myth. Humanity now has fire, cooking, sacrifice, technology; it has agriculture; it has marriage. Sacrifice in future depends on equal parts for all, which are cooked. Cooking is at the centre of the cultural system. The animal, which must be a domesticated animal, the product of agriculture, is carefully cut up, with the parts most associated with life, the marrow in the thigh bones and the vital organs, being roasted in sacrifice to the gods. The mortal flesh and entrails are boiled for human consumption. Hesiod presents the myth of Prometheus in both his *Theogony (Generations of the Gods)* and his agricultural poem *Works and Days*. The myth is thus early (Hesiod is thought to have written the poems in the eighth century BC). It also lies at the heart of Hesiod's accounts of the gods and of farming. Vernant's analysis of the myth demonstrates its power as a culture myth, and this power was felt in later centuries. Homer appears to share the same basic presentation of sacrifice as Hesiod, though he has a number of variations in detail. That sacrifice is based on the killing of the domesticated animals of agriculture is made clear in *Odyssey* 12. Homer describes how the cattle of the Sun god were not domesticated and could not be sacrificed in the normal way. The companions of Odysseus, driven by hunger, ignore this command and begin the sacrifice:

> 'and because they had no barley-meal in the ship, they plucked instead the fresh tender leaves of a tall oak. Prayer over, they slaughtered and flayed the cows, cut out the thigh-bones and covered them with a double fold of fat, then laid the raw meat above. They had no wine to make libation over the burning sacrifice, but instead poured water as they set to roasting the inward parts. When the thigh-bones were quite consumed and the entrails tasted, they sliced and spitted the rest . . . Then the gods began to show signs and wonders to my crew. The beasts' hides began to move; the flesh on the spits, raw or roasted, began to bellow; and there was a noise like the noise of cattle.'

The sacrifice did not work because the companions of Odysseus used natural products, oak leaves and water, in the place of the correct agricultural products – barley grains and wine – as Homer points out. They also used divine rather than agricultural cattle. (Vidal-Naquet 1981)

The Promethean myth gives an account of human relations with the gods and an 'explanation' or 'origin' for the Greek form of sacrifice. Three other myths 'explain' how the Greeks came to have cattle, grain and wine, and the explanation centres on a divine culture hero like Prometheus. The dispute between Zeus and Prometheus was thought to happen at Mekone, a place in the Peloponnese. The other myths that follow emphasize movement, the bringing of foods into the Mediterranean world.

Cattle were first brought to Greece by the demi-god and culture hero Heracles. As one of his labours he was set the task of stealing the cattle of the triple-headed monster Geryon, who lived on an island in the Atlantic. Heracles managed to perform this task, ferrying the cattle to the Spanish mainland in a giant drinking-cup. He then drove the cattle through southern France, round the Italian and Sicilian coastline, through the Balkans to Greece, stopping at many places on the way to sacrifice one of the animals. At each of these places of sacrifice, an altar was set up, which later formed the basis of a settlement. The most spectacular of these many sites was Rome, where the altar in question was the Ara Maxima or great altar in the 'Cattle Forum'. Nearby, Heracles killed the monstrous Cacus who lived in a cave and tried to steal the cattle. As with all the myths now under consideration, the myth of Heracles and the cattle of Gerypon shows how a vital food came to Greece from elsewhere. As too in the other cases, the journey and arrival of the new food was linked with cult and festival. There was no separation of myth and religion (Burkert 1979).

Grain was brought to Greece by Demeter and her consort Triptolemus. Sophocles is known to have written a play entitled *Triptolemus* which seems to have shown the progress of the culture hero through Asia Minor. Only odd words of the play survive, mostly noted by Athenaeus, and they refer to various foodstuffs, some cereal based, such as rice and beer, some not, such as *garum* (fermented fish sauce). Once cultivated cereals were established in Greece, the Greeks honoured Trimtolemus, Demeter and her daughter Persephone at a number of cult centres, the most important of which was at Eleusis. Here the goddess received the first fruits of the harvest. A mystery cult developed, which somehow linked the life of the corn with the life of the human being. A kind of afterlife was on offer to those initiated. The myth of the rape (or abduction) of Persephone was told in an early poem, the Homeric *Hymn to Demeter*. This sets out the relationship between the life and 'death' of Persephone, the growing of corn, and human dependence on the goddesses: when Demeter mourns, famine strikes the population (Foley 1993). The myth of Demeter was also linked to a major festival in Athens and many other towns, the Thesmophoria, which is discussed in Chapter 3. It is clear that with the grain Demeter brought other social benefits, the *thesmoi* or ordinances by which men live, and also the patronage of conception and some control over life and death.

A similar extensive power is seen in our third myth concerning food, wine and Dionysus the god of the vine. In the prologue to Euripides' play *The Bacchae*, the god tells us that he has journeyed through Asia bringing the technology of wine with him. He comes to Thebes, his birthplace, where he punishes the royal family for not accepting his divinity. Other versions of the myth recount the arrival of the god in Attica. Icarius accepted the god's wine, but when he gave it to fellow villagers, they fell down drunk. Suspecting magic, they killed Icarius.

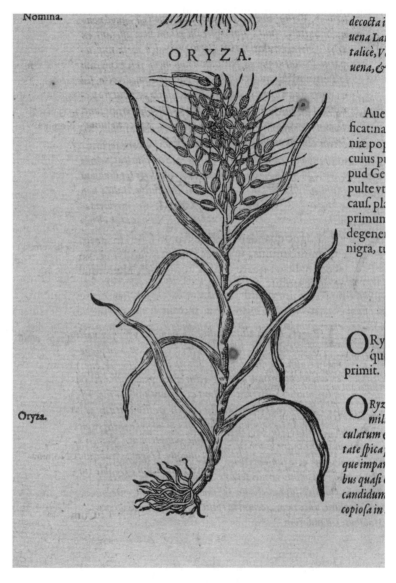

FIGURE 1.3 Rice is a cereal that now belongs to the Mediterranean (for example in Spain and Italy) but in antiquity was seen as an Asian rarity. Nevertheless, it made its way into the pharmacopaea of Dioscorides and Galen, and was even mentioned in Sophocles' tragedy, *Triptolemus*, which was named after the consort of Demeter, goddess of grain. Reproduced by permission of the Dean and Chapter of Exeter Cathedral

His daughter Erigone hanged herself. Death was linked with the drinking of wine; indeed Dionysus was a god of the underworld as well as of the vine. The ambivalent festivals associated with Dionysus are discussed further in Chapter 6. For the present, we note the arrival of wine-making from outside.

These arrivals from elsewhere, cattle, cereals and wine, were fundamental to Greek and Roman culture. But their functions were not the same. Cereals formed the staple food. Animals, especially cattle, held a high status but were eaten comparatively infrequently, by the majority of the population, at least. Wine was a staple drink, but, being inherently destabilizing, had to be treated with respect.

These accounts of the development of civilization and of the arrival of staple foods establish certain basic principles. Food is wrested from the earth only with much agricultural labour. Success is difficult without divine help, but that help is grudgingly given, and only on tough terms. Foods imported into Greece and Italy are a feature not only of trade in the historical period, but also of myth from the earliest times. Developments in food and culture bring benefits and problems. The latter, of course, are inevitable if the pattern of thought of Hesiod's myth of Prometheus prevails, namely that human beings lived in harmony with the gods before that fatal meal.

Scientific and poetic accounts of human development

Hippocrates in *Ancient Medicine* gives a valuable account of the development of medicine (3):

'the art of medicine would not have been discovered in the first place, nor would there have been any research – for it would not have been needed – if for those people who were sick, the same regime and diet was suitable as the food, drink and regime of those in good health, and there were not better options than these. But as it is, necessity herself has forced men to research and discover the art of medicine, because sick people did not benefit from the same food as those in health, nor do they benefit now. From a still longer perspective, I do not think that the diet now in use for those in health would have been discovered if it sufficed for men to eat and drink the same things as the cow, the horse and all animals except man, such as the plants of the earth, fruits, wood and fodder. For they get nourishment from these and grow and lead a life without pain, having no need of any other regime. Now I think that originally men lived on a food of this kind. The way we live now has been discovered and fashioned, developing, it seems to me over a long period. How many and terrible things they suffered from this strong and bestial regime eating raw and unmixed foods with great powers. People would now suffer similar things from these foods, and would fall into strong pain and disease, and would swiftly die. It is likely that they then suffered less from these because they were used to them, but they were violent at that time too. It is reasonable to suppose that most of them died, in particular those with a weaker constitution, while the stronger held out for a longer time. So now, some deal easily with strong foods, and others with great pains and misfortunes. For this reason, indeed, the ancients seem to me to have sought out a food that fitted their nature and to have discovered the food we now have. So from wheat they soaked the grain, winnowed it, ground it, sifted it, kneaded it and baked it, to end up with bread, and from barley they made barley cake. They went through many other procedures with them and boiled, baked and mixed, mingling strong and unmingled with weak, moulding everything to human nature and power.

The Hippocratic author follows a model of progress, basing the advance of medical science on the necessary improvement of the human race as it separated itself in diet from its animal neighbours. This is the reverse model to the decline from the golden age set out by Hesiod and others, for whom work and skills are the necessary evils forced on humanity when Zeus imposed want and powerlessness on them.

With this account of the development of civilization we may compare the comic version given in a late play, fragment 1 of the *Samothracians* of Athenion. There a cook claims that his profession has moved humanity forward from cannibalism to civilized living and good conduct: 'Because of the pleasures I've been speaking of, each person desisted from eating a corpse. They saw fit to live with each other, the people gathered, and cities wen-inhabited – all because of the cook's art, as I say' (lines 34–38, quoted by Athenaeus 14.661c).

The reverse model to that set out by the Hippocratic author is regularly found in Roman poetry. This follows Hesiod's pattern of decline from a golden age. Striking versions are seen in Ovid *Metamorphoses I* and Lucretius *On the Nature of Things V*.

The earth itself, without compulsion, untouched by the hoe, unfurrowed by any share, produced all things spontaneously, and men were content with foods that grew without cultivation. They gathered arbute berries and mountain strawberries, wild cherries and blackberries that cling to thorny bramble bushes; or acorns fallen from Jupiter's spreading oak. . . .

In time the earth, though untilled, produced corn too, and fields that never lay fallow whitened with heavy ears of corn. Then there flowed rivers of milk and rivers of nectar, and golden honey dripped from the green holm-oak. (Ovid 1. trans. Innes)

Lucretrius, writing a poetic cosmology according to the teaching of Epicurus, describes (*On the Nature of the Universe* 5) early human beings roaming like wild animals and living from fruits and berries, with water from rivers and no knowledge of fire.

These are myths of civilization, as the Greeks and Roman conceived it. The myths are not entirely dissonant from some aspects of current scientific accounts. The hunter-gatherers of early human societies are still to be found in Ovid and Lucretius, while the possible movement of agricultural technologies to the Mediterranean from the Near East appears to find expression in the myths of Dionysus and Triptolemus.

The Greeks and Romans were different from other peoples in the Mediterranean, and marked themselves as different with their foods, their relationship to animals and the land, and in their development of the polis or independent city state. The advance to this level of civilization could be celebrated, as in a famous fragment from the *Basket Bearers* of the comic poet Hermippus (63), which imagines Dionysus as a ship's captain bringing all good things to Athens for a dinner and symposium (quoted p. 274 Wilkins 2000, ch. 4). Or arrivals by sea can be presented as a problem. The sea brings dangerous things from outside and threatens the purity of the indigenous people. This is very much the view of Pliny (9.53 and elsewhere), as he surveyed the state of Roman civilization in the first century AD.

What to conclude from these varied accounts? In an essential way, food was at the heart of many cultural exchanges and intersections. Greek was distinguished from foreigner in terms of food. Philosophy identified the importance and also the limitations of food, which needed to be recognized, to prevent its becoming morally dangerous. Plato made the crucial distinction between food that was pleasurable (produced by the cook) and food that was useful. This moral danger feeds through ancient thought to Porphyry and the later ascetics; also through medicine, at least as seen in Galen. Medicine, however, had fostered different perspectives on food and cooking. Cooking was part of the useful process of preparing food for digestion, itself a form of cooking. In the Hippocratic *Art of Medicine*, cooking is part of the civilizing process and fits with the Hesiodic model as a crucial time that separated human beings from animals (though Hippocratic thought is more progressive in its application of the idea than the gloomy Hesiod). Elsewhere in the Hippocratic corpus, the dietary rules of *Regimen II* are developed from the elemental theories based on fire and water in book one. All is derived from fire and water, the cosmos, the world, human beings, animals and plants.

In all that we shall review in later chapters, these positive and negative interpretations will be evident. These thought patterns importantly underlie and inform social and religious patterns seen in Chapters 2 and 3. They also inform much literary expression, which has made a major impact on the reception of eating in the ancient world, in such works as Juvenal, Petronius and Suetonius.

2
Introduction

The separation of rich and poor in society meant differences in quality of diet though not necessarily in taste. The style of cooking and availability of ingredients would have had a common basis. The rural poor would have had access to a starch-based regime, porridges and flatbreads, made more palatable with hedgerow herbs and salads. It is difficult to believe that in times of poverty they would not have drunk fresh milk or churned butter, whatever the general low opinion of such foods. The Urban poor, in Rome at least, lived in tenements without cooking facilities and must of necessity have used the equivalent of fast food from street vendors for a sizeable part of their diet. Animal protein from fish or game would have been an occasional treat rather than a regular staple. This was a diet based on farming and cultivation.

Preferences in cooking styles were a matter of taste and practicality for rich and poor alike. Flatbreads like pitta are better suited to scooping up hummus-style porridges than bread raised with yeast. Olive oil, garum and wine would have been common to most diets. For wealthier people, the meal as vehicle for social pretension, rather than just pleasure or even nutrition, is not new. It has a pedigree which stretches for centuries and excessive or extravagant eating in our period can be compared to Royal banquets in mediaeval times where swan and peacock were on offer in the same way as they can to James Bond's martinis – stirred but not shaken – as unsubtle indicators of sophistication, wealth or power. We tend to share common and unquestioning assumptions on the desirability of rare or recherché ingredients and could well find that those who would nowadays in reality gag at the prospect of fish eggs and fizzy wine will talk reverentially about caviar and Champagne for the days when they win the lottery. Today's rank-smelling white truffle is analogous to Rome's silphium, not just rare and expensive but perceived as an indicator of great taste and discernment.

Of course, there is more than one context to consider even amongst the rich. Parts of society may find any display of extravagance to be vulgar and there have unquestionably periods of history when indulgence may be thought of as weak, in times of war or crisis even unpatriotic. The Victorian era considered it crass even to mention the food being eaten at mealtime; much more important would be to use the correct cutlery and understand which wine was to partner which dish, signs of class familiarity and codes of behaviour that bound the ruling elite together.

These are facets of the same notion, that of shared values amongst those dining. Stern disregard of what is set before you and ostentatious regard for nuances of taste and provenance of the food to be eaten are each attitudes meant to send a message, the first of serious, pious or manly intent, the second of artistic and sensual pretensions. It's Ghandi versus Brillat Savarin but not feast versus famine, for both assume that there is plenty or at the least enough on offer and the means to pay for it. The fraternity of those dining is the core issue and not the menu.

The aesthete, Archestratus, advocated restrained, almost austere treatment of first-rate and carefully sourced ingredients rather than ornate displays of plenty, whereas Trimalchio's dinner shows a taste for excess that is almost Hollywood in its heyday, asking more to be envied than admired. Both can be assumed to be aspirational as outlooks on food rather than completely a reflection of their times.

2

The Social Context of Eating

Boys from Drumchapel don't order prawn cocktail. You'll have the soup.
(Jock Stein)

Regional differences were heavily determined by geographical and climatic factors. I explored some of them briefly in the last chapter. Social and political factors were often equally important determinants. Thus Sparta benefited from the rich valley of the Eurotas valley which appears to have produced specific types of lettuces, cucumbers, figs and other crops. This agricultural wealth seems to have produced luxurious feasting, according to a fragmentary poem of the seventh-century poet Alcman (fragment 19 PMG). But the militaristic political climate of the city state demanded the separation of fighting men from their families and a rigorous regime of austerity. The Hellenistic author Dicacarchus (quoted by Athenaeus 4.141a–d) describes how the mess worked: barley-cake, wine, and a small piece of meat in the infamous black soup are given to all. Olives, cheese, figs, fish, hare or ring-doves may also be provided. Other writers suggest that seasonal foods might also be brought to the mess, and confirm that birds and game were also brought. The *sussitia* or male messes were what caught the eye, as they did in Crete (Athenaeus gives sources for the latter at 4.143a–f). Dicaearchus shows a system in Sparta that used local produce effectively, but was rigidly confined within the social structure. Sparta seems to have been a city state whose food was 'Spartan', in the modern sense, and not luxurious in the Classical period. It was pointedly opposed to luxury, as Athenaeus shows by producing a critique from a Sybarite, whose city epitomized luxury in ancient thought (4.138d). That is not to say that they failed to eat a good diet, since there were clear ideas of the dietary needs of soldiers in antiquity (see below) and we can be certain that the Spartan army did not march on an empty stomach.

Conversely, much of Attica is rocky and infertile, with only limited agricultural land of quality (see Chapter 1). This apparently unpromising agricultural provision did not prevent the development of a great city under tyrannical and then democratic government. Much of this development was based on looking outwards overseas, and bringing to Athens goods that she could not grow for herself. Many cities in the Greek and Roman worlds were similarly shaped both by their social formation and by ideologies based upon those structures. Rome is the greatest example of a city that became a world leader on the basis of military conquest in Italy and overseas, and yet still felt (in some minds at least) that her identity lay in her simple agricultural origins in the Tiber valley.

Political and social structures greatly influenced the foods eaten and styles in which they were consumed. Meat was always a high-status food because of the cost of production, but other foods often played a large part. Also significant were the size and number of houses – what proportion of a city's homes had space dedicated to cooking and to dining? – the shape of rooms, and the types of furniture. Tableware and furniture often contributed to social display at banquets at least as much as new and unusual foods. Social structures dictated which guests were thought appropriate and which not: whether or not women could be invited to a formal meal; whether or not a principle of equality obtained among the diners.

In most ancient cities we know most about the eating habits of the rich, but this chapter will not focus relentlessly on elites alone. For food guaranteed (or not) the biological survival of all, and in a social sense marked the life cycle of nearly all, the rituals of birth, marriage and death. Foods also marked the religious year and the calendar, in public and private feasting which often included all citizens, and sometimes slaves. Status normally determined the quality of food that was eaten, but other factors also came into play, notably the work-rate of certain jobs that required a high-calorie diet. Thus manual workers, slaves, athletes and soldiers required more food than average if they were to serve their social function. Galen shows, as we shall see, that an 'ordinary' person would be made ill by the diet of an athlete or manual worker.

Thus, in Greco-Roman culture, as in most others, the consumption of food was deeply embedded in the social system. Meals revealed status or the lack of it, and were rarely if ever occasions where a person simply refuelled in a socially neutral way. We shall find that poorer people were more likely to eat the products of local agriculture, while the rich were able to supplement the traditional diet with imports and expensive tableware. Other features will be more difficult to distinguish: eating in private and in public are not always easy for us to disentangle. Then, the distinction between sacred eating and secular eating is often blurred. Many ancient texts praise tradition in eating, especially if it is enshrined in religious ritual. This praise often complements denunciation of markets and commercial development. Yet, as we shall see, markets were central to the distribution of food, and commercial activity was built into the supply of foods even to temples. Some of the more extreme comment therefore that appears to be socially directed in fact belongs to the ethical theory of philosophers which is examined in Chapter 7.

This chapter begins with one of the most complete descriptions of a meal that has survived from antiquity. This meal is also, according to Athenaeus 3.126e, the most sumptuous ever seen at that date (about 300 BC). Athenaeus may or may not be right about that, but his statement enables us at least to consider his definition of sumptuousness and to think of any counter examples. Hippolochus the Macedonian gives details of a wedding breakfast in a letter to his correspondent Lynceus of Samos:

> In Macedonia, as I said, when Caranus had his wedding feast, the men invited numbered twenty [or 120]. The instant they reclined on the couches, they were given silver drinking cups, one each as a gift. They were crowned, too, each before entering the room, with a golden headband. The cost of each was five gold staters. When they had emptied the cups, on a bronze plate of Corinthian construction, they were given a loaf of bread as big as the plate. Also chickens, ducks, pigeons, a goose and a vast amount of such things all heaped up. Each guest took it and handed it over, plate and all, to his slaves behind him. Many other varied dishes were served, after which followed a second silver plate, on which again there was a great loaf, geese, hares, young goats, other elaborate breads, woodpigeons, doves, partridges, and a great number of other fowls. 'We gave these too to the slaves', he explains, 'and when we'd had our fill of eating, we washed our hands. Then many garlands of all sorts of flowers were brought in and on top of all this, golden tiaras of equal weight with the first.'

On top of all this, Hippolochus says that Proteas, the descendant of the Proteas who was son of Lanice nurse of King Alexander, drank heavily (he was a big drinker like his grandfather Proteas who accompanied Alexander) and drank a toast to everyone. Hippolochus then writes as follows: 'when we had pleasantly removed ourselves from a sober state, flute girls rushed in along with musicians and sambuca-players from Rhodes. I thought they were naked but people told me they were wearing tunics. They sang an opening song and went away. Other girls came in each carrying two jars of myrrh joined together with a golden strap. One jar was of silver, the other of gold; and was *kotule*-size. They gave these jars to each guest. The next thing to come in was a statement of wealth rather than a dinner. It was a silver plate gilded to a considerable thickness and big enough to take a whole roast pig, and a large one at that. It was lying on its back and revealed its stomach to be full of many good things. Inside it were roasted thrushes, ducks . . .'

The account continues with more drinking, more meat courses, entertainments (including tableaux), and more extravagant gifts. (For translation and notes see further Dalby 1988.) Hippolochus specifically contrasts this feast with the parsimonious fare on offer at the Athenian festivals and schools of philosophy.

The meal is a special occasion. I discuss weddings further below. The time and place are very significant. The end of the fourth and the early part of the third century BC saw dramatic changes in eating that paralleled social and political change. As the city states of the Greek world came to be dominated or entirely governed by the Macedonians and the successors of Alexander, the influence of Macedonian practice was felt. As time went on, and the successor monarchies established themselves and competed with each other in power and magnificence, forms of eating were adapted. In his introduction to this passage (4.128b), Athenaeus tells us that Hippolochus and Lynceus exchanged a number of letters describing banquets attended by the successors of Alexander. In one letter, now lost, Lynceus described the celebration of the festival of Aphrodite at Athens by King Antigonus (a Macedonian nobleman), while King Ptolemy (perhaps Ptolemy II: see Dalby 2000: 374) also dined in Athens. A further letter described a dinner given to the Macedonian ruler of Athens, Demetrius Poliorcetes (or 'Sacker of Cities'), by his mistress, the courtesan Lamia (for this meal, possibly in a brothel, see Dalby loc. cit). The Successors to Alexander were in a political sense spreading their influence over the eastern Mediterranean. But in a wider cultural sense they consolidated that power by travelling to Athens to eat, sometimes at a festival, sometimes at a less religious occasion. This mixture of Macedonian power with festive dining in a Greek polis is comparable to the festival of the Ptolemaia, instituted in Alexandria in honour of the first Ptolemy by Ptolemy II and Arsinoe, but partly based on the model of the Dionysia festivals held in city states such as Athens (see Chapter 3). The Ptolemaia is an event also recorded by Athenaeus, whose possible interest in these events is discussed below.

The Century before the Meal of Caranus

This international dining by the successors of Alexander comes at the end of a century which seems to be very important in the history of ancient dining. At the end of the previous century (405 BC), Aristophanes has Dionysus make a punning remark in his *Frogs* (85), whereby dining with the Macedonians is equated with idealized dining among the blessed departed. A number of lavish meals (whether fictional or not is uncertain) served in Athens in this period reveal Macedonian and Thracian influences. A comic account in a play of Anaxandrides, the *Protesilaus* (fragment 41), boasts an Athenian meal that surpasses a lavish wedding meal for the Athenian Iphicrates, given by the bride's father, the Thracian king, Cotys. Other texts confirm that the Athenian elite were looking north when laying on competitive displays of foods at banquets. The Thracians with their silverware, the Macedonians with their palatial homes, hunting traditions and meat-eating seem to have made an impact on their southern neighbours. Tensions are clear in Athenian literature between an ideology of comparative poverty and simplicity and the competitive desires of the rich to imitate the customs of the emerging power of Macedon. Mnesimachus, another Athenian comic poet of the fourth century, describes a lavish meal in his play *The Horsebreeder*, which seems to show a member of the Athenian cavalry dining far from simply in cedar-roofed halls reminiscent of Macedonian palaces. Also from the same period is the *Attic Dinner* of Matro of Pitane, an epic parody describing in verse an elaborate meal in Athens. These early signs were written much more clearly at the end of the century when the Macedonians controlled the Greek world, and meals were put on in Athens for them, as described by the letters of Hippolochus.

Also influential were developments in Sicily in the fifth and fourth centuries BC. Here too there were courts which gathered both the resources of rich agricultural land and discerning eaters who might eat with pleasure. The Syracusan tyrant Dionysius II was said by Satyrus in his Lives (= Athenaeus 12.541c) to have had a series of rooms in his palace which held thirty couches. In addition to this vast capacity, the tyrant in popular thought had unlimited access to pleasures. Xenophon in his dialogue *Hiero*, named after the fifth-century Syracusan tyrant, brings out (1.17–23) the sated palate of the tyrant, weary of elaborate food (*peritta*) and pungent and tart flavours, and endless access to laden tables, in contrast to the ordinary citizen who only gets treats at festival times. From Sicily come the first cookery books in Greek, those of Mithaecus and Archestratus, and a culture which promoted pleasure. Archestratus offers recipes with the pungent and tart flavours (*oxea* and *drimea*, in fragments 9, 23, 24, 37, 38 Olson & Sens 2000) similar to those mentioned by Xenophon's Hiero. These pleasures appear to have been exported to the Greek mainland, where cooks (some of them Sicilian) appear, for example, in Athens, as reported by Plato (*Republic* 373c4), the Hippocratic doctors (*Regimen* I), Xenophon (*Memorabilia* 2.1.30) and a number of Attic comedies (see Wilkins 2000, ch. 7). These Athenian cooks were not attached to courts but were available for hire in the market place or elsewhere. Rich citizens were thus enabled to serve food of distinction which marked them out from other members of the elite, and allowed an element of competitive display. These citizens could afford to hire additional staff above the slaves and servants normally in charge of food preparation in their households. The hiring of cooks appears to have developed in the fourth century BC, along with other features of luxury noted in Chapter 7.

These cooks have a lot to say for themselves in Greek comedies. They are stock characters like the courtesan and the parasite. They probably reflect a social reality to some extent, but are mainly used by the comic poets to bring together the heat of the kitchen with the rhetoric and brilliance of the dining room. So the cook emerges to make numerous claims about the excellence of his skills, rather as a modern TV chef or restaurateur might do. There is the same combination of provisioning and cooking skills with big claims and big money. But if we consider the patrons of these hired cooks, they are choosing to employ cooking experts in the place of their own slaves, and to display their access to novel and possibly international forms of cookery. Archestratus is a particularly interesting product of this century, at the end of which come the meals of the kings post-Alexander that we have discussed above, and the inauguration of all the other facets of kingly power in the Hellenistic age.

Archestratus came from Gela in Sicily and wrote a poem in epic verse called *Hedupatheia (The Life of Luxury)*. It is humorous but also makes claims to distinction, and speaks to a reader who is imagined to travel throughout the Mediterranean in search of the best fish and other foods. Inexpensive foods are rudely dismissed: he distinguishes his diners from those who eat vegetable side dishes of all kinds (fr. 9 Olson & Sens) and dismisses 'all those other desserts [which] are a sign of wretched poverty, boiled chickpeas, broad beans, apples and dried figs' (fr.60.13–15 Olson & Sens, trans. Wilkins).

Archestratus is part of this apparent expansion in sophisticated eating in the fourth century BC. His poem on cookery and travel was not the first of its kind. Earlier a fellow Sicilian, Mithaecus, had written a cookery book in prose. It is likely, as we have seen, that more pretentious dining developed in the Greek world in the cities of southern Italy and Sicily where the courts of tyrants provided the conditions necessary for the production of culinary literature. Goody (1982) identifies such conditions as an agricultural surplus, a group of discerning eaters who might prefer one mode of preparation over another, and writing. It is probably the last condition that caused cookery books to appear around 400 BC rather than in the sixth century when the rich cities of Sybaris and Croton flourished. Prose treatises were not written on any subject before the mid-fifth century, with Hippocratic medical treatises and scientific philosophical works leading the way. Alongside the texts, these professional cooks were also for hire. There were no restaurants in the ancient world: people generally ate on a reciprocal basis, rather like the aristocratic societies of Europe prior to the early nineteenth century when restaurants were developed. In the absence of the restaurant, people with surplus income in antiquity could hire a chef who would buy, prepare and serve food either with the household slaves or with his own retinue of assistants. The term *hedupatheia*, or 'the experience of pleasure' or 'the life of luxury' – the title in fact of the poem of Archestratus – is first found in the treatises of Xenophon and is related to shopping for fine food and other pleasurable activities. Then, too, the social dangers of 'luxury' or *truphe* are increasingly stressed from the end of the fifth century onwards, particularly in the texts of such fourth-century historians as Theopompus and Timaeus. The Greek world of the fourth century was thus ready for the influx of Macedonian wealth as Philip II and Alexander the Great came increasingly to dominate the Greek cities. Macedonian meals were sometimes identified as militaristic. A fragment (7) of an Athenian comedy, the *Philip* of Mnesimachus (apparently about Philip II of Macedon), appears to describe a Macedonian meal in which spears and weaponry are mixed up with the courses and furniture. It may be, too, that when Archestratus advises a small number of diners in order to avoid what he calls a tentful of mercenaries at table (fragment 4 Olson & Sens), he has Macedonians in mind:

> Everyone should dine at a single table set for an elegant meal.
> Let the total company be three or four,
> Or at any rate no more than five; for after that you would have
> A mess-group of rapacious mercenary soldiers.

Mercenaries were, however, a widespread feature of the unstable Greek world in general in the fourth century BC.

Archestratus emphasizes fish. He belongs to the world of elite eaters and the high-protein diet. But it is an elegant elite that praises the simple elegance of bread, barley preparations, the best fish with restrained flavouring. Dismissed are Sicilian cooks (the ones I linked with the tyrants' courts perhaps) who added cheese flavours to fish. As in many modern cuisines therefore, there were layers of good dining. Some concentrated on the display of wealth, such as Caranus; others on rich and complex flavours (those criticized by Archestratus); while others sought elegance and simplicity (see further Wilkins & Hill 1994: 21–4, Olson & Sens 2000: lii–lv).

Simplicity as a subset of elegant dining is an important feature of formal eating in many periods, including the present, as Shaun Hill discusses in his introduction. Simplicity feeds through also into much literary representation of food. As we shall see in Chapter 9, Aristophanes represents the rural way of life as idyllic and untainted by the corrupting money of the city, while the moralizing poetry of Horace, Juvenal, Ovid and pseudo-Virgil locates good eating among the Roman peasantry.

The Centuries after Caranus

Having examined briefly the century before Alexander, I now consider first the impact of these developments on Rome, and then the picture that Athenaeus is drawing for us with all this material. This will consolidate our emphasis on dining among the elite, which makes an impact in most cultures far greater than is warranted by their proportion in the population. I then turn to the majority of the population.

The lavish courts of the Hellenistic kings, such as the Seleucids and the later Ptolemies, continued to put on extravagant displays, which included banquets. The competitive nature of such feasting is brought out, again by Athenaeus, when a new player emerged, the growing city of Rome. In the second century BC, Rome was able to conquer Macedon, and the general Aemilius Paulus put on impressive games. Not wishing to be outdone, reports Athenaeus (5. 194c–195f, quoting Polybius), the Seleucid monarch Antiochus IV Epiphanes put on a splendid festival in the royal park at Daphne near Antioch. There was a great display of Thracian, Macedonian and Roman weaponry, followed by sacred images, sacrificial animals, women in litters adorned with precious metals, costly oils of saffron, fenugreek and other plants, and banquets of 1,000 or 1,500 triclinia (couches grouped in threes).

Such shows contributed to the displays of wealth seen in later Roman triumphs. On the one hand these were considered un-Roman (see Chapter 7) but on the other they heralded the ever-greater processions of wealth and banqueting in Rome that eventually brought the imperial forms of dining of Augustus and his successors. There are two points to add, which are dealt with later in this chapter. First, much of the discussion so far has concerned rulers: we must consider too the competitive elites within Greek and Roman cities. Second, banquets and other forms of eating are often a sub-set of other displays of wealth, such as a palatial home, gold and silverware, or a vast retinue of slaves. Competitive dining may be satisfied by these related displays of wealth rather than developments specifically concerning the food itself.

Athenaeus on the Greco-Roman Fusion

We can trace the Greek influence on Rome in another way, through the presentation of Athenaeus. The letter by Hippolochus that records the meal of Caranus is a very valuable document. It is preserved by Athenaeus partly for its rarity (we might compare his unique preservation of Archestratus and Matro and a number of comic texts that describe banquets), but that rarity is significant. Many texts do not describe at exhaustive length the great series of dishes served at formal meals. The details pall after a while, unless they have the added spice of a satirical tone or some other narrative device. This is what Petronius aims for in the dinner of Trimalchio discussed in Chapter 9; a less than omniscient narrator adds further comedy to the absurdities of the host. Indeed there is a similar element in Hippolochus' own narrative, where he is not the omniscient narrator but is in need of the opinions of others (on the subject of the musicians' see-through clothes). But what details we are given! There are many courses of meat and fowls. This is not paralleled often in texts from the Greek cities in earlier periods, but is found in Roman meals, including the dinner of Trimalchio. There is a roast pig stuffed with birds, pulses and seafood. The stuffing of one animal with another also appears in Roman banquets. There is much reference to bread and cereal products. Perhaps because the meal of Caranus is a wedding, there are many gifts for the guests. This is clearly marked and extensive. It is underlined by a number of references to the wealth on display and on offer. This is a distributive meal which requires further discussion, since the distribution of food, whether by the city state or individual benefactor, was at many periods a form of self-definition and political influence. Then there is much emphasis on the furniture and table furniture, the size of dishes and the metal from which they were made. The room in which the meal takes place is specially contrived to reveal features previously hidden by fabrics. In the Roman period, mechanical versions of this contrivance were a regular feature of lavish meals, as reported by Seneca and Petronius, and as used by Nero in his Golden House. This too requires further analysis. There is much entertainment during the meal. There are comparisons with the frugality of Athens. There are several new beginnings, when water and garlands are brought in. This too I discuss below. Then, most significantly, the guests are given wine as soon as they arrive. This parallels Homeric practice, but it is conventionally thought that drinking (at the symposium) followed the food part of the Greek meal, or the *deipnon*. I discuss below the probable ordering of food and drink at the Greek meal. At all events, the Macedonian practice parallels Roman practice, and that followed by Athenaeus at the meals for his wise diners in the *Deipnosophistae*. Athenaeus does not explicitly say that Roman dining practices were strongly influenced by the Macedonians rather than the smaller Greek states, but he perhaps implies as much by placing the meal of Caranus at the head of his book on meals (book 4). The cook of the Deipnosophistae also serves a stuffed pig very similar to the one served by Caranus (9.376c–d, noted by

Dalby 1988), though there is a possibility that this may be a literary allusion by Athenaeus rather than a reflection of Roman practice.

Athenaeus also draws attention, as we have seen, to the contrast with Athens and compares the influence of Macedon on the competing kings of the Hellenistic world, many of whom had been Macedonian generals and were the successors to the power of Alexander the Great. The final striking feature of the meal of Caranus is the trumpet blast at the conclusion of the meal, which Hippolochus notes is a Macedonian practice at large meals (there are twenty diners at this meal). There is a similar use of the trumpet at the meal of Trimalchio, and the practice is attested elsewhere in Roman culture, particularly in a military context. We noted at the beginning of the chapter the unparalleled sumptuousness of the meal of Hippolochus. That sumptuousness (*poluteleia*) is precisely the distinctive feature of the meals offered by Larensis, the Roman host of the Deipnosophists at Athenaeus' fictional meals at the end of our period. On these issues in Athenaeus see further pp. 27 and 274–5, and Dalby 1996: 152–83.

The Eating and Diet of the Majority of the Population

The demographic structures of ancient cities and rural areas are varied, complex and changed over time. For the purposes of this book they are best reviewed in the essays collected in Garnsey (1998), with the accompanying bibliography. Ancient texts often divide populations comparatively, into the richer and poorer or better or worse members of society. In this book, when reference is made to urban elites, what is meant is less than 10 per cent of the population. As for the other 90 per cent+, some of this number lived in considerably better circumstances than others, in both town and country. It was generally the case that when food supplies to the population were threatened, which was not rare, as both Galen and Garnsey (1988, 1998) make clear, food shortages tended to hit the countryside before the town and the poorer before the richer. As far as the elites were concerned, the main dangers of food shortages were not to their food supplies but to political stability.

The majority of ancient populations lived the hard life of the subsistence farmer or landless labourer, which was insufficient to guarantee enough food for the family unit in all years. This majority of the population enjoyed food that was in modern terms 'organic' and 'pure', but with the major downsides that supplies were not guaranteed and that quality might often be poor. Thus Galen tells us that peasants in Mysia sent their wheat to the cities while the farmers themselves ate the cheaper and inferior grains. Galen tells us furthermore that certain foods were avoided in general, and fed to animals. However, they became human food when shortages struck home. He thus draws important boundaries between human and animal foods. If the peasants sometimes ate animal food, did that make them closer to beasts themselves in the eyes of city dwellers? In some people's eyes this certainly was the case. These issues are explored in Chapters 4 and 7.

Poorer citizens in towns also ate less well than the rich. Distinctions were often pointed out, as Juvenal does in an extreme form in *Satire* 5. The poor were more likely to eat out in public places, or at least to buy take-away food. They were less able to buy slaves who might prepare the food and had less space in which to organize the cooking of food, particularly if they lived in Roman insulae, or apartments. There is plentiful evidence of bars for take-away food and drink in Pompeii and Athens, together with textual evidence for the bars sometimes combined with shops, or *kapeleia*, in Greek cities (Figure 2.1). These have been well discussed in Davidson 1997, though in Chapter 6 I challenge some of the conclusions he draws.

In Greek and Roman culture, the food of the rich was not utterly different from that of the poor, as is the case in a number of cultures. To be sure, some imports in the Roman Empire were likely to be restricted to the rich, such as Indian spices, exotic birds and expensive fish. But poor people had locally grown spices such as thyme and coriander, local birds such as thrushes and blackbirds and shoaling fish such as sardines and anchovies. A striking example of the rich eating superior versions of the diet of the poor is provided once again by the poem of Archestratus. In fragment 5 Olson & Sens (2000), Archestratus declares, on the subject of bread:

> The best to get hold of and the finest of all, cleanly bolted from barley with a good grain, is in Lesbos, in the wave-surrounded breast of famous Eresos. It is whiter than snow from the sky; if the gods eat barley groats then Hermes must come and buy it for them from there. (trans. Wilkins)

Wheat is mentioned later in the fragment. But Galen and many ancient texts declare barley far inferior to wheat, principally because it

FIGURE 2.1   Bars on street corners are plentiful in the streets of Pompeii and Herculaneum and were doubtless also found in many other ancient towns. The pitchers built into the counters contained wine (hot and cold) and also food to be taken away. The choice of food on the premises or to take away is not exclusive to the modern world.

lacks gluten to allow the making of good bread. In fourth-century Greece, then, the rich were not urged merely to eat the superior grain, wheat, that the poor could not afford. They might also choose barley, which the poor enjoyed in mashes, porridges and flat cakes, but which the rich could enjoy for flavour, but in a highly refined and expensive version. The rich certainly did not want to avoid cereal products, as is clear at the meals of Caranus, Philoxenus and Matro; that is not to say that they did not wish to enjoy a superior version to which the poor could not aspire. Cereals are discussed further in Chapter 4. (For the meals of Philoxenus and Matro see Dalby 1987, Wilkins 2000, Olson & Sens 1998.)

A second example of the rich eating the same flavours as the poor is provided by imported silphium. Archestratus (fragment 46.14) criticizes cooks who use silphium and cheese to flavour expensive fish. A poorer person might have a head of local garlic to flavour sardines

(Aristophanes *Wasps* 679). (For the flavours of Greco-Roman food see p. 3 and Wilkins & Hill 1992.)

Archestratus identified vegetables, chick peas, beans, apples and figs as signs of poverty. This is a somewhat extreme formulation. But there is some echo of this in a fragment from the play *The Olynthian Woman* of the fourth-century comic poet Alexis (167):

> My husband is impoverished, I am an old woman, and we have a daughter, another child (a son) and this good girl here. Five of us altogether. If three of us have dinner, the other two must share with them a small barley-cake. We wail unmusical sounds whenever we have nothing. Our skin gets pale when we have no food. The portions and the whole of our life are: a broad bean, a lupin seed, some vegetable leaves, < . . . > a turnip, some *ochros* (a pulse), vetch, a Valonia acorn, a tassel-hyacinth bulb, a cicada, a chick-pea, a wild pear, and the 'mother's care', planted by a god, a dried fig I mean, invention of a fig tree in Phrygia. (trans. Wilkins)

Paupers are rare in comedy, though the food of the poor is sometimes referred to in passing, such as mallow in the *Wealth* of Aristophanes, for example (see pp. 136–7). But in that passage, there is a sharp reminder that the diet of beggars is under discussion rather than what a poorer citizen might expect.

Alexis here, however, coincides with the comments of Archestratus as far as the chick pea and fig are concerned. We may note that the impoverished family has no meat, no fish, and a high level of cereal and pulse, which is nutritious in modern terms, but lacks the status-quality of richer neighbours who might afford small fish and a little meat. The hungrier members of the family (and note there is no gender division here in the distribution of food) eat the staple barley-cake or *maza* in small quantities, while the other three have more varied nutrition. It coincides with the prescriptions of Galen six centuries later, as far as the vegetables and pulses consumed are concerned, and also in including the acorn and the locust or cicada. Pulses such as chick peas, chickling vetch and the other vetch known as *ochros* are part of the standard diet for Galen, while acorns are not. Like bitter vetch and tares, these are animal food. Acorns, says Galen, come in the category of famine food (2.38): 'once, when famine took hold of our land, and there was an abundance of mast and medlars, the country folk, who had stored them in pits, had them in place of cereals for the whole winter and into early spring. Before that, mast like this was pig food, but on this occasion they gave up keeping the pigs through winter as they had been accustomed to doing previously. At the start of winter, they slaughtered the pigs first and ate them; after that they opened the pits and, having suitably prepared the mast in various ways, ate it (trans. Powell).' This passage is discussed further in Chapter 4.

Acorn-eating was an emergency measure, as discussed by Mason 1995 and others. Acorns came further down the list of emergency foods than some other nuts, such as the chestnuts widely used in Europe and mentioned in Chapters 1 and 4. In this respect the family of Alexis' play have been reduced to animal food. The cicada is an interesting further element. There is evidence that cicadas and locusts were eaten in Greece: Aristophanes mentions them in a fragment (fr. 53) and in his *Acharnians* alludes to their crunchy texture. Such references are rare, though Aristotle, rather in the style of Galen, notes the way that country people catch them for eating purposes. It seems likely that locusts were eaten but not seen as a delicacy. They were on the fringes of the diet like other items eaten by the poor. We might compare foods that were shared with animals, though we should bear in mind that there is much overlap between human and animal foods. Note that the Greek staple of barley was considered animal food by the Romans and by Galen. Also comparable are snails and wild greens, which the Greeks still eat and which were eaten by all classes in antiquity. Galen does not actually mention cicadas or locusts. He dismisses wood grubs and other insects caten by the Egyptians, but his silence on locusts may indicate their lack of importance in the diet, or Galen's failure to notice them, or lack of interest on his part.

A hierarchy of foods clearly emerges from Galen's review of the diet, from the most refined foods of the urban elites to the foods normally reserved for animals, which the poor were forced to eat at times of shortage. Within these parameters there was much variation. Galen says that all the Greeks eat snails every day. The context is a comparison with the Egyptians who eat wood bugs, snakes and reptiles. Galen appears to be considering the Greek equivalent of unusual items in the diet. But he is also explicitly considering an item that is difficult to classify. It is, he says, neither winged nor aquatic, nor even obviously terrestrial. We might take this extraordinary statement about all the Greeks to mean that the snail was a staple of the mass of the population. Archaeological evidence for molluscs, both terrestrial and marine,

FIGURE 2.2   Although the locust was sometimes identified as the distinguishing food of distant peoples, Aristotle and others attest to the consumption of insects in Greece. Locusts were used in medicine, and, like the camel, indicate a wide dietary range in antiquity. Reproduced by permission of the Dean and Chapter of Exeter Cathedral

suggests that they were also consumed on palace sites (Karali 2000). As with barley, we may safely assume that molluscs were eaten by all classes of people. They were, in the words of Richard Maybe, 'food for free', but special specimens might be collected and served to rich diners. Athenaeus preserves a story about Apicius sailing to Libya to try their prawns, only to discover the prawns of Minturnae back home were better. Patience Gray (1986) offers striking testimony on snails and on the diet of the poor in general in different parts of the Mediterranean in the modern period.

Meat consumption was certainly lower for poorer citizens, since the price of meat was of necessity higher than that of fruits, vegetables, grains and pulses because of the inefficient use of energy in raising animals. For the majority of citizens, life was a vegetarian life for much of the year, with meat provided by the city state on festival days, and

supplements from wealthy citizens when they wished to feed the populace for certain political ends. Aristophanes represents such feeding of
citizens in his *Knights* as the corrupt feeding of a rather gullible child.
It became rather more extensive in the Hellenistic period through
public benefaction and the distribution of food by Hellenistic and Roman
rulers. (See further Schmitt-Pantel 1992, Veyne 1976, Donahue 2005.)

It might be thought that the organic diet of fresh food for the majority
of the ancient population was healthy if not of the highest quality.
Quality counts for much, both in self-esteem and in health concerns,
as Galen and Juvenal make clear. We might think that Juvenal is
exaggerating in his contrast between the diet of the rich Roman patron
and his poor client in *Satire* 5:

> My lord will have his mullet, imported from Corsica or from the rocks
> below Taormina . . . But what's in store for you? An eel, perhaps (though
> it looks like a water snake), or a grey-mottled river-pike, born and bred
> in the Tiber, bloated with sewage. (trans. Green)

However, the broad picture of the poor fish of the Tiber is supported
by Galen (Wilkins 2004). Juvenal highlights the low self-esteem of the
client, Galen the damage to his digestion.

This theme is taken further in two striking passages in Galen's *On
the Powers of Foods*. Everyone has a different constitution in Galen's
system, but nevertheless he did manage to make some generalizations
about the peasant diet. These should be compared with the overview
of the human diet discussed in Chapter 8. First, the dangers of eating
cheese with bread:

> If one also adds cheese to the bread, as holiday-makers [viz people
> on feast days] among our country folk usually prepare it (which they
> themselves call unleavened), there is certain harm for everybody, even if
> some of them are very strong in body constitution, such as those who
> are by nature the best reapers and ditch-diggers. For these people are
> observed to concoct unleavened breads better than the strongest athletes
> (as they also do beef and the meat of he-goats). What further need is
> there to mention sheep and female goats as well as these? In Alexandria,
> they eat donkey meat as well, and there are also some people who eat
> camel. For while custom contributes to their concoction, of no less
> importance is the small amount taken and the depletion of the body as
> a whole that necessarily accompanies those who toil throughout the day
> at their proper activities. For the depleted flesh snatches up from the
> stomach not only half-concocted but even, when they work after a meal,

sometimes absolutely unconcocted chyme. This is why these people later suffer very troublesome illnesses and die before they reach old age. Ignorant of this, most people who see them eating and concocting what none of us can tackle and concoct, congratulate them on their bodily strength. Also, since very deep sleep occurs in those who undertake much hard labour, and this helps them with concoction to a greater degree, they are consequently less injured by harmful foods. But if you were to force them to stay awake for more nights in succession, they would immediately become ill. So these people have but this one advantage in the concoction of harmful foods. (Galen 1.2, trans. Powell)

This valuable passage demonstrates the difference between the labourer's constitution and that of his rich counterpart; the apparent strength of his digestion, but the cost in disease and early death, and in the dangers of country food after cooking. It is not merely a matter of poor ingredients but unwise combinations. On the positive side, though, we might note that Galen attests to their meat-eating, though not to its frequency. Galen has more to say on the hazards of country cooking in a passage on wheats boiled in water (1.7):

But once when walking in the country far from the city, with two lads of my own age, I myself actually came upon some rustics who had had their meal and whose womenfolk were about to make bread (for they were short of it). One of them put the wheat into the pot all at once and boiled it. Then they seasoned it with a moderate amount of salt and asked us to eat it. Reasonably enough, since we had been walking and were famished, we set to it with a will. We ate it with gusto, and felt a heaviness in the stomach, as though clay seemed to be pressing upon it. Throughout the next day we had no appetite because of indigestion, so that we could eat nothing, were full of wind and suffered from headaches and blurred vision. For there was not even any bowel action, which is the only remedy for indigestion. I therefore asked the rustics whether they themselves also ever ate boiled wheat and how they were affected. They said that they had often eaten it under the same necessity that we had experienced, and that wheat prepared in this way was a heavy food, difficult to concoct. (trans. Powell)

In this scene, the peasants have access to the premier cereal, wheat, but all the same are not able to prepare it in the ideal way. They therefore benefit less from it than if it were in the ideal form of leavened bread. Necessity forces them to refuel even before the fuel can be prepared as needed. Peasants are thus liable to suffer from lower quality and less appropriate preparation. Compare Garnsey (1999). We might note, too, for the discussion of gender later in this chapter, that women bake the bread, but it is the men who talk to the three strangers when they appear in the fields, and who cook the emergency boiled wheat.

Galen's anecdotes offer valuable testimony to the eating practices of the poor. A final report from Galen will add a further dimension. In his discussion of milk (3.14), he illustrates the dangers of unwholesome milk:

> In an infant, when the first nurse had died, and another who was full of unhealthy humour was providing the milk for him, his whole body was obviously infected with numerous ulcers. When famine had taken hold in the spring, the second nurse had lived on wild herbs in the field. So she and some others in the same country who had lived in the same way were filled with such ulcers. We observed this in many others who were living in a similar way in the area. (trans. Powell)

The wet-nurse, a poor woman who was feeding the baby of a wealthier mother, was suffering from malnutrition, the chronic state of the poor in many Mediterranean countries in the early spring before the new season's crops became available. Time and again Galen refers to the pressure, on the rural population in particular, when winter stores had run down and the poor were forced to turn to animal food. Garnsey (1999) comments on endemic food shortages in antiquity. This is paralleled in the modern period by Gray (1986), Camporesi (1993) and Helstosky (2004), among others. The last (p. 11) quotes a Neapolitan commentary of 1884 on the urban poor: 'One woman dispenses charity in a most ingenious fashion. She herself is poor and eats only boiled maccheroni seasoned with a little bit of sharp cheese, but her neighbor, who is very poor, has only a few morsels of dry, hard bread to eat. The woman who is less poor gives her neighbor the water in which her maccheroni was cooked, a whitish liquid that is spilled onto morsels of bread, making them softer and giving them at least a flavour of maccheroni.'

On eating out among the poor, Heltosky (2004: 16) quotes the same source, Matilde Serao, *Ventre di Napoli*: 'With one or two *soldi*, one could afford a piece of boiled octopus, or snails in broth, or hot foods like maccheroni, served at the numerous *osterie*: "in all the streets in the worker's neighborhoods there were osterie that have stoves set up out-of-doors. Here the maccheroni is always boiling and there are pans containing tomato sauce and mountains of grated cheese . . . the portions are small and the buyer fights with the owner because he wants a little more sauce, a little more cheese, and a little more maccheroni".' Food shortages were noted in Chapter 1 in the reign of Louis XIV in France. Food supplies could not be guaranteed to the whole population in countries such as Greece, Italy, France or Britain until the twentieth century. Note that the ulcerous nurse in Galen's story, whose condition is not easy to specify (see Powell 2003: 181), was one of a number of people observed. The cause of the problem was 'wild herbs', in other words plants not 'softened' or cultivated by the process of agriculture. To be sure, many ate raw or wild plants in antiquity, and rich people like Pliny and Musonius Rufus encouraged it, as we shall see. But these non-farmed products retained something of the rawness of nature noted in the Hippocratic text on the *Art of Medicine* (quoted in Chapter 1) and were risky for people with humoural imbalance (see further Chapter 8).

The endemic risk of food shortage in the spring prompted a form of literature little found in the modern world, namely fantastic products imagined to exist in the land of Cockaigne (as it was called in its mediaeval version). In this land, rivers flowed with wine, barley-cakes and sausages, and fish and birds begged to be eaten. Athenaeus discusses a number of comic examples in Book Three (267e–70a): see Wilkins (2000). Comedy is a significant genre, for this is dramatic literature presented to mass audiences, often of more than ten thousand people. It would be less likely to succeed in a society such as Western Europe or the United States, where there is a surfeit of food. The endless descriptions of a food paradise where there is no need for the hard labour of agriculture or for slaves (the food produces and serves itself) speak as loudly as Galen of a world in which the poor at least frequently go hungry. Comedy also provided descriptions and lists of rich men's feasts for audiences to hear with mouth-watering relish. How this may have been heard by less privileged theatre audiences is considered in Chapter 9.

The human life-cycle

Discussion of the rural poor, at the opposite pole of society from the urban elites, gives a gloomy picture of ancient eating. It is certainly a gloomier picture than the one currently held of the Mediterranean world in northern Europe. We can lift the gloom somewhat by repeating that some of the population outside the elite did not survive merely at subsistence level. The standard protagonist in the plays of Aristophanes, for example, is a citizen of moderate means, and the antisocial farmer of Menander's comedy *Dyscolus* lives a Spartan life by choice. Cnemon fails to exploit the economic value of his farm. The pessimistic picture is also tempered by festivals in the religious year and by the key points of birth, marriage and death in the human life-cycle. Communal sacrifice to the gods often brought distribution of meat and other foods to all participants either at civic or at local level (see Chapter 3), and most families observed feasts for the birth of children or their integration into the community. Marriages were important occasions for feasting among the very rich, as shown in the Macedonian wedding quoted above, as also for much poorer families. A somewhat idealized rural marriage is described by Dio Chrysostom in his *Euboaean Oration* (7.65–80). The family feasts, with the men reclining on a rustic couch (*stibas*), and the bride's mother sitting down. There is much detail about arrangements for the food, seating arrangements of the diners, and the roles of bride and groom. The status of these people is hard to judge, because the issue lies at the centre of Dio's speech. I discuss a marriage in Chapter 3 between a rich urban family and a comparatively wealthy farmer's daughter.

Special diets

Certain people required a special diet. Manual workers have already been mentioned. If they did not receive adequate calories, the work could not be done. Some slaves were in a similar position. In a well-known passage in his work *On Agriculture* (56: see Dalby 1998: 140–1), Cato the Elder stipulates that the working slaves should receive a greater ration than the overseer: the need for energy outweighs status. The diet of slaves in general varied greatly. Some dined with the rest of the family, as noted in Chapter 7, for example, in the albeit unusual case of Cato the Elder. Others ate 'slave *maza* (porridge)' in the phrase of Aeschylus or 'slave bread' in the phrase of the archaic poet Archilochus. The relative merits of these diets we are not able easily to evaluate, as discussed in Chapter 4.

Other categories in need of a high-calorie diet were soldiers and athletes. There is rich evidence on the military diet, much of it gathered in the excellent article of Davies (1971), who details all categories of food and a wide range of primary sources and locations across the empire. He shows that the Roman army was well fed, that the logistics of provisioning were vast, and that a well-balanced diet was achieved. He particularly stresses the meat content of the diet, with fish and game also in settled conditions. Good generals and emperors ate the same food as their troops. Davies draws extensively on letters and graffiti from across the empire from Syria to Britain. He concludes (1971: 137–8), 'perhaps the best tribute to the army of the Principate, on campaign or in peace-time or even during the rare mutinies, is that there is no recorded complaint about the Roman military diet'. Armies that were not well fed did not perform well; discontented armies might turn on the emperor in the imperial period. Where the citizen soldier in the Greek world was thought to have a Spartan regime in his three days' rations (the regular, if misleading message from the plays of Aristophanes), Roman soldiers appear to have eaten better than average. Galen remarks that the Roman army did not recommend barley, because it provided inadequate energy in comparison with wheat (a claim not accepted by modern science: see Chapter 4). In the current British army, battlefield provisions of food are set at 4,000 calories a day, twice the standard male requirement. When Alexander's army was on the march, great feasts were eaten on frequent occasions in great tented dining halls (Plutarch). We saw too, in Chapter 1, the retinue of cooks who followed the Persian king and his generals on campaign. An army of occupation also, such as soldiers in Britain, at Vindolanda on Hadrian's wall, for example, enjoyed both local meat and some imported goods. Soldiers might therefore be the harbingers both of Roman government and other accompanying forms of civilization that spread to Britain in the wake of the armies. Olive oil and wine are two examples, but others include rabbits, rocket, and a wide range of fragrant plants. The same applies to other parts of the Roman Empire. We might compare the campaigns of Alexander which brought foods back to the Mediterranean from the East, and the campaigns of Romans in Asia Minor. We discussed Lucullus' introduction of the cherry into Italy in Chapter 1.

Athletes too, again in the ancient world as in the modern, needed high-energy diets. The Hippocratic doctors recognized the high-protein diet needed by athletes, and frequently noted the instability of such a regime, which could easily crash into bad health (Jouanna 1999: 331–2). Galen, who began his medical career in a gladiatorial school, finds that the two 'strongest' foods, wheat and pork, are essential for the athlete. An ordinary person, like Galen or his reader, could not possibly support the high-energy intake of the athlete, who is in a category apart, like the manual worker (*On the Powers of Foods* 1.2). These comments complement moral criticisms of athletes by the poets Xenophanes and Euripides, the latter calling an athlete the 'slave of his jaw and the victim of his stomach' (quoted by Athenaeus 10.413c –414c). The most famous athlete of antiquity, Milo of Croton, in anecdotes at least, lived up to the Galenic prescription (Athenaeus 10.412e–f): 'Milo of Croton, as Theodorus of Hierapolis says in his work *On Athletic Contests*, used to eat twenty pounds of meat and as many of bread, and he drank three pitchers of wine. And at Olympia he put a four-year-old bull on his shoulders and carried it round the stadium, after which he cut it up and ate it all alone in a single day' (trans. Gulick).

Eating alone

The key to ancient eating was commensality, sharing the table with others. Eating was not mere refuelling, it was an affirmation of family, kinship or civic and religious bonds. The spectre of the man who failed to eat with others was, like Milo of Croton, a grim reminder of social deviance. The tyrant was the example of the solitary eater: Xenophon's Hiero, noted above, makes this very point. The tyrant has all pleasures available to him, and as in Athenaeus' presentation of the Syracusan tyrant Dionysius II, enjoys both lavish banquets and as many virgins as he can abuse. Braund (1996) reviews the evidence. The tyrant is the bad ruler in ancient thought, with his appetites perhaps most powerfully presented in Plato's *Republic*. We should bear in mind, though, that royal courts, whatever their political deficiencies, were also generators of innovation. This is seen in the Persian king and elsewhere. The Sicilian courts seem to have developed Greek cooking and cookery books. Furthermore, Hellenistic courts promoted scientific and medical research, partly through fears of poisoning, and so stimulated, directly or not, the search for new products that might save the life of the monarch, but might also become the sensational new foodstuff. The diffusion of the citron might be an example of a food which spread westwards under such stimuli. On the similar transfer from the new world of tomatoes, chocolate and the potato to European courts, initially for their medical and other qualities and only much later as foodstuffs, and then foods for the masses, see Chapter 1.

Public and Private Space

In ancient cities from early times, the marketplace, or *agora* in Greek, *forum* in Latin, was the focus for political gatherings, and also for the exchange or purchase of goods, including foods. The marketplace in Athens in the fifth and fourth centuries BC sold many different foods, as did markets and fairs throughout the Greek and Roman worlds (Frayn 1993, Thompson & Wycherley 1972, Wilkins 2000). A city's ability to attract many goods for sale was a sign of prosperity particularly noted for Athens by Thucydides and Xenophon, and for Rome by Aelius Aristeides, though other authors deplored commercial activity (as discussed in Chapter 7). There were specialist meat markets, fish markets, and markets for other categories of product.

Also in public areas were civic buildings in which dining took place, both daily dining for state officials, such as the tholos, thesmotheteion and many other offices in Athens, and buildings for honorific dining. In Greek cities such buildings were the prytaneia, which contained the sacred hearth of the city and in some ways represented the city's identity (Miller 1978). Honorific dining in the prytaneion of Athens, for example, was reserved for the descendants of the tyrant-killers, Olympic victors, and other distinguished citizens, along with foreign guests. Athenaeus tells us (4.149d–e) that in his native city of Naucratis in Egypt, on the authority of Hermeias in book 2 of *On the Gryneian Apollo*, there were special regulations for eating. The meal in the prytaneion on the feast day of Hestia prytanis and at the Dionysia, following appropriate prayers and libations, was served to diners on couches and consisted of wine, two types of bread, pork, a vegetable, eggs, cheese, dried figs, a flat cake and a garland. There were fines if the meal was more extensive than this; extra food could not be brought in; leftovers were fed to the slaves of those present. On other days, fish was allowed in the prytaneion. No women were allowed, except a piper.

Much eating in antiquity took place in the private space of the home, whether royal palace or more modest dwelling. Some homes had sufficient space to dedicate a room to dining, but others, the vast majority, did not. Larger homes with more slaves might have kitchens. Roman aristocrats, from the emperor down, had extensive kitchens; many smaller homes had none (Ellis 2000: 27–8, 158–9). Greek and Roman ovens, for example, might be built into a kitchen but more often were a portable item that could be set up outside when weather

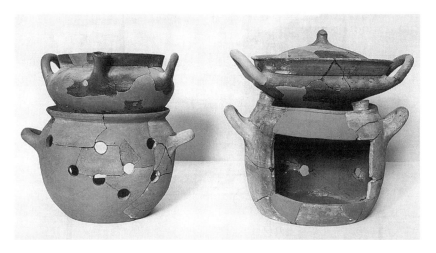

FIGURE 2.3   Most Greeks and Romans did not have dedicated kitchens. If they cooked at home, they used small portable stoves and pans, like these from the Athenian market area, which could be taken outside where possible. The small size of the utensils and absence of gas and electricity does not necessarily imply less sophisticated cooking than in a modern kitchen. Reproduced by kind permission of the American School of Classical Studies: Agora Excavations

permitted (Sparkes 1962, Liversidge in Flower & Rosenbaum 1958: 29–38). Even where families were wealthy enough to hire cooks, the cook often expected to bring his own slaves and his own utensils. There seems to have been much variation in this regard. In Menander's *Dyscolus*, for example, the cook brings furniture but needs to borrow cooking pots. Special arrangements had to be made for the reception of guests who were not kin, especially in cities like Classical Athens where the segregation of women was practised. Such segregation could be achieved in a number of ways. If it was a large house, a special room, or *andron*, might be provided. Meals could also be provided alfresco (see below). In Menander's *Dyscolus*, segregation is achieved in the open air. Eating also took place in public areas, in state buildings and religious precincts. Religious festivals were probably the main focus for such eating. Public occasions could also be celebrated in the home: the Rural Dionysia in Attica appears to be an example, where the community celebrated the festival, but each family used their own home to do so (Parker 1987). There were also many different kinds of meal to be catered for. The inscriptions of Asia Minor and Rome

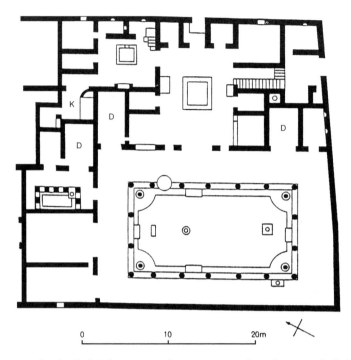

FIGURE 2.4   In classical Athens, many homes seem to have been small. In later centuries, richer citizens throughout the Roman empire built large town and country houses which had indoor and outdoor dining facilities. Often, as here in the House of the Vetii at Pompeii, more than one dining room appears to have been needed. D = dining room, K = kitchen

studied by Schmitt-Pantel 1992 and Donahue 2005 record an enormous variety of meals and entertainment offered by politicians and individual benefactors. These might include a little sweet wine and light entertainment, religious feasts or political rallies. Such public feasting constituted a major form of patronage and redistribution. Variety is seen too in the supreme example of the Roman emperor. Suetonius describes the eating habits of the emperor Augustus at private dinners (*Aug.* 70), at political meals (74), at festivals such as the Saturnalia, and finally in the informal eating that he enjoyed when alone. In the last instance, he snacked on the hoof, very much in the modern fashion (see pp. 271–2). Almost all free people in antiquity ate sometimes more formally than on other occasions, perhaps once or twice a year, perhaps daily if they were rich and powerful.

There were also shops and bars which offered food and drink on a commercial basis, either to eat in or take away. These *kapeleia, popinae* or *tabernae* were often viewed with grave suspicion by the rich: Theopompus denounces the demagogic bars of Byzantium; Juvenal sneers at the bars of Rome. Elsewhere, bars are often identified with prostitution. Galen suggests human flesh was served at certain inns (*On the Powers of Food* 3.1). On the other hand, Varro in his work on agriculture identifies a wayside inn as a desirable commercial option for the farmer if the farm lay beside a busy road. Many of these distinctions probably looked different from the perspective of citizens outside the elite. There is plentiful evidence for bars and taverns in Pompeii and Herculaneum (Laurence 1994). They are to be found on many street corners. They seem to have been important for the provision of food and drink (hot or cold in both cases), and for providing flexible modes of eating, whether indoors or outside. Travellers as well as local citizens needed food and sometimes accommodation at the larger-scale inns. We should imagine a wide range from the large inn to the small take-away stall. (See further Kleberg 1957.)

In addition to the built environment, open spaces also provided many opportunities for eating al fresco. Notable examples are described in many different texts. Tents were set up at the Thesmophoria festival to provide shelter for an all-women celebration of Demeter and Persephone. Characters in a comedy of Aristophanes, the *Women Celebrating the Thesmophoria*, speak of being tent-mates, the women living and eating together rather than in their own homes and families (see further Chapter 3). Tents with impressive designs on the fabric are set up for a special communal feast at Delphi in the *Ion* of Euripides (see Schmitt-Pantel 1992). The Persian kings travelled round their empire in tented cities, and Alexander had vast tented dining rooms during his invasion of the East. The Greco-Roman adoption of tents seems to be related to these models, which were created by the original nomadic lifestyles of the Near-Eastern kingdoms, and the demands of military campaigns.

The Romans also had a liking for dining in the garden. Examples are to be found among the rich citizens of Pompeii, and emperors too had numerous possibilities for al fresco dining. These combined with the decoration of rooms inside, which gave impressions of the natural world, with vistas, sea-scapes and still-life frescos. Claridge (1998: 290–2) describes Nero's fantastic Golden House. A mosaic at Palestrina illustrates an open-air meal in the Nile Delta.

Furniture

At all periods, furniture and the tableware and equipment associated with eating are of the greatest importance. Later authors noticed that the Homeric heroes sat on chairs at mealtimes, and did not recline. The couches on which diners reclined appear to have come into the Greek world in the archaic period, and are certainly attested on Corinthian vases from the sixth century onwards (Murray 1990).

Dining on couches raises issues of central importance to our study of ancient dining. This is one of those practices (mentioned in Chapter 1) that moved eastwards across the Mediterranean. The Assyrians, the Persians and other eastern peoples seem to have developed reclining at table as part of royal and aristocratic dining that possibly derived from their nomadic lifestyle. The Assyrian King Ashurbanipal is pictured on a famous relief, now in the British Museum, reclining at dinner with the head of an enemy displayed in a nearby tree. Several passages in the Old Testament confirm the evidence of Greek authors and reliefs that the Persians reclined at mealtimes. In Esther 1, for example, we read of the great feast of the Persian king at which couches (or beds) were provided in a great courtyard in the garden for a range of his subjects. The Greeks picked up the practice either directly from the Assyrians or indirectly diffusion by through the world of the Persian Empire. This was dining in style, and many elites in the Mediterranean strove to imitate it in order to display their international networking to the peoples at home in the Greek cities or elsewhere. Some texts, which we shall see in Chapter 7 and which I discussed in Wilkins (2000), portrayed the Persians as supremely luxurious and effeminate. But the Greeks and later the Etruscans and Romans were deeply influenced by the practices of the most powerful empire in the archaic and Classical Mediterranean. Other practices derived from the Persians included representations of meals. The Persian king is rarely shown eating. Drinking, certainly, sometimes with food to hand. But rarely eating. Much of Greco-Roman art and literature similarly privileges drinking wine over eating food, as if food were too gross a material to weigh down the royal or aristocratic representation. Contradictory representations of the Persians as the Greek world absorbed these influences into their own are not just ambiguities or ambivalent responses to a powerful neighbour, but derive from the place of eating and drinking within Greco-Roman and wider Mediterranean culture. Questions attached to the Great King of Persia are no different from

FIGURE 2.5   Ashurbanipal, the King of Assyria, feasts with his queen. He is
reclining in the manner that was adopted by the Greeks, Etruscans, Romans and
other Mediterranean peoples. His wife sits with him but does not recline. He is
represented on a higher plane than his courtiers, indicating that a hierarchical
principle predominates over the theoretically equitable arrangement of the
Greek (but not the Roman) symposium. The head of an enemy is displayed
in a tree. Copyright of the Trustees of the British Museum

ambiguities around the Hellenistic courts or at the court of the Roman
Emperors. Should the Augustus represent all the wealth and diversity
of Empire, or should 'tradition', simplicity and restraint prevail? The
question is still alive today.

The couches appear to have been part of the oriental influence on
archaic elites, who competed to show off themselves dining in this new
style. As time progressed the style filtered down through the classes,
so that by the late fifth century it was well known in the Greek cities.
I argue in Wilkins (2000) for familiarity with reclining at symposia. It
seems to me that the furniture and dining styles were subject to aristocratic refinement but that reclining and the sharing of wine mixed with
water was widespread through all classes. All classes of men of status,
that is. Women of status are not believed to have reclined, certainly
not in the presence of men, at least, unless the occasion demanded it –
such as a wedding – and segregated reclining was possible. Representations from funerary reliefs, where men are reclining at mealtimes in
death, show the mourning widow sitting beside the couch. Courtesans
sometimes reclined; women of status did not. Poorer people were liable
to recline on a straw mattress or equivalent, called a *stibas*, which

FIGURE 2.6   The Costume Banquet, from El-Jem (ancient Thysdrus) *c.*200–220
(mosaic) Musee National du Bardo, Le Bardo, Tunisia Lauros/Giraudon. The
mosaic represents a group of diners in an amphitheatre. They chat in colloquial
terms, like the freedmen in the *Satyricon* of Petronius. These lower-class
drinkers contrast with many of the mosaic images found in rich villas. Photo:
www.bridgeman.co.uk

is attested in all periods. In the fourth century BC, Plato mentions it in
his ideal *Republic* (p. 195), and Menander mentions one at a rural
sacrificial picnic in *Dyscolus* (quoted in Chapter 3). It is found in Dio
Chrysostom's description of a rural wedding in the second century AD

THE SOCIAL CONTEXT OF EATING

(Oration 7), and in mosaic representations of dining from North Africa.

We are sometimes given details of how many couches were to be found in a room. Archestratus says that three to five diners suffice, but elsewhere we have much higher figures. Athenaeus mentions the matter at *Deipnosophistae* 2.47f, quoting for example a seven-couch room from comedy by the Attic fifth-century poet Phrynichus, and Xenophon has a similar room for his *Symposium* set at the house of the aristocratic Callias. In the wedding feast of the Macedonian Caranus quoted above, there is textual uncertainty over whether there were 20 or 120 diners on couches. We have also seen figures of 30 couches to a room for Dionysius II and of 1,000–1,500 triclinia in Hellenistic Antioch.

Similar developments are seen in Italy, with reclining being introduced to the Etruscans and other Italic peoples, including the Latins and Romans (see Rathje 1990). In descriptions of Greek and other Eastern influences on the Romans as they absorbed the Eastern Mediterranean in the third and later centuries BC, furniture as much as new foods seems to have made an impact along with works of art and other booty captured in war. Such imports marked out successful competition among the Roman elite, just as it had done for their Greek counterparts in the archaic period.

As far as tableware is concerned, vases made of pottery made a huge impact, together with associated plates and dishes which show that food as well as wine was served on decorated tableware. Metalware made an even bigger impact. We can see this in the Corinthian ware and gold and silverware used by Caranus in the Macedonian meal described above, and in many Greek and Roman examples, not least the meal of Trimalchio. He too is proud of the weight of his Corinthian bronze.

With this furniture went the larger architecture of the dining room. First its characteristic shape to house the couches, either in Greece or Rome. Then wall decorations such as frescos, special shapes for *cottabos* (the wine-flicking game), and floor mosaics, which in the Hellenistic and Roman periods became common in wealthy dining rooms and enabled the decorators to echo the events on and around the table. Hippolochus emphasized the wealth of the meal of Caranus. This could also be brought out in later periods in themes in mosaics, whether the wealth of the Nile or the wealth of the sea. The connection between the sea and wealth is seen particularly memorably in the mosaics of Roman villas in North Africa (modern Tunisia), which, though miles from the sea, have rich images of seafood on the floor.

Private eating

Most eating in antiquity took place on private occasions. Feast days organized by the city or by wealthy individuals were special occasions, which contrasted with private occasions. Private meals took on different forms, according to occasion and time of day. The number of meals per day varied but there is much evidence for light meals eaten at breakfast and/or lunch times, with one larger meal later in the day. This was the meal to which outsiders might be invited and which was the occasion for more ambitious eating. This is also the meal that was likely to be recorded in literary sources. As we have seen, Suetonius records that Augustus entertained formally on such occasions, in contrast to his private eating arrangements when he was alone, at which he often ate in transit and with much informality. Similarly, Plutarch records that Cato the Elder often ate with his slaves when at home, and drank the same wine as they did. The biographers remark on the preference for simplicity in these powerful leaders, partly because they consider it unusual and partly because they believe it reveals a tough moral character. But these and other leaders ate with all the standard trappings of rank and hierarchy when they thought it right. Such occasions were likely to be special versions of the main meal of the day.

We would thus expect relatively unspectacular eating in the private meals (breakfast and/or lunch) and higher-status foods and tableware – and if appropriate the presence of guests – at the *deipnon* or *cena*. The Hippocratic author of *Regimen III* (68) dispenses with the minor meals altogether and recommends only one meal a day. Diocles of Carystus, writing in the fourth century BC, allows lunch and dinner (fr. 182.5–7 van der Eijk 2000), with meat and fish reserved for the latter occasion. Mealtimes give shape to the day just as religious festivals give shape to the year. The prescriptions of doctors are unlikely to apply to the mass of the population. Galen, for example, describes a *deipnon* he shared with farm workers which consisted of wheat that was boiled because the bread had run out (see p. 58). The meal is prepared on the spot, and its other components (if any) are not mentioned. This is a meal of the most basic kind; Galen ate it because he was travelling and hungry. A richer picture of village life in Asia Minor may be found in Mitchell (1993).

Richer people were more likely to invite guests more often, poorer people much less frequently and possibly only on special occasions such as marriages and family gatherings. Our sources assure us that different conditions obtained for Greek and for Roman formal dining. Among the Greeks, equality obtained across all the diners, while the Roman *cena* or *convivium* was hierarchically organized to emphasize the patronage that the rich man was dispensing. It is also said that there were clear gender differences, with women of status present at Roman dinners, but not at Greek. These claims deserve some investigation, not least because a number of our sources, among them Athenaeus, operate in a fusion of Greco-Roman practice.

Food and Social Status

The principle of equality at the Greek dinner was not as strictly observed as might be supposed. Where Roman society had its clients attached to an influential patron, Greek cities had the institution of the parasite or flatterer. These were people at table who were not present as of right, but had as it were to sing for their supper. Xenophon portrays one such in his *Symposium*, in which Philip arrives hungry and uninvited and expects to earn his meal by telling jokes. When his witticisms appear to be unappreciated he falls silent, since the strategy appears to have failed. If he can't entertain, then he does not eat. Later in the proceedings, he does a grotesque parody of a dance performed by one of the female entertainers. Our best commentators on everyday life in fourth-century Athens, the comic poets, abound in parasites who abased themselves in various shameless ways in order to earn their meal. Athenaeus collects many examples in book 6 of his *Deipnosophistae*. The comic poet Eupolis also wrote a play entitled *Flatterers* for the fifth-century stage, in which a group of idle people were portrayed as scroungers from the tables of the rich Callias. This form of patronage is portrayed in a more positive light in Plato's *Protagoras* and Xenophon's *Symposium*, in both of which Callias entertains Socrates and other philosophers at home. Parasites were indeed present in a sense in the *Odyssey*. The suitors of Penelope were men of status and not parasites. But they were eating the cattle of King Odysseus on a non-reciprocal basis in which they repaid the meals with nothing. They also maltreated a social level below that of parasite, the beggars, who had a right to beg for food from the tables, even though they could not sit at table as of right. The suitors abused both the household of the absent Odysseus with their non-reciprocal consumption of animals and the beggars, in attempting to deny them food that was not even their own.

There were other ways in which elite status could be displayed, most notably the sponsoring of sacrifices and distributions of food to the population. This is a feature of the Hellenistic Greek cities, and is widespread in Republican and Imperial Rome, as Donahue (2005) has documented (see pp. 65–6). In Rome, meals both public and private were often organized on a severely hierarchical basis. This is clear in distributions of food by the emperor in big arenas, where different categories of citizen received different portions, and in the entertaining of poorer clients by rich patrons. I quoted above (p. 57) a particularly graphic example of this in the fifth satire of Juvenal. A host might also display his wealth and beneficence by entertaining vast numbers, as many Roman emperors did, and as we saw above from Dionysius II of Syracuse and Antiochus IV Epiphanes in Antioch. Such lavishness was not necessarily a good idea, Plutarch advises, in *Table-Talk* 5.5. In this regard, we should bear in mind that entertaining on such a vast scale was always the exception rather than the rule, and that even among the elite, such scenes as Pliny dining with his wife (see below) were more normal than the great feast of beneficence.

Food and Gender

Women of status were present at the Roman dinner, especially at court and other state occasions, but they do not seem to have been as numerous at the dinner as men. A clear distinction between Greek and Roman practice is made by the Roman biographer Cornelius Nepos (preface 6–7):

> for which Roman is ashamed to bring his wife to the formal meal (*convivium*)? Or whose female head of the family does not hold first place in the house and move about in public? Greek practice is very different. For a Greek woman is not admitted to the *convivium* unless it is a family meal, nor does she take her seat unless it be in the inner part of the house.

This statement appears to hold good for the Greek evidence. Fragment 186 of Menander describes a family meal: 'it's a job to be plunged into a family dinner-party, where father will have the cup and lead the talk; and after words of advice to the young man is in a jocose mood; then comes mother after him; then the old aunt mutters some nonsense aside, and a hoarse-voiced old man, the aunt's father; and after him an old woman who calls the youngster dearest while he nods assent to them all' (trans. Gulick). Comic texts from the fifth and fourth centuries attest a shared occasion but different arrangements for male and female guests at weddings (Euanggelus fragment 1): 'I told you, four [. . .] tables of women and six of men, a full dinner and lacking in nothing . . .' (see Wilkins 2000: 60). Similar arrangements are described by Dio Chrysostom at the wedding in Euboea in the second century AD (mentioned p. 61). Weddings are semi-public occasions for which evidence is available. I am not aware of any evidence for private meals that contradicts the statement of Nepos, who speaks of women of status, of course, and not slave women and *hetaerae*, who were present at the Greek symposium, as discussed in Chapter 6. Four hundred years earlier, Herodotus appears to anticipate the evidence of Nepos. At 5.18.2–3, Herodotus has some Persian envoys ask Amyntas the Macedonian to bring wives and concubines to join the meal, as is the Persian custom. They are told that that is not the custom in Macedonia (and by implication in Greece). Plutarch (*Table-Talk* 1.1 = 613a) reports Persian practice differently, claiming that concubines but not wives were present at their symposia.

The Roman evidence for women at meal times is comparatively plentiful. Valerius Maximus gives an idealized account (2.1) of women seated at the *cena* beside their husbands who reclined. Juno and Juppiter were imagined to dine likewise. But human beings no longer followed the practice in his own day, Valerius implies. In the past too, women drank no wine. This picture of Republican virtue may be no more than a pious generalization that fits the moralizing discourse of the period. Quiet virtue was also possible under the emperors. Pliny the Younger describes an evening at home with his wife and friends (*Letter* 9.36):

> if I am dining alone with my wife or with a few friends, a book is read aloud during the meal and afterwards we listen to a comedy or some music. (trans. Radice)

The love poets attest women at dinners, who might be seduced from their husbands (McKeown 1987). This evidence is difficult to read since the genre seeks to destabilize accepted patterns of behaviour, and it is often unclear quite what the status of the poet's girlfriend might be. Satire too has women at dinners, in a hostile presentation in Juvenal *Satire* 6; and in a less venomous description in Petronius, *Dinner with Trimalchio*. At the highest social level, emperors' wives and senators' wives dined at the imperial court (Suetonius *Caligula*).

We might expect some help in this regard from Plutarch and Athenaeus, the writers of the second century AD who fused many aspects of Greco-Roman behaviour in their intellectual world. But on the subject of women at formal meals in their own period, they have little to offer. There art no female Deipnosophistae.

It is worth making some general points. Much of the Greek evidence comes from Classical Athens, which appears to have had stricter sexual segregation than many other cities, with the possible exception of Miletus. There is little evidence that such strict segregation applied to all classes of free women. There were female bread-sellers and fish-sellers in the market, for example (see Wilkins 2000). But there are few counterexamples either (see, for example, Galen's anecdote about peasants boiling wheat above). Women could eat and drink with each other. Some comic evidence is gathered in Wilkins (2000). When we read in Plato's *Symposium* that the piper is not needed, and can be sent to entertain the women if needed, we have no idea of the circumstances or manner of eating of such women and their friends. The women we do know about are the companions or *hetaerae*, the escorts at symposia who figure widely in comedies, vase paintings and in the pages of Athenaeus. The latter records many witty sayings of these women in book 13 of the *Deipnosophistae*. The ubiquity of the courtesan at the Greek table only serves to emphasize the absence of the woman of status. Yet all such women ate every day, with their families, friends and kinsmen.

Other approaches may be helpful. Dalby (1993: 176–81) has suggested, using the comparative evidence of the Sarakatsani shepherds of north-western Greece, that women tended to feed their men first, and themselves afterwards, on less good food. This is a useful way forward but there is little ancient evidence to support it. Dalby's attempt to use a scene in Aristophanes' *Wasps* is not convincing. Archaeological evidence, however, appears to suggest that in Mycenae and Bronze Age Crete, on the basis of chemical deposits in bones, men ate more fish and meat respectively than women (Tzedakis and Martlew 2002). Garnsey (1999) also surveys a different range of archaeological data and concludes that women, especially those of childbearing age, were more likely to suffer malnutrition than men. In a rare comment, Galen says women and children eat jujubes, a bad food in his view.

We have discussed so far women as consumers of food and drink. As far as the preparation of food is concerned, it is certain that women prepared food more often than men, unless the household could afford slaves. There is a good deal of literary and visual evidence for this, some of which is collected in Wilkins (2000a). Pherecrates, the comic poet, in fragment 10 of his *Savages*, has a character imagine a world in which there are no slaves. So it is the women who have to get up early and grind the corn for the day, just as 600 years later it is the women in Galen's anecdote who bake the daily bread. Such activity confirms the general picture of men out in the world working either as manual workers or in more refined activities, and women at home in charge of the household stores. This is the message of the sober *Oeconomicus* of Xenophon, and also of the playful comedies of Aristophanes, *Thesmophoriazousai* and *Frogs*.

Order of the meal

It is often said that the Greek *deipnon*-symposium was divided into the food part of the meal (the *deipnon*) and the drinking part, the symposium. This is broadly true in Greece, and much less the case in Roman dining. Two texts from about 400 BC shed some light on the issue. A gastronomic poem, the *Deipnon* or *Dinner* of Philoxenus, describes an elaborate meal which concludes with the phrase, 'when they had had their fill of food and drink'. The tables are then changed, and the symposium or drinking session begins. Evidently, the guests drank as necessary during the meal, but there was a clear division before the symposium started, with clean floors, new tables, new garlands, prayers and libations. A new start, but there had been wine before, and more food would follow during the symposium, when the second tables or dessert courses were routinely served. In Rome, drinking begins the meal (this can be seen clearly in Trimalchio's dinner and in the meal of the Deipnosophistae), and follows at the end. The two qualifications that need to be made to the Greek pattern is that no one was likely to eat a large meal without the possibility of liquid refreshment if needed; and secondly that a number of texts make clear that wine was drunk at an earlier stage. At the beginning of *Odyssey* Book Three, Telemachus and the disguised Athena are given innards of sacrificial animals and wine when they arrive, and then more meat and the glorious feast a little later. In Book Four, they are welcomed by Menelaus and have their fill of food and drink, and then have a drinking session to follow. In *Iliad* 9, the embassy to Achilles eats and drinks. Wine is the first consideration, then food, the chine of a hog, then 'when their thirst and hunger were satisfied', they drink toasts and continue. We should thus think not so much of an exclusive division between the eating and drinking parts of the meal (and indeed in many sources, from Xenophon onwards, the terms *deipnon* and symposium cover both parts of the event). Rather, there was a new start at the beginning of the symposium, with new garlands, new tables, new prayers and a new start to the mixing bowl or crater. This picture is, however, contradicted by Plutarch in his *Table-Talk* (8.9 = 733f–734a). He claims that the order of the meal had changed from earlier times, with oysters, sea urchins and raw vegetables served at the beginning rather than at the end of the meal. He claims also that current drinking at the beginning of the meal was unknown in earlier times, where nothing was drunk before the dessert course. Plutarch may be right, but I doubt that no drinking took place at an earlier stage. A case in Galen supports this. Watching a man eat a standard meal, he tries to work out why apples and pears upset him (*On the Powers of Foods* 2.21). The man has a bath, drinks some water, and eats fenugreek and radish with normal starters; drinks some sweet wine; eats mallow with oil, *garum* and wine, with fish, pork and chicken; drinks a cup or two of wine, and then eats two sharp pears.

It is often difficult to define the precise order of a formal meal, and given the variety of cities, eating practices and time scale under review in this book, nothing definitive is likely to emerge. Certain points can, however, be made. There were differences over time, as Athenaeus notes (confirming Plutarch) at 3.101b: 'All the ancients however did not serve before the *deipnon* either sow's wombs or lettuce or anything else of that kind, as now happens. Archestratus the inventive chef at least speaks of them after the meal and the toasts and the anointing with myrrh' (trans. Wilkins). Athenaeus then quotes Archestratus fr. 60 Olson & Sens (2000), which is a very good survey of second tables. Athenaeus remarks further that in the dinner given by the courtesan Lamia to Demetrius Poliorcetes in Athens, fish and meat were served first, as was the case with the dinners of King Antigonus and Ptolemy II also mentioned on p. 44. It is difficult to say what was served first in Archestratus, given the fragmentary nature of the poem and disputes among the editors over the ordering of fragments within the poem. He announces in fragment 9 Olson & Sens: 'Bulbs. I bid farewell to vinegar-dishes of bulbs and plant stalks, and to all the other side dishes.' There could, however, be some similarity between the appetisers and the 'second tables' that were served during the Greek symposium. So too at the meal of Trimalchio, small fish items come at the beginning and end of the meal. Athenaeus presents a number of foods that seem to have moved their customary place between the beginning and end of the meal or vice versa. These comments of Athenaeus and Plutarch exhibit a desire to reconcile ancient and contradictory evidence.

3
Introduction

The constraints imposed on diet by religion are similar to those imposed by military and social bodies. They seem to be an exercise in cementing the ranks of the believers, providing a sense of group cohesion and belonging rather than anything remotely connected with core beliefs and philosophy. Even so, as symbols of the religion, they acquire a significance beyond what may appear necessary or sensible. Perhaps it is easier to demonstrate devotion through such obvious means as, say, avoiding non-kosher or halal food or forgoing meat during Lent, than it may be to comply with strictures on the brotherhood of man or turning the other cheek. More likely, though, is the attraction of a communal show of unity and brotherhood in the face of outsiders.

It is generally abstinence that is called for, fasting as part of some regime of mortifying the flesh, and the objectives are self-discipline and self-control. The appeal for societies dependent on military strength or concerned about continuing separate identity is not hard to see, for the interests of god and state are rarely at odds with each other.

The followers of Pythagoras comply with these rules in that they are bound together by the avoidance of flesh and, a touch more bizarrely, the bean family. Vegetarianism, though, has in common with Buddhism, and for the same reasons, the notion that life is sacred of itself rather than submissive to the state's or society's greater need. This would have been more contentious than any dietary regime and the offering of anything less than animal life at the altar of the gods would have seemed inferior and absurd. In times of danger a bunch of celery will never have quite the impact of slain goat.

The ritual slaughter of animals, their cooking and distribution was in Greece closely connected with religious ceremony and would again be an exercise in reinforcing social order more than anything gastronomic. Christianity has little in the way of foods that you are required to eat rather than required to avoid. The host, the sliver of bread which symbolizes the body of Christ, is the main exception, and is delivered only to true believers who have prepared themselves through penance to receive it. However, the dedication of a bout of greed or overindulgence to the gods is nothing new.

Feasting tends to follow the fast, Easter Day after Lent, Id after Ramadan. Christmas may have little left to connect it with the birth of Christ but that is the excuse for three weeks of overeating and drinking across much of the wealthy world. It is difficult not to assume that things were ever so.

Food and Ancient Religion

I f we ask what religion had to do with food in antiquity, the answer is threefold. First, the religious festivals shaped the year of the community. Festivals also marked the life-cycle of the individual, with the appropriate feasts to mark birth and integration, marriage and death. Calendars survive from the Greek and the Roman worlds (Parker 1996, Burkert 1985, Mikalson 1975, Beard, North & Price 1998: 60–77). Many festivals and smaller rituals entailed (among other things) the offering of animals or other foods to the gods, a number of whom were responsible for the success or not of the flocks and the harvests. At those festivals, human beings often ate with the gods, and enjoyed a special meal. Second, the religious festivals were linked with the power and social structures of the community and reinforced the social order. Third, eating in a religious context was often considered 'traditional'. Sometimes such ancient rites were in need of explanation, giving rise to a branch of literature that consisted of answers given to questions a reader might ask. We shall see examples in Ovid and Plutarch. Religion's roots in the past did not preclude new gods and new rituals to meet change over time.

I begin this chapter in the modern Mediterranean world, with a scene which illustrates how society organizes itself around religious markers. Such markers were likely to have been more prominent in the ancient world.

On a hot August Sunday in 2003, some thirty or forty Cretans met for lunch in family groups. They had chosen a picnic spot in the shady wooded gorge of St Antony of Patsos, in the Amari valley. They brought barbecue charcoal and plenty of meat, and cooled wine in the stream. Salads and other dishes were also prepared. It was a genial occasion with family and friends on the weekend after the Feast of the Assumption, a festival in the Orthodox calendar which focuses on home and family. Numerous visits were made to the small shrine of St Antony, which was cut into a cave in the wall of the gorge. At the entrance to the shrine hung crutches, a zimmer frame and other thank offerings for cures effected by the saint. A little further inside, a rocky ledge supported candles and offerings, apparently of olive oil, in Fanta and Coca-Cola bottles, and beyond that was the shrine itself with altar, incense and icons.

This holy spot in pre-Christian times housed the cult of Hermes Kranaios, probably Hermes of the spring, after whom the water source is still named. Votive offerings to Hermes and an inscription naming the god have been found, the offerings dating from 2000 BC, the inscription from the first century AD.

For those not participating in the picnic, a taverna beside the road leading to the gorge offered lunch on a limited commercial basis. Cooking was conducted on two small rings powered by bottled gas. Tables were set outside in the shade of walnut trees. Demand was such that the waitresses (who were also assistant cooks) were not able to supply all that was needed. So it was that most tables provided their own informal waitress, while a man from another table, possibly the owner, retired into the kitchen and fried pork chops on the tiny gas rings.

A number of points can be drawn from this lunchtime scene. The first is the continuity of cult at this valuable spring. In a hot island, with August temperatures over forty degrees centigrade, water comes at a premium. It is sought by both human beings and plants, and provides drinking water, supports agriculture, and may offer therapeutic properties. At springs all over Greece, Pan, Hermes, the Nymphs and other deities were believed to protect the water source, and were propitiated by the human population. Offerings were made both in thanks for benefits received and in the hopes of benefits to come. An offering of oil, honey or barley-cake was as likely to be made as an animal sacrifice. A meal can be informal and portable – as is the case with the modern picnic. It can include hot food, and informal furniture. It may be a special occasion despite the natural surroundings and the distance from home. The participants may all share one purpose; or there may have been many purposes for the gathering. Then, the meeting was private, and non-commercial. The commercial setting was provided by the taverna; but here too, I have suggested, there was a fusion of commercial and personal activities.

These meals can be interpreted in several ways by a contemporary observer. Important elements would appear to be kinship and community, tradition as provided by the festival, and the shrine located in the landscape. Food was available on a commercial and non-commercial basis. Its consumption was pleasurable both for the taste buds and for the human eater as a social being. I have concentrated on eating at the human level. Of course, 'religion' in the modern and ancient world embraced gods and divine forces with elemental powers, with explanatory myths attached to them and with demands for worship and respect from their human subjects. St Antony of Patsos is a modern example of a local cult in a remote part of a Greek island. In antiquity, there were thousands of such cults throughout the Mediterranean world, many with their particular cult practice and mythical narrative. At such places, and at the great sanctuaries of Olympia, Eleusis and Delphi, the Greeks and Romans honoured their gods and tried to secure their support for agriculture, for the survival of the community, or for a specific enterprise. In many cases, worship included blood or non-blood sacrifice and a meal shared between the worshippers and the god. Beside most temples (the major remains of religious precincts still visible today) we should imagine an altar for the offering of sacrifice, and buildings (or a space for the erection of temporary buildings) for dining after a sacrifice.

For an ancient version of the lunch at Patsos, we may usefully compare a meal described in a comedy by Menander, his *Dyscolus (Bad-Tempered Man)*, which was written in Athens in 316 BC. The play is set in the remote village of Phyle in northern Attica. A mother has organized a rural sacrifice at a shrine of Pan and the Nymphs (no doubt a water source), because she seeks to avert nightmares sent to her by Pan about her son's safety. She brings her wealthy urban family to the countryside and they sacrifice a sheep to the gods, with the help

FIGURE 3.1   This sketch by Francois Lissarrague from a vase painting illustrates
the dismemberment of the animal in sacrifice. Note the scattered parts of the
animal, nearly all of which were eaten in sacrifices to the Olympian gods.
The operation is overseen by an ithyphallic Herm, marking the spot as ritually
protected. From F. Lissarrague, *The Aesthetics of the Greek Banquet* (Chicago)
by kind permission of the University of Chicago Press.

of a hired cook who brings furniture and picnic equipment with him.
He brings rugs (*stromata*), apparently to make *stibades* or rustic couches
(405–21). He has brought some pots and pans, and expects to borrow
others locally (504–21). Sacrifice is followed by lunch (*ariston*, 554–
62), and later there are plans for a symposium for the men and an
all-night revel for the women (855–9). Tensions are felt between the
male and female participants, between the rural and urban participants,
and to some extent between the servants and masters. It is a less
relaxed occasion than the picnic I observed, because the plot requires
it to be an informal engagement feast. But there are striking similarities.
A sacred grove is the setting; people set out from home and cook meat
in the countryside. They take with them urban comforts; the meal
integrates and brings together disparate elements. In this case, as often
in Greek comedy (which is discussed at greater length in Chapters 7
and 9), there are concerns about the excesses of youth, about the
young man spending money about town and not being a respectable
husbander of the family resources. But the ritual consumption of meat
and wine at the end of the play brings all together in the correct way.

Sostratos, the rich young man in question, satirizes his mother for her fanatical sacrificial activity (260–3): 'my mother is planning to sacrifice to some god, I don't know which, and she does this on a daily basis. She goes the rounds of the whole deme sacrificing.' Notable here is the frequency of the offerings and the mother who is at the centre of this sacrificing: wealth allows multiple private sacrifice, and being female is no obstacle – an important corrective to some of the points made about gender in Chapter 2.

The play also puts on stage an example of the comic cook, who enters carrying a sheep for sacrifice and slaughters it as the first stage of providing a meal for the people present, which will be followed by the symposium and all-night festival (on the latter see p. 130). The upper class woman engaged him in the marketplace. The occasion combines religious activity with commercial expertise (the term for cook, *mageiros*, is complex, as explained in Chapter 1). This is notable for us as observers of ancient society, but it is also an issue in the play. The misanthropic Cnemon after whom the play is named denounces the worshippers as pleasure seekers who only give the gods cast-offs from the animal that are inedible for human beings. He says (447–53),

> how these thieves sacrifice! They carry in their beds and their wine jars, not for the benefit of the gods but of themselves. The incense is holy and the sacrificial cake. The god got that as a whole offering on the flames. Then they offer the tail end and the gall bladder to the gods – because they're inedible – and themselves wolf up everything else.

The play shows this antisocial critic being punished for his failure to recognize the reciprocal basis of society. That is not to deny that he has a powerful point. Pleasure and sacrifice were not separated. We might add that the gods were offered animals at the time of year that suited human agriculture (Jameson 1988) and religion is built into the human cultural order. A purist such as Cnemon is therefore well placed to bring out this point. At the same time, the satire highlights the close interrelation between religion, food and social exchanges. These are further illustrated by the *mageiros*, or cook. Cnemon criticizes this hireling from the city. He is not alone in doing so, for the cook is a stock figure of Athenian comedy (Wilkins 2000). But *mageiroi* are also to be found in inscriptions setting out regulations for religious festivals (Berthiaume 1982), and in the Spartan messes, which were far from luxurious. They should then be placed on a scale running from strictly religious official through meal-provider in institutions to celebrity for hire in a private home, the caterer who would bring aspects of a modern restaurant – the latest in dining – to the rich man's banquet.

Comedy is a problematic source for ancient life, but this ancient picnic is suggestive in a number of important respects. People in antiquity often ate informally, away from home. There were small sacrifices made for family reasons, in addition to the great festival sacrifices in the large cities. Men and women ate together, under certain social codes. Much can be said about the formal and informal eating of the majority of the population, even though most of the evidence which follows is drawn from the eating for display of the rich and famous.

Major and Minor Shrines

Large cities had a proliferation of cultic activity. At civic level, as seen for Athens in the Panathenaiac regulations quoted below, a number of altars of the god might be used at the same time. Then at local level, complementary rituals were celebrated. The *demes*, or local districts of Athens, held festivals to local gods, and small-scale sacrifices to local heroes. I quote part of one such calendar from the Attic deme of Marathon:

> In the month Skiraphorion, before the Skira [festival]. To Hyttenios, fruits in season, a sheep, 12 drachmas. To Kourotrophos, a pig, 3 drachmas, priestly portion 2 drachmas, 1 obol. To the Tritopateres, a sheep, priestly portion 2 drachmas. To the Akamantes, a sheep 12 drachmas, priestly portion 2 drachmas.
>
> The following in alternate years: first set – In Hekatombaion, to Athena Hellotis, an ox . . . (trans. Rice & Stambaugh)

Alongside, and sometimes in combination with these political units, local groups of *orgeones* or *thiasoi* met together to sacrifice to a local deity and feast together. Athenaeus explains (5.185f–186a), 'the lawmakers gave thought to dinners (*deipna*), and set up dinners of the tribe (*phyletica*), of the deme (*demotica*), as well as of the *thiasos* (worshippers of Dionysus or another god), of the phratry (kinship group) and finally of the so called *orgeones*.' Much is known of these groups from inscriptions (see, for example, Ferguson 1944 and Parker 1996: 333–42). One set of regulations from central Athens prescribes,

Decreed by the *orgeones*: the Host (*hestiator*) shall offer the sacrifice on the 17th and 18th of Hekatombaion. On the first day he shall sacrifice a suckling pig to the Heroines and a full-grown victim to the Hero and he shall set up a table, and on the second day, a full-grown victim to the Hero. He shall reckon up his expenses and spend no more than the revenue. [He shall distribute] the flesh as follows, to the *orgeones* present (a portion), to sons a portion not exceeding a half, and to the womenfolk of the *orgeones* [if an ox were sacrificed], – to free matrons a portion equal to (that of the *orgeones*), to daughters a portion not exceeding a half, and to one female attendant (for each matron) a portion not exceeding a half. [He shall deliver] the portion of the woman to the man (i.e. husband, guardian, master). (trans. Ferguson)

This was an annual sacrifice made to the hero Echelos, possibly from the fifth century onwards. It was made by a group of men who shared the meat afterwards. Men had to be present to qualify. Their sons and female dependants also qualified, the women, though, only if an ox rather than a pig was sacrificed: with an ox there was clearly substantially more meat. This evidence for the women (who are of reasonable means if they can afford a slave) shows that they qualify for meat sometimes but not always, and depend on their husband or guardian to get it. Ferguson suggests that normally women probably did not attend the sacrifice.

A second set of regulations (Dittenburger *Sylloge* III 1097.30) concerns a sacred precinct that was let to a tenant when the *orgeones* did not need it. In the sacred period in Boedromion, the tenant provided a kitchen (*optanion*), dining couches and tables for two *triclinia* (two groups of three couches, enough for between a dozen and thirty diners). The diners sacrificed and ate the meat on site: it was not allowed, this time, to take it away. These regulations show the social and religious dimensions fully enmeshed together, and complement nicely the evidence from Menander above and the Panathenaia inscription below. Dining couches and tables belonged firmly to the religious world as well as to the world of the private house, while the kitchen is often better attested in cult sites than in private dwellings. An inscription from Eleusis, for example (IG 2 2 1679.189), mentions building work (in stone) to an *optanion*. This indicates a substantial structure rather than the temporary kitchens apparently often used in private houses.

Rome too enjoyed such groups of diners to local divinities, which were integrated into the major festivals and political feasting of the city (Donahue 2005, Beard, North & Price 1998: 292–4).

A similar picture of small-scale sacrifice in a larger context emerges at the great cult site of Olympia, as described by Pausanias in his *Description of Greece* (5.15). There is a massive altar of Zeus (5.13), built up with a great mound of ash from sacrificial flames, with special regulations for use during and outside the games. The ash comes from the altar of the *prytaneion*, where a fire burns permanently. For most Greeks and Romans, at an international level, the special occasion of the games was the focus of attention. There was extensive sacrifice, and much emphasis on the links with Heracles, the mythical meat-eater (see Chapter 1). Meat, as we saw, was particularly necessary for athletes, and Milo of Croton's eating feats are linked with Olympia. But for the local people (of Elis) a different and complementary pattern of cult emerges. There were monthly sacrifices on all the altars in the complex sanctuary, 'in the ancient manner'. These were non-blood sacrifices of incense, wheat cakes mixed with honey, and olive twigs, together with wine libations (except for the Nymphs and the Mistresses, who received no wine). Libations were offered to Greek and Libyan gods at the great shrine of Ammon, with which Olympia had links. There were also libations for heroes (deified human beings) and their wives. It was in the prytaneion of the Elians (the sacred hearth of the community, like the prytaneion in Athens and temple of Vesta in Rome) that the community honoured the Olympic victors in a special dining room (*hestiatorion*).

Conservatism and Pleasure

We return now to the relationship between religion and the commercial world which could potentially add pleasure and luxury to the religious experience – the point highlighted by Cnemon above. In many of the texts considered in Chapters 7 and 9, implicit contrasts are made between tradition as endorsed by religion and new, especially external pressures, brought by commerce and the market, which promote change and by implication moral danger. Ovid gives a good example of this in *Fasti* 6, on the goddess Carna. The goddess loves traditional emmer wheat and bacon and hates fish and foreign birds. In stressing traditional, agricultural production she preserves Rome's ancient, Republican, identity. While this perception is important and often made, as we shall see, we must always stress the existence of the opposite, the important connections between religion and the commercial world. Thus sacred land was rented to farmers; animals were bought for sacrifice; the sale of meat and hides raised further revenue; and city treasuries were often held in temples, such as the Athenian Parthenon. Furthermore, sacrifice helped to express the wealth and power of a city or an individual, as much as it expressed tradition and an established agricultural base. If the city of Athens had the resources to sacrifice several hundred cattle at a single festival, which its own farmland could not sustain, that was a considerable statement of wealth.

To the commercial argument, we can add that pleasure cannot completely be excluded from the experience of sacrifice. Meat, if eaten rarely, was likely to be intensely desirable at ancient feasts, as was the experience of community among the worshippers, especially if augmented by wine which was often drunk at times of festivity.

We should remember also that, conservative though ancient religion might be in several respects, both Roman and Greek cities were open to many new cults and religious practices. Thus to Athens came, for example, the cult of Adonis, of Bendis, of Isis and of Cybele. To Rome came the cult of Isis, and in the crisis years of the third century BC, cults from the Greek world that included Apollo and the Great Mother, Cybele. The introduction of Syrian, Thracian, Egyptian, Phrygian, Egyptian and Greek cults respectively reflects both a population in need of these gods and the identity they supported (immigrant communities in many cases), and also in Rome's case, a need for the support of foreign gods.

The evidence of *orgeones* applies also to these foreign cults. The cult of Bendis arrived in the Piraeus in the fifth century BC. By the third century, it was incorporated with state cult. The polis provided the animals, some of which were supplied for a fee to the *orgeones*. The *orgeones* feasted on the meat, and the polis claimed the hides. Ferguson (1944: 101–3) calculates that probably 100 cattle were sacrificed (a hecatomb), providing meat for a vast number. The feast of Bendis was both a polis festival and a feast for the *orgeones*, who may have eaten together privately. Ferguson conjectures that the meat may have been carried home raw. It was possible for those who were not *orgeones* to sacrifice in the shrine, but portions of the sacrificial victims had to be given to the priestess and priest, gender difference in the official being marked by female and male animal victim. This is a vivid illustration both of the integration of foreign cults into Athens, and the large numbers who benefited from the meat of sacrifice.

With the foreign gods, also, came foreign customs and in some cases foreign foods. The cult of Adonis, for example, was linked with herbs and perfumes (see below). Perfumes give a graphic material illustration. Perfumes such as frankincense and myrrh were imported from Arabia and Africa to the Greco-Roman world (Miller 1969: 102–5). The incense was included in standard Olympian sacrifice, and represented the fragrant, ethereal part of the sacred meal which went up to heaven in scented smoke suitable for the gods. The mortals by contrast ate the wet, meaty, mortal part of the animal, which reflected the mortal nature of human beings. But perfume might also be linked with eastern ways and extravagance. Athenaeus has various tales about perfume-sellers for example, in his twelfth book, on luxury. Archestratus fragment 60 includes perfumes in the pleasures of the symposium. And Ovid comments in the *Fasti* (1.337–46),

> Of old the means to win the goodwill of gods for man were spelt and the sparkling grains of pure salt. As yet no foreign ship had brought across the ocean waves the bark-distilled myrrh; the Euphrates had sent no <frank>incense, India no balm, and the red saffron's filaments were still unknown. The altar was content to smoke with savine And the laurel burned with crackling loud. To garlands woven of meadow flowers he who could violets add was rich indeed. (trans. Frazer)

Perfumes thus performed an ambiguous role. They reappeared at the symposium, where, like flowers, they played an ambivalent part. Both Athenaeus (15.669f–686c) and Plutarch (*Table-Talk* 3.1: 645d–648a) present arguments for and against the use of flowers in garlands at mealtimes. Was it part of sacred practice? Or luxurious? A link with the natural world and thereby the gods of nature such as Dionysus? Or disgraceful extravagance? It was of course potentially all of these things, and therefore a fruitful area in which to place ideological markers.

Perfumes and garlands played a part in the sacrificial part of the ceremony. Both animal and priests were garlanded. Perfumes and garlands also reappear at the symposium, as we have just seen. We should bear in mind that when a sacrifice is mentioned in a text, unless it is a 'holocaust' or entirely burnt animal (normally sacrificed to the gods of the dead), the sacrificial animal was divided between the participants, and a *deipnon*, of a formal or informal kind, followed. (It was possible to have a *deipnon*, without a preceding sacrifice, since meat could be bought at market. That may be where much of the meat described in Greek comic texts or Roman satirical texts in fact came from. But the normal expectation, especially in the Greek world, was that meat, which was eaten rarely, came from sacrifice.) Thus the shared meal followed the act of sacrifice and the symposium followed the meal.

The symposium, the third element in the sequence sacrifice–*deipnon*–symposium, was in its turn a pleasurable activity, as well as a ritualized occasion. At the end of the *deipnon* – the starters and the main courses of the Greek meal – the tables were replaced, water was brought for washing the hands of the diners, and a new start was signalled by libations and prayers. These were prayers to Zeus, Dionysus, the goddess of good health Hygieia, and other sympotic gods. Libations were made in neat rather than mixed wine, and a hymn was sung at the end (see Athenaeus 15.701f–702b). These religious rituals framed the drinking rituals and other social rituals which are described in Chapter 6.

Menander strikingly addresses the issue in a fragment of a lost play whose title also suggests indulgence:

> Then do we not do business and sacrifice in similar ways? Where for the gods I bring in a nice little sheep that I've bought for ten drachmas, for a little less than a talent I can get pipe-girls and perfume and harp-girls [. . .] Thasian wine, eels, cheese and honey. It follows that we get a blessing worth ten drachmas, if, that is, good omens have accompanied the sacrifice to the gods and we offset these benefits against the expense on these luxury items. But how can this not be a doubling of the evils of sacrifice? Now if I were a god, I would never allow a loin of meat to be put on the altar unless the dedicator did not also consecrate an eel: in that way, Callimedon would be dead, one of the kinsmen of the eel. (*Drunkenness* (*Methe*) fragment 224)

Callimedon was a politician of the fourth century BC, who was attacked in other comedies also for his weakness for expensive fish (see Chapter 5). The speaker puts together the sacrifice and symposium in the sequence we have just followed, and then compares the prices for a small sacrifice and a slap-up meal (there are 6,000 drachmas to the talent). The joke lies in the hypothesis that you get what you pay for, and if you pay less for the sacrifice, the gods reciprocate with less. That is not the standard approach to religious offerings (compare Porphyry 2.15–16), but the speaker touches on an uneasy ambiguity in values.

Passages such as this are particularly striking, for they reflect on the ambiguous nature of Greek sacrifice. First, there is an uneasy relationship between the human and divine, which is at the heart of Hesiod's classic accounts of the myth of Prometheus. Then, sacrifice, as we have seen, is built into the human social system, so there are inevitably aspects which appear to focus on human well-being rather than the strict demands of religion, if defined in a fundamental way. Sacrifice and other religious offerings also lead to meal times and social gatherings of eating and drinking which are inherently pleasurable – socially pleasurable, and pleasant too to the taste buds. Religion is mixed up with entertainment, and with political life. A sacrifice might be followed by a meal in an office of the Athenian democracy, for example. Would that be problematic? It might be, if excesses were detected. One of the legal speeches of Demosthenes (54) refers to groups of citizens who parodied religious rites at symposia, and the affair of the Mysteries in Athens in 415 BC concerned fears of conspiracy against the democracy expressed in the parody of rituals at private symposia (Thucydides Book 6.27–9, Andocides *On the Mysteries*).

Similar questions might arise over the influx of wealth into Rome in the second century BC. Polybius (31.26.1–5) describes the riches of Aemilia, wife of Lucius Aemilius. She, we are told,

> used to display great magnificence whenever she left her house to take part in the ceremonies that women attend, having participated in the fortune of Scipio when he was at the height of his prosperity. For apart from the richness of her own dress and of the decorations of her carriage, all the baskets, cups and other utensils for the sacrifice were either of gold or silver, and were borne in her train on all such solemn occasions, while the number of maids and men-servants in attendance was correspondingly large. (trans. Paton)

What is wrong with the expression of wealth on a religious occasion? Literature offers no shortage of criticisms of such phenomena. Plutarch, for example, writes (*On the Love of Wealth* 527d),

> Our traditional festival of the Dionysia was in former times a homely and merry procession. First came a jug of wine and a vine branch, them one celebrant dragged a he-goat along, another followed with a basket of dried figs, and last came the phallos. But nowadays this is disregarded and gone, what with vessels of gold carried past, rich apparel, carriages riding by, and masks. (trans. Csapo & Slater)

This brings us to the crucial dangers of pleasure in ancient thought, which are explored in Chapter 6.

We return to the ambiguous figure of the *mageiros* (cf. p. 28). The man who cuts the animal's throat is not a person of high status. But he performs a religious task, albeit an arduous and bloody task. He might also sell meat after sacrifice. Religious and commercial are, once again, not separated. And – still the *mageiros* – he might hire himself out to cook specialist meals, luxury meals, for people with surplus income. In Sparta, meanwhile, the *mageiros* supervised the communal meal (Molpis, *On the Spartan Constitution*, quoted by Athenaeus 4.141e).

We have seen numerous questions about religion within human society. What did the gods themselves want from sacrifice? Why did they need sacrificial offerings? To be sure they demanded honour from their human dependants. But why the meat of sacrifice? As we have seen, the human participants received the mortal parts of the animal, and the gods the smoke of the burnt marrow and vital organs – the life force of the animal. But why did they require that sustenance? If a god is complete, as Heracles assumes in Euripides' *Heracles* (1345–6), then he or she needs nothing. Aristophanes pursues this idea in his *Birds*. As is standard in comedy, a very materialist approach to the gods is adopted. The birds take over the zone of the air between the humans on the ground and the gods in heaven, thus preventing smoke from sacrificial cooking reaching the gods. They are in this way starved into submission. Interesting philosophical questions on why the gods would or would not welcome certain types of sacrifice are presented by Porphyry, *On Abstinence* 2.

As we come to explore some ancient festivals, we shall see that they often seem to reinforce strongly prevailing social structures and ideologies, but at the same time have many contradictory features. These puzzling elements reflect the complex religious histories of the cities (which is a matter for specialist studies such as Deubner 1932, Parker 1996, Burkert 1985 and Robertson 1993), but also the powerful collocation of related ideas, such as wine and death in the Anthesteria or babies and corn in the Thesmophoria. Festivals often contain negative as well as positive features: they can be a time for holiday, drinking and licence; at the same time for sexual assault and the ritual rehearsing of dark aspects of the human and natural world.

Festivals

Festivals in the Greek and Roman cities brought a sense of solidarity and identity, promoted usually by sacrifice and the shared activity of imploring the god for support and offering something of value (normally the life of an animal). First, I explore the role of food in a number of Greek festivals, which brought together much of the citizen body in an affirmation of civic identity. In Athens, the Panathenaia honoured Athena, the city's principal divine protector. The festival consisted of competitions (with the famous Panathenaic jars of oil as prizes), dances, all-night festivals, and as a centrepiece the offering of a new robe to the statue of the goddess and the sacrifice of cattle. An inscription from Athens in the fourth century BC (*Inscriptiones Graecae* II^2 334) sets out in detail how the meat is to be distributed.

> In order that the procession may be equipped and marshalled in the best possible way each year for Athena on behalf of the Athenian people, and that all the other necessary arrangements may be made for the festival as it is being properly celebrated on every occasion for the goddess by the *hieropoioi* [sacred officials], it is voted by the people, in accordance with the resolution of the council: when the *hieropoioi* make the sacrifices, they are to distribute the portions of meat from two of them, that to Athena Hygieia and that in the old temple, performed in the traditional way, in the following proportions: five shares to the *prytaneis*, three to the nine archons, one to the treasurers of the goddess, one to the *hieropoioi*, three to the board of generals and division-commanders, and the usual shares to the Athenians who participated in the procession and the maidens who act as *kanephoroi* [basket-bearers]; the meat from the other sacrifices they are to distribute to the Athenians. From the 41 minas which represent the rent of the sacred land, the *hieropoioi*, along with the cattle-buyers, are to buy the sacrificial cattle; when they have conducted the procession, they are to sacrifice all these cattle to the goddess on the great altar of Athena, except for one which they are to choose ahead of time from the finest of the cattle and sacrifice on the altar of Nike; all the rest of the cattle bought with the 41 minas they are to sacrifice to Athena Polias and Athena Nike and distribute the meat to the Athenian people in the Kerameikos in the same fashion as in the other distributions of meat. They are to assign the portions to each deme in proportion to the number of participants in the procession from each deme . . . (trans. Rice & Stambaugh)

These regulations clearly bring out the link between participation and the allocation of meat. Even in a democracy, officials must have their special portions. Most of the officials hold political posts, but the basket bearers were girls who carried in their baskets grain – to sprinkle over the animal's head – beneath which was concealed the sacrificial knife. Since it is a large festival, sacrifices take place at different altars,

FIGURE 3.2   The Parthenon frieze includes a number of cattle processing to the altar, some of which appear restive. The cattle are present on this great imperial monument to demonstrate the piety of the Athenians and their ability to make costly offerings to the city's goddess. Beef was distributed to all participating citizens after the animals had been offered in sacrifice to Athena. Copyright of the Trustees of the British Museum

and the meat produced has different destinations. The Panathenaic procession wound its way from the *pompeion* at the Dipylon gate in the Kerameikos through the Athenian agora to the temples on the acropolis. The meat for the people is then distributed at the Kerameikos. The journey of the robe and of the animals and their meat thus traverses spatially the heart of the city. Fisher (2000: 362–3) suggests that citizens picnicked on this meat in the Kerameikos area. Note that the method of distribution of the meat was standard and not peculiar to the Panathenaia.

The City Dionysia reflected the democratic structure of the city also. The cult statue of Dionysus was brought from the northern borders of Attica to the heart of the city, the agora or marketplace. Thence it travelled to the temple of Dionysus to the south of the acropolis. Here, according to Aristophanes at least (*Frogs* 16–18), the god could observe the tragedies and comedies in the theatre. I comment in Chapter 9 on the sacrifices and use of festivity that the god and the rest of the audience witnessed in the plays themselves. In the city, there were mass sacrifices. Demosthenes tells us that the streets were filled with the smoke of sacrifice (*Against Meidias* 51–4). Inscriptions recording the sale of cattle hides in the fourth century BC suggest that between 106 and 274 cattle had been sacrificed in the year 333 (IG II² 1496.80, Csapo & Slater 1994: 113, Rosivach 1994). These are major sacrifices in a region that cannot easily raise cattle. We might compare the hecatomb at Olympia, an international gathering of all Greek states, to judge what the city of Athens was trying to do. While the city offered these cattle to Dionysus, the citizens reflected on their eating and drinking culture as presented on the dramatic stage. The city also affirmed its power by displaying to all in the theatre the treasure contributed by allies to the empire and the orphans of Athenian soldiers killed in action. The festival allowed the city to display military and economic power alongside dramatic and religious rituals representing her place in the order of things.

The principal festival in Sparta and other Dorian cities was the Karneia (Burkert 1985: 234–6). As with the Thesmophoria, normal state business (including warfare) was suspended during the festival. Demetrius of Scepsis tells us (*The Trojan Battle-Order*, book 1, quoted by Athenaeus 4.141e–f) that nine groups ate a sacrificial meal together in nine tent-like structures called 'sunshades', 'in imitation of their military life-style'. This ritual meal represented the military structure, and accompanied dances for boys and girls, and a special foot race, featuring *staphylodromoi*, or 'grape-runners'. Some scholars (reviewed by Burkert) have interpreted this race as a ritual representation of the hunt for a victim (whether animal or god) in certain harvest rituals.

There were festivals especially for women. These are particularly instructive for this study since they show women coming together in groups to eat and perform other activities away from the family unit in which they are frequently confined in ancient accounts. Three that deserve mention here are the Thesmophoria, held from an early date in a number of Greek cities, the Adonia, a festival that came to Greece from the Near East, and the Agrionia, a festival of Dionysus. The first was held in honour of the goddesses Demeter and Persephone. It promoted the fertility of both women and cereal plants, and combined elements of fertility and infertility, eating and fasting in striking ways that illustrate those complexities often found in Greek and Roman festivals. The women left their homes and shared tents with each other on the Pnyx hill (in the case of Athens), that is, the hill where the all-male citizen assembly normally met but suspended business during the festival.

On the first day of the festival, it seems, the women baled up from a pit the rotting remains of pigs thrown there in a previous festival. These remains were linked with the earth and, according to one source, were spread on the fields as fertilizer for the grain. The women also made in dough models of snakes and the male organs. On the second day, the women sat on branches of the chaste tree (*agnus castus*) and fasted: these were two forms of natural contraception. On the third day, these negative aspects were transformed into positive celebrations, focused on roast pigs. Burkert (1985: 242–6) comments extensively on the Thesmophoria and its relation to the myth of Demeter and Persephone, most famously seen in the Homeric *Hymn to Demeter*. Pigs are particularly associated with these fertility goddesses in other rituals also (in addition to their being the most frequently sacrificed animal).

The rituals of the Thesmophoria festival have several instructive elements. First, this pattern of not-eating at a festival followed by feasting is echoed in the Hyakinthia at Sparta, where the death of the hero is recognized at the outset by not eating bread or cakes, not wearing garlands and not singing songs. On the final day, they sacrifice many animals, and give dinners at home to their acquaintance and their slaves (Polycrates, *On Sparta*, quoted by Athenaeus 4.139d–f). Second, fasting at the Thesmophoria is typical of Greco-Roman practice. It was limited and specific. A number of commentators associated the Jews with fasting, which makes a striking point. The Jews did indeed fast, in a distinctive and controlled way. It was never life threatening, unlike the extreme fasting of some ascetic early Christians (Grimm 1996). Third, sacrifice for women only is found elsewhere, for example in a story about Tegea in Pausanias (8.48.5): 'the women offered up a victory sacrifice on their own, without the men, and they did not share any of the meat of the victim with the men'. Fourth, a striking inter-pretation of the Thesmophoria is offered by Detienne (1994 [1977]), who contrasts this festival of conception and reproduction (with its rotting pigs and dank things of the earth) with the Adonia, the festival of courtesans and lovers in honour of the consort of Aphrodite. The

Adonia was celebrated in private houses, and reflected the beautiful but short life of Adonis in myth with the ritual of the 'gardens of Adonis'. Pots were placed on the rooftops of 'hot' plants, herbs and spices that would germinate quickly, live briefly and die in the heat like the mythical fragrant but short-lived god Adonis. Such plants contrast with the cereal grain that is placed in the ground and grows slowly over the long term. This brilliant contrast places women, reproduction, social space and plants in Greek culture in a very clear conceptual perspective that is a triumph of structuralist thought. (There are a few counter cases: a citizen girl attends the Adonia, in Menander's play *The Samian Woman*, for example and gets pregnant.) Detienne shows how the lesser plants (than meat, grain and wine) were celebrated in Greek religion and myth: he has other chapters on myrrh, spices and lettuce.

Plutarch describes the female festival of the Agrionia as it was celebrated at his native city of Chaeronea in Boeotia (*Table-Talk* 8 = 717a). 'The women search for Dionysus as though he had run away, then desist and say that he has taken refuge with the Muses and is hidden among them, and then after a while, when their dinner is over, quiz each other with riddles and conundrums.' Plutarch's explanation for the ritual is this: 'when drinking we ought to engage in conversation that has something speculative, some instruction in it, and that when conversation like this accompanies indulgence in wine, the wild and manic element is hidden away, benevolently restrained by the Muses' (trans. Minar, Sandbach & Helmbold). There are three related features of the Agrionia that are important for this book. This is one of a number of Dionysiac rituals in which the disruptive fertility god drives women out of their houses, in which society encloses them for the purpose of producing babies, food and clothing. He drives them out to the hillsides where (in other versions) he makes the natural world miraculously produce milk and honey in contrast to the main crops of agriculture. Second, these Boeotian women celebrate a *deipnon* after their hunt for the god is over. This is evidence for women's *deipna* to add to the evidence in Chapter 2. Third, Plutarch interprets the ritual as an analogy for conduct at the symposium. We can add that here is also evidence for women playing what are otherwise interpreted as sympotic games. Authors such as Athenaeus might lead us to think that only courtesans played such sympotic games. These games are not only sympotic games; they are part of a festival, and are an example of the combination of religious festivity with what might from a modern perspective be seen as secular eating and drinking.

This combination is seen too in feasting at the Rural Dionysia in Attica, where the festival is celebrated in the home as well as the community (see p. 65). We might also note that Plutarch's after-dinner conversations recorded in his *Table-Talk* (nearly one hundred in all) are sometimes set at festivals, sometimes on special occasions such as the arrival of a friend, or the return of Plutarch himself to his home, and sometimes not specified. One is set at Corinth during the Isthmian games, another during the Anthesteria festival celebrating the opening of the new vintage (3.7). Meals eaten at festivals are not distinguished from those enjoyed on other days, beyond a linking of conversation with an element of the festival.

In many ways religion, as expressed in these festivals and other rituals, reinforced the power structures of ancient cities. These structures took different forms. Human beings were subject to the power of the gods, which they understood only imperfectly. The gods provided the means of survival, but expected to be honoured in return. Hence the elaborate system of sacrifice in which human beings offered first fruits, animal and other sacrifices to the gods. The life of an animal was normally the most valuable offering that could be made. Within human society, cities organized sacrifices and complex rituals within festivals in order to sustain their social and political systems. Individuals might offer sacrifices on behalf of themselves or their families; groups of people might combine to honour a local god or hero, a whole city might undertake a sacrifice, or a group of cities, indeed the whole Greek world might participate in an international religious festival such as the Eleusinian Mysteries or the Olympic Games.

Festivals and sacrifices within city states closely reflected their political structures. In the democratic city of Athens, we are told by a hostile source, pseudo-Xenophon or 'The Old Oligarch', who wrote in the late fifth century, the Athenian people had organized feasts and sacrifices in such a way that ordinary people could enjoy them as easily as the wealthy class. He writes (2.9),

the Athenian populace realizes that it is impossible for each of the poor to offer sacrifices, to give lavish feasts, to set up shrines and to manage a city which will be beautiful and great, and yet the populace has discovered how to have sacrifices, shrines, banquets and temples. The city sacrifices at public expense many victims, but it is the people who enjoy the feasts and to whom the victims are allotted.

Festivals the author has in mind presumably include the Panathenaia and in particular the City Dionysia, described above.

In Rome too, there were great festivals and sacrifices. An inscription (ILS 5050 = Beard, North & Price 5.7b (1998: 140–4)) records Augustus' celebration of the Secular Games in 17 BC. This was a continuation of a centennial event under the Republic. There are sacrifices to the Fates, Juppiter and other gods; sacrifices of animals and different kinds of sacrificial cakes; shows and banquets, and prayers for the people, with provision for men and women. There were also games, plays and processions. As in Greek festivals like the Panathenaia and Dionysia, athletics, plays and shows were as much in evidence as sacrifices and banqueting. This was seen also in the Roman triumph, which welcomed home a victorious general with his army and booty, and integrated him back into Rome with sacrifice to Juppiter Capitolinus and a banquet with the Senate (see Beard, North & Price 5.8 (1998: 144–7). There were also many smaller festivals, a number of which were closely linked to the agricultural year and to certain related activities, which included the opening of the new wine, the feast of ovens in honour of bread-making, and the feast of Carna, which is described in Chapter 5.

Ovid tells us, too, about the Cerealia, which was celebrated in April, linking it to the myth of Demeter and Persephone/Ceres and Proserpina (*Fasti* 4.393–402):

> Next come the games of Ceres. There is no need to declare the reason; the bounty and the services of the goddess are manifest. The bread of the first mortals consisted of the green herbs which the earth yielded without solicitation; and now they plucked the living grass from the turf, and now the tender leaves of tree-tops furnished a feast. Afterwards the acorn was produced; it was well when they had found the acorn, and the sturdy oak afforded a splendid affluence. Ceres was the first who invited man to better sustenance and exchanged acorns for more useful food. (trans. Frazer)

As with the Thesmophoria, the sacrifice at the festival is linked with the pig, and the plough-ox is explicitly excluded. The goddess, in line with her antiquity, is said to like what is old, and to be satisfied with little (a piglet rather than an ox), provided it is pure.

Other examples are the Fornacilia, the Feast of Ovens (*Fasti* 2.512–32), which promoted good baking, and the Vestalia (*Fasti* 6.249–468). The famous Vestal Virgins prepared special cakes of grain and salt for the guardian of the city's hearth (the Roman version of the Greek *prytaneion*), all the ingredients for which came from prescribed areas and were prepared in traditional modes.

Athenaeus' Deipnosophistae offer a final example of a festival. One of their meals coincides with the celebration of the Parilia in Rome. Ovid, *Fasti* 4.721–806, provides the details of this festival of shepherds. Beard, North & Price 5.1 (1998: 116–19) show how an agricultural festival in which the blood of animals was not spilt was converted into the birthday celebration of Rome with full blood sacrifice. Here is religious innovation at work, to reflect the transformation from pastoral community to world power. Athenaeus describes the festival and its reinvention for civic purposes (8.361e–f):

> While much talk of this nature was still going on, right then was heard all through the town the ringing notes of flutes, the crash of cymbals and the beating of drums, accompanied by voices in song. It so happened that it was the feast of the Parilia, as it used to be called, though it is now called the Roman Festival, instituted in honour of the Fortune of Rome, when her temple was erected by that best and most enlightened of emperors, Hadrian. That day is celebrated annually as especially glorious by all the residents of Rome and by all who happen to be staying in the city. (trans. Gulick)

The diners of Athenaeus, being more talkers than doers, reflect on various kinds of civic festivity, apparently as their contribution to the festive day. Athenaeus is once again performing that function which is so vital for this book, bringing together the Greek and Roman worlds. He combines the evidence of Greek literature with the Roman world (the subject of their conversation) outside the dining room. In many ways there were strong similarities between the Greek and Roman worlds: the Romans indeed sometimes sacrificed by the Greek rite, sometimes by the Roman. Greek Heracles became Roman Hercules. He had brought cattle to the Classical world, as we saw in Chapter 1: Rome was one of his foundations, Olympia another. There were also great differences, but much variation was to be found also within both Greek and Roman cultures. Plutarch explicitly addressed Greekness and Romanness in a Greco-Roman religious context. Among his 113 'Roman Questions', he asks (109–10 = 289e–290a),

> Why is it not permitted for the priest of Jupiter, whom they call the Flamen Dialis, to touch either flour or yeast? Is it because flour is an incomplete and crude food? For neither has it remained what it was,

wheat, nor has it become what it must become, bread; but it has both lost the germinative power of the seed and at the same time it has not attained the usefulness of food . . . Yeast is itself also the product of corruption, and produces corruption in the dough with which it is mixed; for the dough becomes flabby and inert, and altogether the process of leavening seems to be one of putrefaction; at any rate if it goes too far, it completely sours and spoils the flour.

Why is this priest also forbidden to touch raw flesh? Is this custom intended to deter people completely from eating raw meat, or do they scrupulously repudiate flesh for the same reason as flour? For neither is it a living creature nor has it yet become cooked food. Now boiling or roasting, being a sort of alteration and mutation, eliminates the previous form; but fresh raw meat does not have a clean and unsullied appearance, but one that is repulsive, like a fresh wound. (trans. Babbitt)

Among the 'Greek Questions', Plutarch asks (46 = 302b) why the people of Tralles call vetch the purifier and use it for expiations and purifications. This intellectual approach to ancient religions, which in an early form of social anthropology, offers tentative explanations to puzzling religious phenomena, highlights rituals which are specific to a particular city (a recurring theme of this chapter), and covers a wide range of social practice, including foods and cooking. The interrogative format resembles the approach used by Ovid in his *Fasti*, whose principal focus is Rome, but with much Greek ritual and mythology also present. Some aspects of ancient religion were so strange that bizarre explanations were often needed. This is particularly so in the riddling responses of oracles and in the foundation myths for some cities. Ephesus would be founded, according to an oracle, 'where a fish might indicate and a wild boar lead the way' (Athenaeus 8.361e). At Phaselis, meanwhile, a town in southern Asia Minor, the sacrifice of salt fish commemorates the salt fish used to purchase the territory by the founder from a local shepherd (Athenaeus 7.297e–f). Athenaeus found these two stories in local histories (Creophylus, *The Chronicles of the Ephesians* and Heropythus, *The Chronicles of the Colophonians*). They illustrate, if nothing else, the diversity of religious practice, and the complex relationship between the human and animal worlds in antiquity, which is discussed further in Chapter 7. This relationship was often given material commemoration through the foods eaten and the cooking method specified.

Many festivals brought together government leaders and the inhabitants of the city. We saw in Chapter 2 the great festivals put on by early Hellenistic monarchs, such as the feast of Antiochus IV at Daphne. This was a display of royal power designed to compete with the games put on by the Roman general Aemilius Paullus. But the gods were included in the procession. Polybius tells us (31.3 = Athenaeus 5.195a–b), 'it is not possible to enumerate the quantity of sacred images; for statues of all beings who are said or held to be gods, demigods, or even heroes among mankind were borne along, some gilded, others draped in garments of gold thread. And beside all of them lay the sacred myths pertaining to each, according to the traditional accounts, in sumptuous editions.' (trans. Gulick) Next in the procession, Polybius tells us, came hundreds of slaves carrying gold and silver vessels. This was a display of power and wealth, with every imaginable god encouraged to take part. The gods may in some cases have been unwilling participants, since some of the funding for the procession came from raids on temples.

The most famous description of a religious procession in the Hellenistic period comes from the work on Alexandria by Callixeinus of Rhodes. This is an account of the festival organized by the second Ptolemy, Philadelphus, and his wife Arsinoe in honour of the first Ptolemy, Soter, and his wife Berenice. The procession and associated activities are a representation of the power and international range of this Successor kingdom. There is a special marquee for the main party, which houses 130 couches, 100 silver tables, and is strewn with flowers (though it is winter) to reflect the fertility of Egypt. There are representations of symposia, tragedy, comedy and other Dionysiac activity inside. For other attendees, soldiers, artisans and visitors, there is separate provision for feasting. The procession itself honoured first the dead couple, then all the other gods, and in particular Dionysus. There were people dressed as Sileni and other worshippers; perfumes such as frankincense and myrrh; and people representing time and the seasons. There were representations of wine and special wine containers; many animals, such as camels, rhinoceros, and birds; many people from exotic places to the east and the south; women representing the cities of the Greek mainland and Asia Minor. There were representations of the victories of Alexander, and great displays of gold.

This description is preserved by Athenaeus (5.196a–203e), who comments that Philadelphus surpassed many kings in wealth, thanks to the riches provided by the Nile and its delta. We have here apparently a procession in honour of deified kings, which is built around the recognition and worship of Dionysus, the god whose triumphal journey through Asia was echoed by the conquests of Alexander. Much of the procession honours distant places, to which the royal couple are now shown to have access. It is a demonstration of power and influence, and may be closely compared with such processions in Athens. As mentioned above, in the Panathenaia Athena was honoured with a procession and sacrifice. The Alexandrians organize their distribution of meat with particular reference to the royal family and their guests. There is separate provision for 'soldiers, artisans and visitors'. Athens, wishing to reflect its own social structure, divided up the meat according to who was in the procession and who had participated from each of the constituent demes of the polis.

The triumphal arrival of Dionysus in the Ptolemaia is an expanded version of the arrival of Dionysus into Athens from overseas, represented in the Anthesteria and possibly other Athenian festivals of Dionysus. The idea that a god came from elsewhere and is represented as doing so is common (see Chapter 1 on Dionysus, Triptolemus and Heracles). Comparison between the Ptolemaia and Athenian festivals of Dionysus show very well how religious processions reflect the social and political structures of the city. A further striking comment on festivity in Alexandria is provided by Athenaeus 7.275f, who has preserved an extract of Eratosthenes' treatise on the Ptolemaic queen, *Arsinoe*: 'Ptolemy founded all kinds of festivals and sacrifices, particularly those connected with Dionysus; and Arsinoe asked the man who carried the olive branches what day he was then celebrating and what festival it was. He replied: "It is called Flagon-bearing [*Lagunophoria*] and the celebrants eat what is brought to them while they recline on beds of rushes, and each man drinks out of a special flagon which he brings from his own house." When he had passed on, she looked at us and said: "That must indeed be a dirty get-together. For the assembly can only be that of a miscellaneous mob who have themselves served with a stale and utterly unseemly feast."' Athenaeus' speaker Plutarch adds, 'But if she had liked that kind of festival, the queen would, of course, never have grown tired of getting up the very same offerings which were customary at the Feast of Pitchers [*Choes*]' (trans. Gulick). Arsinoe might well sneer at the food of the people after the remarkable foods on offer at the Ptolemaia. But we should note here three things. First, the integration of a version of a widespread polis festival, the *Choes*, second day of the Anthesteria, into the cult of the Ptolemaic kings. Second, the differentiation of rank even in a festive context (implied by Arsoinoe's stance). Note that the populace reclines on rush beds (*stibades*): as discussed in Chapter 2, reclining was a widespread practice: it was just the gold and ivory that distinguished reclining among the rich. Third, Dionysus in the city state was precisely a god who mixed people up together and dissolved hierarchies (Seaford 1994). Arsinoe's distaste for this is interesting, because in the Hellenistic and Roman period Dionysus was increasingly appropriated for the festivals and displays of the rich and powerful, as Plutarch, for example, reveals in his *Lives* of Alexander and Mark Anthony.

Food Offerings

The main food at festivals was meat, at least the most prestigious food, that is. It is best illustrated by the Panathenaia inscription quoted above, by the hide figures for the Dionysia, and by the great sacrifices at Olympia. Animal sacrifice is the most important because of the cost of the offering, and the patterns of thought attached to the taking of life. Detienne and Vernant, as we have seen, stress the issues of definition (between human, animal and god) and identity (in terms of agriculture, gender and civilization, as defined by the use of fire in settled communities). Others stress the guilt felt at the taking of an animal life. For the best summary of the Greek sacrifice, see Burkert 1985: 55–68).

There were also many other festival foods and food offerings, in profuse variety throughout the myriad communities of the Greco-Roman world. Galen mentions cheese bread on festival days in Mysia (see p. 57 above). An *'obelias'* or 'spit-loaf' was served at the Dionysia. Special meals were served on holy days in the prytaneion at Naucratis, as discussed on p. 64).

We turn now to rituals that specified bloodless offerings. We noted above a number at Olympia, which complemented the animal sacrifices of the festival period. Another striking example was the altar of Apollo Genetor in Delos, where wheat, barley and cakes were offered, and there was no use of fire and no killing of animals. This was, according to Diogenes Laertius, *The Life of Pythagoras* 13, the only altar at which Pythagoras worshipped. Pythagoras is difficult to distinguish from his followers, and much of his thought centred on numbers, music and mystical ideas. But an important part of his teaching – and the part often picked up by satirical commentators – concerned his dietary restrictions. Excluded were meat, some fish, and beans. Diogenes Laertius (14), along with many other ancient commentators, explained these restrictions by the belief in the transmigration of souls. This belief is eloquently expressed by a fictional declaration against meat-eating by Pythagoras in Ovid's *Metamorphoses* 15. Porphyry sets out the Pythagorean case extensively in *On Abstinence* (translated in Clark 1999). Diogenes Laertius explains Pythagoras' motives as follows (13):

> his real reason for forbidding animal diet was to practise people and accustom them to simplicity of life, so that they could live on things easily procurable, spreading their tables with uncooked foods and drinking pure water only, for this was the way to a healthy body and a keen mind (*psuches*). (trans. Hicks)

There are many critiques of the thought of the Pythagoreans. Diogenes echoes the beliefs of his age in the early third century AD. His probable contemporary Athenaeus, as we shall see in Chapter 9, attributed similar ethical goals to Homer's portrait of his heroes in the *Iliad* and *Odyssey*. Detienne (1994 [1997] 37–59) has written an excellent critique of the food restrictions among the Pythagoreans, bringing out both the political aspect of the cult and the connection between purity and antiquity. (He discusses the polar contrasts of meat-eating and vegetarian offerings in the context of Milo at Olympia, where there were also ancient vegetable offerings (see above).) Purist followers of Pythagoras removed themselves from the Greek city states of southern Italy and opted out of the sacrificial system and therefore of civic life and identity. Other followers of a less monk-like disposition compromised and refused to eat certain animals and certain fish only – in order not to opt out completely. Parts of the animal that they did not eat were those most associated with life, the brain, the bone marrow, the vital organs. They also only ate the 'guilty' animals, the pig, which trampled the grain of Demeter, and the goat which grazed on the vines of Dionysus.

The followers of Pythagoras, along with the Orphics, a related group of mystics, best illustrate the practice of food taboos in the Greco-Roman world. As Detienne shows, meat is socially the most striking taboo in antiquity: strict Pythagoreans simply excluded themselves from the civic community whose religious identity was founded on animal sacrifice. The connection between beans and the transmigration of souls was also known in Egypt. In general almost no food was taboo, unlike in the Jewish code of the Old Testament: see Parker

(1983: 357–65). The Greeks and Romans normally did not eat food dedicated to the dead, such as dogs sacrificed to Hecate. Certain fish were also off-limit. Athenaeus gives evidence for the religious status of red mullet (7.325b–c):

> Apollodorus also, in his treatise *On the Gods*, says that the *trigle* is sacrificed to Hecate because of the associations of the name, for the goddess is tri-form. But Melanthius, in his work on the Eleusinian Mysteries, includes the sprat with the *trigle* because Hecate is a sea-goddess also. Hegesander of Delphi declares that a *trigle* is carried in the procession at the festival of Artemis because it is reputed to hunt sea-hares relentlessly and devour them; for they are deadly. Hence, inasmuch as the *trigle* does this to benefit mankind, this huntress fish is dedicated to the huntress goddess. (trans. Gulick)

These attestations demonstrate that fish were not completely excluded from Greek religion – far from it. Nor were restrictions on fish confined to marginal sects such as the Pythagoreans. In Attica, the women of Eleusis celebrated a feast at the festival of the Haloa, which included 'every sort of food, except those forbidden in the Mysteries – pomegranates, apples, eggs and fowls and certain specified kinds of fish. When the banquet was ready the magistrates departed leaving it to the women. The Scholiast explained the rich feast as demonstrating that it was in Eleusis that mankind had learned humane eating' (Parke 1977: 98). This evidence for a rich feast, exclusive to women, with dietary restrictions and an aetiological explanation, is characteristic of the Greco-Roman cities. This happens to come from Eleusis, a major city in the religious firmament. Despite cases like this, Parker (1983) concludes that food taboos were limited.

Two further categories of offering to the gods remain to be considered. These are the offering of first fruits, or the best part of the harvest, to the god who was thought to have provided (Burkert 1985: 66–8 offers many examples). Literature abounds in warning tales of communities who failed to sacrifice to agricultural gods. In the classic myth of Meleager, first seen in *Iliad* 9, Artemis takes offence when she alone of the gods fails to receive a harvest-offering from King Oeneus. She sends a monstrous wild boar to devastate the crops. In the historic period, inscriptions record offerings made by farming communities. Here are details of the dues collected by the sanctuary of Eleusis in about 420:

The Athenians shall bring first fruit offerings to the two goddesses from the fruits of the field following ancient custom and the oracle from Delphi: from one hundred bushels of barley, no less than one sixth of a bushel, from one hundred bushels of wheat, no less than one twelfth of a bushel . . . The demarchoi shall collect this in the villages and deliver it at Eleusis to the sacred officials of Eleusis. Three corn silos shall be built at Eleusis . . . the allied states shall also bring first fruit offerings in the same manner . . . They shall send them to Athens . . . The city council shall also send notice to all other Greek cities . . . and shall urge them to make first fruit offerings if they wish . . . And if one of these cities brings offerings the sacred officials shall receive them in the same manner. Sacrifice shall be made from the sacred cakes according to the instructions of the Eumolpidae, and also a sacrifice of three animals (trittoia) beginning with an ox with gilded horns, for each of the two goddesses from the barley and from the wheat, then for Triptolemus and the god and the goddess and Euboulos each a perfect victim, and for Athena an ox with gilded horns. (trans. Burkert)

The inscription vividly shows the integration of protection for the harvest with the powerful cult (and associated myths) of Demeter and Persephone at Eleusis. Also clearly spelt out are the demands of national and international politics in Athens, the city which controlled Eleusis and the Mysteries. The Eumolpidae too were an ancient and influential family of priests in Eleusis and Athens. The inscription mentions both ancient custom and the construction of new silos (Burkert notes that the silos had already been built at this date). This illustrates how religion was both rooted in the past and tied to contemporary demands. It is very frequent for offerings to consist of honey and other cakes (see Chapter 4).

The grain harvest did not provide the only 'first fruits'. We know also of thank offerings to Poseidon for the delivery of a shoal of tuna: Athenaeus (7.297e) tells us of the sacrifice of the first fish caught at Halae in Attica, on the evidence of Antigonus of Carystus, *On Diction*. A second category of non-sacrificial animal was also sacrificed. Hunting was a popular practice in every period, and was especially pursued by the ruling class. Large animals caught might be sacrificed to the gods of wild places, Artemis in particular. This form of sacrifice, since it did not come in the category of farmed animal required by normal sacrifice – the standard contract with the gods of civilized agriculture, we might say – should be seen as a thank-offering and a precaution in case a god of the wild took offence. Burkert (1985: 58 and 149–52) has much to say on the subject.

Finally, how did the gods eat? I noted above that strictly the gods needed nothing. Accordingly, myths told of the gods eating the special foods of nectar and ambrosia which generate not blood in the veins but divine *ichor*. This can be seen, for example, at a feast of the gods in *Iliad* book 1 or in the description of Calypso in *Odyssey* 5. The gods ate in similar social contexts to human society, with couches and drinking cups, and disputes. There is a rich mythical tradition of the bloody marriage-feast among the gods. Examples are provided by the battle of the Lapiths and centaurs (a wedding feast overwhelmed by drink and lust) and the marriage of Peleus and Thetis, which in many accounts is seen as a tranquil prelude to the Trojan War. These events were imagined in many artistic and literary versions. For many, the strangest form of divine eating in antiquity was (in Greek) *theoxenia* and in Latin the *lectisternium*. In this format, the gods, rather than being remote, Olympian recipients of the sacrificial smoke, were present in effigy form at the human feast. Burkert (1985: 107) describes such festivals at Sparta and Delphi in the Greek world. For the Romans, Livy records the first *lectisternium*:

> When they managed to find neither the cause nor any means of ending the incurable plague of that winter, the Sibylline Books were consulted by decree of the Senate. The *duoviri sacris faciendis* celebrated the first *lectisternium* ever held in the city of Rome, and for eight days they appeased Apollo and Latona and Diana, Hercules, Mercury and Neptune, with three couches spread as magnificently as it was then possible to furnish. The rite was also celebrated in private houses. (Livy 5.13.5–8, trans. Beard, North & Price 2: 130)

The gods were desperately needed in the city to cure the plague. The best way to make them present (truly to inhabit their statues, we might say) was deemed to be at a banquet on a lavish scale. This was no moment for antique simplicity, indicating, once again, that religion and society were closely associated and that there was no necessary division between social lavishness and religious simplicity. Eating in a religious context may be lavish or not, according to the cult, the god and ritual in question and the political circumstances. We might compare the cult statue of the god, which might be an ancient carving in wood (Dionysus carved from fig-wood, for example), or a massive statue in gold and ivory, such as the Zeus at Olympia.

4
Introduction

Starch is central to our diet. A piece of meat or fish may be the focal point but it is the starch element that fills you up, that stops you feeling hungry, and that is core to the meal, whether it be fish, meat or vegetarian in style. Once eaten, the carbohydrates in starchy foods quickly convert into glucose, the body's main fuel, and circulate through the blood to all the body's cells. The body uses carbohydrates first, before fats or protein, so they will always give a quick lift to energy levels.

It is also a democratic aspect of the diet as both rich and poor alike will rely on it to form the base of their mealtime regime. Nowadays this could be chips or rice, but in the period before Colombus this would mean cereal crops such as wheat and barley either made into porridge or baked as bread.

Porridge has a deeply unappealing image. Made from oats, it forms the traditional breakfast in Scotland, where it is considered part of the country's heritage, but is little eaten by choice elsewhere. American grits made from corn may have the same reputation in southern states. However, wheat, milled into semolina which is made into a porridge, gnocchi alla romana, in Italy in the same way as cornmeal polenta, can be prepared in various guises, many of which are both interesting and exciting to eat. The porridge, once cooled and set with cheese and spices, for instance, can be grilled or griddled to give a totally different style and texture to the dish, a surprising take on what can constitute porridge.

The style and quality of bread are heavily dependent on the type of cereal used. Wheat is the top cereal, always the most sought after and most expensive. No other flour will make anything other than flatbread for they will not contain sufficient gluten to raise a loaf. Breads made from rye form dense heavy loaves that have wonderful sweet, sour notes as well as distinctive texture but lack the subtlety and class of white wheaten bread whether raised or flat. Barley makes passable porridge and can be cooked into a faux risotto but is really best made into beer.

It is possible to contend that the quality of a country's bread is indicative of its attitude to food generally. If the building block of our diet is treated with respect then there is hope for all the rest. Sadly, Britain and the United States come off badly in this respect and the industrially produced loaf, packed with inferior fats to improve 'mouth feel' and prolong shelf life, has dominated the market and been assimilated into the national consciousness as archetypical. In France and Italy bread is still largely in small-scale and careful production. Even Eastern Europe produces better bread from inherently inferior grains to give first-rate pumpernickel and rye sourdough breads.

Perversely, it is the enthusiasts who are returning brown and wholegrain flours to a position of superiority, through the organic and wholefood movements. These would have seemed strange indeed to those in Rome and Greece who spent ingenuity and resources tracking down the finest wheat and sifting it to a bleached whiteness – proof positive that good food and good cooking are as much cultural as they are a result of the lottery of climate and soil conditions.

Staple Foods:
Cereals and Pulses

> Besides, the bread sold in their market is famous, and they bring it in at the beginning and the middle of a banquet without stint. And when they are tired and sated with eating, they then introduce a most delightful allurement in what is called smeared brazier-bread. It is a soft and delectable compound dipped in sweet wine, with such harmonious effect that a marvellous result comes to one whether he will or no. For just as the drunken man often becomes sober again, so the eater of it grows hungry again with its delicious flavour. (Lynceus of Samos)

In the first three chapters, we have reviewed cultural factors in the understanding of food in Greek and Roman thought, social factors, and the place of food in religious thought and practice. In this and the next chapter, we come to examine some of the foods themselves, first cereals and plants, and then meat and fish.

Many ancient texts divide the diet into its cereal base, or *sitos*, and its plant and animal proteins or *opsa*. These *opsa* have been discussed by Davidson (1995, 1997), who shows that there was much concern in literary and philosophical texts to maintain the right balance between *sitos* and *opsa*; that the highly flavoured, tasty additions should not take over from the bland cereals as the dietary base. This was only a danger to the rich few, who were able even to contemplate eating more meat than barley-cake.

Certain principles governed the presence of any particular food in the Greco-Roman world. Regionality was always an important factor. Fish-eating was only a possibility for the mass of the population if they lived by the sea. If they lived in an area such as mainland Greece where barley grew better than wheat, they were less likely to eat wheat than barley. Agricultural methods of production and political control of distribution were also important factors. Large cities such as Athens in the fourth century BC and to a much larger extent Rome in the imperial period were better able to import animals for sacrifice or other purposes and grain than were ordinary smaller communities. For much of the ancient population, there was no obvious possibility of choosing a food that came from another continent or that was available across the ancient Mediterranean in the way that products such as pasta, sweet corn, wine and beef-burgers are now marketed. These markets depend on mass production and low unit cost to achieve international distribution. This did not occur in antiquity, except on a small scale, in comparatively luxurious foods. It happened to spices, which were light to transport and high in value. It happened to fermented fish and fish sauce, and to wine. A rich eater could choose to drink an imported wine rather than the local product. But for the majority this was not an option.

That lack of choice in comparison with the modern consumer, however, masks an important feature in antiquity – the movement of foods. As we have seem, p. 14, farming technology probably moved west to the Mediterranean from the Fertile Crescent. At a period before the classical period in Greece, the domestic fowl had travelled from the forests of Thailand to Greece and Italy, and the pheasant had arrived in Greece. By the first century AD, the rabbit and the damson plum had arrived in Italy and the citron was well known. The lemon and aubergine were almost certainly not known in the Mediterranean until the post-Classical period, and rice probably had to wait until the Arabic presence in Europe to become more than an exotic curiosity. This was a continuous process, that benefited the rich more than the poor, but nevertheless affected everyone.

While it is not entirely clear that cereal, wine and olive technology moved westwards rather than developing independently in a number of sites in the eastern Mediterranean, it is widely believed to be the case. It was believed in antiquity, which explained the arrival of wine in the Greek world with the mythical arrival of Dionysus from Asia and of cereals with the journey of Demeter and Triptolemus through Asia Minor.

This phenomenon is mirrored in the arrival into Europe of foods from the Americas at the time of the Spanish conquest. Turkeys, chocolate, vanilla, tomatoes, chillis, maize and potatoes arrived at the courts of Europe and were objects of royal interest before they settled down as food for the common people.

The movement of foods coincided with the movement of people, so that while some enjoyed exotica imported into their city, others encountered them in foreign places. Homer's *Odyssey* illustrates the phenomenon at an early date.

Trade brought to cities both exotica such as perfumes and spices and additional supplies or variants on what was locally available, such as wheat, wines and other essentials. Exotic imports were likely to attract the attention of competitive members of society, members of the wealthy elite in particular who might wish to display on social occasions food items that marked them out as being part of a knowledgeable international network. Imports of goods that were also locally available might be required if a poor harvest threatened indigenous supplies, or if an imported variety was perceived to be of finer quality. Thus a number of literary passages identify the finest products of particular places (see Chapter 9).

Cereals, together with beans and pulses, were the basis of the ancient diet. These formed the *sitos*, the staple of the diet, to which protein supplements, whether meat, fish, vegetables or fruit, were added. These supplements were known in Greek as *opsa*, in Latin as *pulmentaria*.

Cereals and pulses provide the majority of the body's energy requirements, as well as essential proteins, vitamins and minerals. For daily calorie requirements, Wills (1998: 12) gives figures of 1,940 for women under 50 and 2,550 for men. These figures are lower than those used by Foxhall and Forbes (1982: 48–9), which derive from the Food and Agriculture Organization of the United Nations. According to the latter, a very active male requires 3,337 and a very active female 2,434. Much of the ancient population – outside the leisured elites – could be counted as very active. We do not know how often they failed to gain their annual energy requirements, but Galen and Garnsey give good evidence that there were frequent shortfalls. This should not, on the other hand, be exaggerated. Foxhall and Forbes (1982: 66) report a post-war study of peasants in Crete which showed a standard diet of olives, cereal, pulses, wild plants, herbs, fruit, and a small amount of goat's meat, goat's milk, game and fish. This diet, not unlike the diet of much of the ancient population, provided some 2,550 calories a day, with more needed in the villages than the towns because of the heavier labour of farmers. Richer people also ate more meat and dairy products than their poorer counterparts. The researchers found these energy levels to be adequate, with no evidence of malnutrition. The Cretan study of Allbaugh (1953) and the ethnographic studies in the Argolid, on which Foxhall and Forbes base their study, provide invaluable comparative data for the ancient world.

We should bear in mind that while cereals might often appear bland and unappealing, particularly in the form of 'porridge' which is much present in ancient sources, there are many possibilities for variation in preparation. Galen comments on this, and on flavourings that might be added. We might compare, from the modern world, the differences between wheat in the form of bread and pizza; cakes; pasta, cracked and bulgar wheat and semolina (see Davidson 1999: 843 and *Larousse gastronomique* 1293–4). Ancient porridges sound unappetizing, but might be similar to Italian polenta, only made of wheat or barley rather than maize, which was not available in antiquity.

In many cities, the provision of grain was one of the primary duties of the authorities, failure in which might lead to civic disorder. There is a long history of grain shipments to Rome and other important cities from net exporting areas, and indeed of a two-way flow of grain as traders met different patterns of shortage according to agricultural and climatic conditions (Braund 1995 on the Black Sea in the fourth century, Garnsey 1988, Rickman 1971). The grain supply was something that potential benefactors could do something about, for the benefit both of the citizens and of themselves. It was important, too, to keep on side divine benefactors, as can be seen in the festivals of Demeter/Ceres and Persephone/Proserpina in many parts of the ancient world, and in the dedication of the first fruits of the harvest to these goddesses, as was discussed in Chapter 3. This daily need for cereals and pulses was recognized in medical texts, with both the Hippocratic *Regimen II* and Galen's *On the Powers of Foods* starting their account and devoting much space to the subject. In general there seems to have been a gradual development in the processing of cereals, such that new forms of wheat, for example, became more widespread during the period under investigation. Sallares (1991) studies bread and durum wheat; commercial bakeries grew up in large cities such as Athens and in Rome (Pliny 18.107, Curtis 2001: 367); there were developments in milling technology, as Pompeii vividly attests. A good deal is known about the milling of cereals on both a domestic scale and commercially. (See, for example Sparkes 1962 and Curtis 2001.) Much of the hard work of milling was performed by women (Wilkins 2000) – and, wherever possible, by slaves.

There might appear to be a distinction between Greece, the producer of barley and barley porridge or *maza*, and Italy, the producer first of

FIGURE 4.1   Women pound the grain with pestles in a mortar. This image on
a Boeotian vase anticipates daily scenes of women pounding cereals in many
modern countries. The work was hard and normally performed by women, or
slaves if they could be afforded. Smaller querns were also used (see Sparkes
1962), as were commercial, animal-powered mills, the latter particularly in
the Roman period. Moralists thought that food should be prepared at home.
Reproduced by permission of Staatliche Museen zu Berlin

far, or emmer-wheat porridge, and later of bread and durum wheats. The richer land of Italy could sustain the better cereal, which in nearly all ancient authors is considered better in a variety of ways. There are several important modifications to be made to this picture. Over the Greco-Roman world as a whole, there is no doubt that wheat is a superior cereal, since the gluten which naturally occurs in the grain enables bread to be made, through its ability to trap the gas produced by the yeast organism. Barley, in contrast, is much less successful a cereal for bread, and is better suited to barley-cakes, flatbreads (see further Braun 1995) and in particular the preparation known in Greek as *maza*. Foxhall and Forbes (1982) are particularly informative on the qualities of barley. It is not always the case that wheat was preferred to barley, as Archestratus shows (fragment 5, quoted in Chapter 2). But this is generally the case. Galen notes that the Roman army was prejudiced against barley, believing it to impart less strength to the body. (An impressive counter example to such a belief is the provision of barley to the Athenian rowers on an emergency mission from Piraeus to Mytilene on Lesbos. In Thucydides' account (3.49), the barley seems to meet the extreme demands for energy that the journey implies. The men ate as they rowed, and the food was a mixture of barley flour, honey and oil.)

Galen's treatise on food is particularly valuable in this area, for it covers a wide range of cereals and locates them across a wide social and geographical area. Thus in his native area of Mysia in Western Asia Minor, the standard grain seems to be a primitive wheat, while elsewhere it is millet or oats and in Thrace it is *briza*, or rye. Galen, unlike such authors as Archestratus and Athenaeus, was interested in the diet of the wider population, and noted the cereals that the peasantry normally ate, together with comment on the forms of processing and cooking and also on cereals that they might resort to in times of hardship. Galen's evidence is useful for its broad social reference. It also helps us to place cereals in a large framework, which includes religion and the place of human beings within the natural world. (See Baudy 1995 on the Eleusinian Mysteries; Chapter 3 above, on the Thesmophoria festival, links agricultural and human fertility.)

Cereals, like meat, were thus tied into the religious and social system. The support of the gods was necessary to ensure a reasonable harvest, and in most communities the hierarchy of grains set out by Galen (or a similar one) broadly followed the human hierarchy of wealth and status. Grain-eating was an essential activity of civilized people – the 'milled life' was in fact a term in Greek for the civilized order – and all the hard work necessary to prepare and grind the grain was performed largely by women or slaves. Marriage ritual reinforced the connection between the processing of grain and women's work. In Greece, a barley parcher was given to a new bride apparently by Solon: see Braun 1995: 27; in Rome, the ceremony of *confarreatio* combined a bread offering with a marriage contract (Garnsey 1999); and in Macedonia, a loaf was shared equally between bride and groom.

Status was often crucial. A rich citizen who was in a position to compare his or her own city with others might prefer a style of bread from further afield. It has often been noted (for example, by Goody 1982) that Athenaeus mentions some 74 types of bread. Athenaeus reflects the cosmopolitan overview, which can survey the whole Empire for the finest product in any category. Given the extent of that perspective, of course, 74 is a low figure for an area running from Spain to Iran and Russia to North Africa: there was undoubtedly much local variation (either in technique or terminology) that did not register in the cosmopolitan centres. Our sources give us, however, a fair range of breads and cakes, from the perspective of specialist bakers, techniques, region and (extensively) terminology. Greek breads may thus be compared with Roman, African with French. It is a mark of status to buy bread rather than make it in the household. We shall see Plato's and Livy's comments on such 'luxurious' developments in Chapter 7. If bread is to be home made, then a specialist baker could be employed. Both Hippolochus and Athenaeus note the excellence of Cappadocian bakers, and Galen mentions Cappadocian wheat (Dalby 2003: 74). The point is important whatever the 'real' skills of Cappadocians with flour.

Equally crucial, however, are geography and climate. A market might demand wheat, and a city such as Rome might be able to guarantee supplies in all but the worst harvests because of its domination of supply over a wide area from North Africa to the Black Sea. But for many people, other cereals kept hunger at bay better. These cereals might be a local speciality, such as those reviewed by Galen. There might also be a mixture of cereals, or a mixture of cereals and beans. Camporesi (1993: 100–1) notes that in Italy before the twentieth century, white bread was the preserve of the rich and the city dweller, while farm workers and artisans ate black bread, and the poorest bread made from bran alone. Wheat and bean flour might be blended to make a good peasant bread; barley might be used when the wheat was exhausted; vetches, oats, sorghum, rye with mixed grains and

FIGURE 4.2   Models of figures preparing and cooking food are found in parts of the Greek world, such as Boeotia and Rhodes. This Boeotian figure monitoring the oven is comparable to literary accounts, and the oven itself is found elsewhere in the archaeological record: see Sparkes 1962.

millet were also used. Camporesi's summary of cereals used for bread in Italy has much in common with Galen's list for Asia Minor and the Black Sea.

Camporesi reviews also the boiling of grains with milk to make polenta or porridge. Maize is the cereal generally so used in contemporary Italy, but other grains listed by Camporesi are millet, melic, barley, vetch, buckwheat, oats, spelt and 'panic'. These foods, made by boiling flour in water or milk, were widely used in Greece in particular, and could produce 'porridge'; dried porridges that could be reconstituted in thick soups, or flatbreads cooked in the hearth. Galen offers good evidence for this practice in Asia Minor, as applied to wheat flour and, as we shall see shortly, to acorn flour.

On a number of occasions, Galen, in the first two books of his *On the Powers of Foods*, discusses a hierarchy of cereal and other food plants, as far as consumers were concerned. He does not do this for animals and fish, probably, I believe, because these formed a less significant part of the staple diet of the majority of the population. First for Galen is wheat. This is the favoured grain of people of status, and is taken by peasants to town since it gains a higher price, and they can eat lesser cereals. Then come barley, lesser wheats, vetches and tares. At this stage, the food is fit only for animals. (The crucial word here is 'only', for many foods might be grown for animal or human food, according to circumstances. In the modern world, barley and maize have this dual use.) What constitutes a preferred cereal is determined by geography and social, cultural and medical factors. Will a gladiator be able to fight if he is fed on too few calories? Manual workers require more energy than citizens of higher status but less active lives. Should this energy come from 'better' cereals? Herodotus notes that the Persians considered the Greek diet inferior because it had little interest in cakes: from this perspective, the cereals are better prepared with honey, nuts and other attributes of cakes.

The bottom line, however, is to eat enough calories per day. Galen has a number of cases where famine strikes and enforces different cereal choices from the normal or the desirable. At 2.38, he considers wild plants:

> People in the country regularly eat wild pears, blackberries, mast and *mimaikyla* (as the fruit of the strawberry tree is called), but the fruit of the other trees and shrubs is not eaten very much. However, once when famine took hold of our land and there was an abundance of mast and medlars, the country folk, who had stored them in pits, had them in place of cereals for the whole winter and into early spring. Before that, mast like this was pig food, but on this occasion they gave up keeping the pigs through the winter as they had been accustomed to doing previously. At the start of winter they slaughtered the pigs first and ate them; after that they opened the pits and, having suitably prepared the mast in various ways, they ate it. Sometimes, after boiling it in water, they covered it with hot ash and baked it moderately. Again, on occasion, they would make a soup from it, after crushing and pounding it smooth, sometimes soaking it only in water and adding some flavouring, sometimes pouring in honey, or boiling it with milk. The nutriment from it is abundant, like nothing that has been mentioned in this work up to the present in this section of the book. For mast is just as nourishing as many cereal foods.

Of old, so they say, men supported life with it alone – the Arcadians for a very long time although all present-day Greeks use cereals. (trans. Powell)

Galen's comments are impressive: his understanding of the storage strategies of peasants is approved by Gallant (1991) and Garnsey (1999:40–1). His data on acorn-eating accords closely with Mason (1995), whose cross-cultural studies of acorn-eating corroborate Galen's comments on acorns as animal food, nutritional value, cooking methods and taste (bitterness caused by the presence of tannins). He also corresponds with her findings about the attribution of acorn-eating to primeval people, and to people in neighbouring villages (but not to the community of the witness him- or herself). Credibility is important, since Galen might be suspected of a condescending, distant view of peasants that has little to do with their daily lives long-term. Such is certainly the case with most ancient texts, technical and literary.

Galen follows the medical orthodoxy and places wheat and barley at the top of the list of human nutrients. Medicine, as part of the civilized world, accepted the supremacy of cereals to feed the population, over trees that might supply acorns or chestnuts. For the doctors, such foods were staples only in certain regions, and in times of food shortage. Consideration of staples, of course, leads to discussion of the whole population, and not just the privileged elites who could enjoy a high-protein diet. Galen's testimony, for what it is worth (I believe that it is worth a great deal), gives much attention to the mass of the population. He attests, for example, in times of shortage, the transfer of acorns from the usual use – animal food – to emergency use (human food) under duress – a shortage of food. The pigs were eaten early (as noted in Chapter 5), and the acorns eaten 'in place of cereals for the whole winter and into early spring'. We shall see other cases in Galen where the cereal base of the peasants' diet was most under attack in the Mediterranean spring. The peasants have thus, as often, been forced to resort to foods of lower choice. These are foods that were once acceptable but are no longer, and foods that were normally fed to animals. The hierarchy of foods reflects status – wheat in the cities, declining to barley and millet if under compulsion. But city authorities might resort to importing from abroad before that stage. Acorns are an extreme example, in terms of the *social* organization of the human diet. *Nutritionally*, says Galen (supported by Mason 1995, incidentally), the acorns are superior to all other such foods (including the ones normally eaten by these peasants, like the strawberry tree) – with the exception of chestnuts. (We might compare Galen's treatise *On the Thinning Diet*, where, medically, wild foods and mountain foods are preferred over the rich foods of the agricultural plains.) Then, in terms of energy transfer, it is much more efficient for human beings to eat the plant rather than feed the plant to the animal and eat the animal. These are all factors in peasant survival. Ancient peasants were forced down this hierarchy of foods more often than they would wish; they almost certainly ate less meat and fish than they would wish (given these are high-status foods). But these choices were not always, or necessarily, detrimental to health.

Camporesi (1993: 98) describes a similar practice in upland Italy. Drawing on an eighteenth-century source, he describes the use of wild and cultivated chestnuts, and the consumption of chestnuts eaten fresh, roasted or boiled, cooked in the ashes or in the oven. Wild chestnuts might also be dried, ground into flour and made into cakes. Camporesi's source, the Tuscan Saverio Manetti, claims that the poorest peasants in the regions of Pistoia and the Casentino district eat chestnut products exclusively as their bread staple. Similar dependence on chestnuts was also to be found in upland areas of France, the Limousin, for example, until recent times.

Galen notes the stimulus of famine to enforce acorn-eating, while for Manetti, chestnut-eating (an inferior nut in Galen's view) was endemic among poorer peasants. Such dietary constraints demonstrate the vast gulf between the foods of the rich elites of the city, who could choose which type of wheat bread they might prefer, and the perilous diet of the poorer peasantry. Country dwellers were inevitably more affected by seasonal factors than city dwellers. Galen frequently remarks on food shortages among the Asian peasantry in the lean months of the Mediterranean spring (see Chapter 2). Camporesi's assessment of the agricultural worker's diet in the region of Ferrara is similarly grim (1993: 81): 'there was practically no variation from day to day; the food was not only poor but debilitating and depressing, monotonously repeated month after month. The absence of bread was inadequately compensated for by the cheaper polenta; bread returned in the summer, when the extra energy needed for heavy farm work made its calorific value absolutely necessary. In that season, the peasants' diet improved and bread and ministra appeared on the table, though the latter was still the same old pasta and beans with a little seasoning. Foods such as tuna in oil, cheese and water melon eaten with bread also partially substituted for the bad water of the lowlands and for wine, which was often unavailable. Even without the evidence of calorific tables, it is clear that this type of diet showed a negative nutritional balance, especially in the winter . . . The latter was a long season of hunger, poverty and debt, at the end of which the poorest peasants and day-labourers were exhausted, in a dreadful psychological and physical state.'

This gloomy conclusion from an author who honours the old forms of food preparation over the mass production of modern Italy is similar to the remarks of another enthusiast for the old ways of the Mediterranean kitchen. Patience Gray describes winter on a Greek island as follows (1986: 189): 'On Naxos, on a restricted winter diet, everyone suffered from appalling pains in the liver region, deriving not only from monotonous diet but also from impure water and the terrible north wind.' Galen has an example of damage done to women's health by the eating of wild plants in the spring (quoted in Chapter 2).

I have noted elsewhere Galen's comment (*On the Powers of Foods* 1.2) that manual workers appear to have huge appetites and to be able to eat rapidly foods that upper class people would not be able to manage – but only at the cost of painful illness and early death. The grim life of the rural worker was alleviated by season, as Camporesi notes, and to some extent by festivals and special occasions in the life-cycle such as marriage. Here, a little meat might be eaten, or special foods, such as cheese-bread, which is the subject of Galen's text at the moment he speaks of peasants eating rapidly and unwisely. The peasants enjoyed the variety but did not benefit medically, if Galen is to be believed. Richer members of rural and urban communities doubtless fared better. There were many gradations and much variation across the Roman Empire between the extremes of the rural labourer and the rich elites who controlled local and international politics. Many might afford breads and porridges made from cereals and beans higher up the hierarchy, and also might be able to afford street food, including some incorporating small quantities of meat and fish, if they had sufficient means – as I explore in the next chapter.

We have seen in earlier chapters the importance of cooking in many areas of ancient thought. This is particularly important in the processing of cereals, as Galen himself demonstrates in his anecdote (see p. 58) about wheat flour boiled in water. This is the cooking method employed for the acorns and chestnuts discussed above, but this time used to cook high-status wheat. Galen's questions to his hosts when he suffers terrible ingestion as a result of eating this porridge reveal that they boil wheat as a rapid source of food when the bread runs out. This highlights the important point that preparation is often as important as the cereal or legume employed. Preparation of cereals is particularly time consuming since the outer husks often need to be removed before the grain can be ground into flour. This, as we have seen, was the work of slaves, and often of women. The women of Athens are freed from these arduous and time-consuming labours in two passages of Aristophanes, while his fellow comic poet Pherecrates has a character remark (fragment 10 Kassel-Austin) that the village echoed early in the morning to the women grinding grain in their mills (see p. 77). Aristotle remarks (Politics) that in poorer households, women perform the duties of the slaves. See Wilkins (2000a).

The preparation of cereals varied greatly. Braun (1995) provides an overview of bread-making and *maza*-production in the ancient Mediterranean, adding a useful review of Jewish practice in the Old Testament to complement the evidence of classical authors for the Greco-Roman world, and for Galen in particular, who considers also Asia Minor, Egypt and occasionally Syria. Wheat was sometimes finely ground, to make the best bread-wheat. But it could also be in a rougher form, the archaic groats, perhaps equivalent to modern cracked, or bulgar, wheat. Or it might have a grainy quality as in semolina. It could also be prepared as a porridge, like *maza*. Galen leaves us in no doubt that wheat boiled in a pot is far inferior to wheat made into bread. Different forms of bread-baking, too, produced very different products. These differences included texture and no doubt taste, and also medical effects. Galen rules as follows (*On the Powers of Foods* 1.2):

> Among the Romans, as also among just about everybody else over whom they rule, the purest bread is called *silignis*, and the next is called *semidalis*. While *semidalis* is an ancient Greek name, *silignis* is not Greek but I cannot give it any other name. Now *silignis* is the most nourishing of them; next is *semidalis*; and the one in the middle, wholemeal, is third. Fourth is the group from unwinnowed grain, of which the bran loaf is the worst. It is indeed the least nourishing, and of all the breads it moves the bowels most. The best-concocted breads are those that have been most leavened and very well kneaded, and baked in an oven with moderate heat. Greater heat scorches at once when first applied, and produces a pottery-like appearance on the outside; and the loaf turns out to be of poor quality on two counts, with its inside raw and inadequately baked, and its crust overbaked, dry and like pottery. (trans. Powell)

Galen's comments are similar to those of Diphilus of Siphnos and Philistion, two Hellenistic doctors quoted by 'Galen', one of Athenaeus' semi-fictional Deipnosophists (3.115c–f). Philistion praises fresh bread over dry; declares that bread baked in the ashes (*enkruphias*) is heavy and indigestible; and bread baked in a small oven (*ipnites*) or stove (*kaminites*) is indigestible. Bread in a brazier (*escharites*) or in a flat pan (*tagenistes*) is oily and indigestible. Best is the bread from a large oven (*klibanites*). These terms based on the baking environment are widespread. For a review see Dalby (1996: 91). In this medical analysis, expressed by Galen himself in *On the Powers of Foods* 1.2, the bread from a large oven is best. This view may well have been shared by those Athenians who bought bread from bread-sellers, or went to the Athenian version of Poilane, Thearion; also by the Romans who frequented commercial bakers from the second century BC onwards, in Rome, Pompeii and elsewhere. Here is a case of medical opinion and popular taste running counter to the fears of the moralists.

For those who could not bake bread, 'many people in the country in our region', Galen describes (1.5) wheat flour boiled with milk. There was also (1.6) coarse-ground wheat flour (*chondros*) boiled with water and eaten with a wine and honey mixture or wine alone, either sweet or astringent. Oil, salt and vinegar might also be mixed in. There were also rural dishes of einkorn boiled with *siraion* or salt and emmer mixed with must, sweet wine or a wine and honey mixture (1.13).

On the preparation of barley, Galen mentions (1.9–10) that bread can be made from it – and is vastly to be preferred – but that *maza* is the main product. What is meant by *maza*? It is, literally, a kneaded loaf. It won't be leavened much, if at all. It is a method for the incorporation of barley or other flour with liquids and possibly flavourings. So there could be a wet version, which is sometimes translated as porridge – a mix of wet cereal with honey, milk or other liquids, especially *siraion*, or concentrated must. Or it could be dried, broken up and kept for some years (Foxhall & Forbes 1982: 66). Or it could be a 'flatcake', as in many forms of *plakous*, or cooked into a sweet cake.

If the porridge form is chosen, vinegar can be added, oil at the beginning of the cooking, salt too (shortly before eating). The only other things to add are leeks and some dill. Galen criticizes, for medical reasons, other ingredients which cooks add, namely boiled grape juice or must (for *hepsema* and *siraion* see Dalby 1996: 89), honey and cumin. There were clearly both sweet and savoury versions of this 'mash' or 'porridge', the staple barley product, and the default if the barley grain was not to be made into flatbreads or cakes.

Other cereal preparations mentioned by Galen are oats (1.14), which are eaten in Asia boiled with water and sweet wine, *hepsema*, or a wine and honey mixture. There is boiled millet in rural communities in Asia Minor (1.15), mixed with pork fat or olive oil. Alternatively, it might be boiled with milk. It was also eaten in parts of Italy where it was a more successful crop than wheat or barley. Rye (*briza*) was made into a dark bread in Macedonia and Thrace. Galen (1.13) found it malodorous.

The hierarchy of cereals that I have discussed is based on a number of considerations. The first is that a large perspective is implied, so that wheat, barley, rye and so on can be set side by side and considered. Such an overview is likely to come from a writer or scientist in a large urban or intellectual centre, such as Rome, or in Galen's case Rome and Pergamum. This view is completely different from that of the farmer living in a community and trying to grow the best cereal for that soil and that climate. If, in the Black Sea region, millet or rye might be more likely to succeed, then it will be grown. There is also the issue of growing more than one crop in order to manage risk more effectively. Further, discussion of breads should consider non-wheat flours. The evidence for chestnuts in Camporesi supports this. Athenaeus mentions *etnitas*, a pulse-based flour, in book 3.

Secondly, authors assume that wheat is the best cereal. This again is often the overview. It is striking that Hippocratic doctors from *Regimen II* to Galen are clear that wheat is superior to barley, in strength and nutrients. Barley, though, had other qualities and was essential in the doctor's armoury for the production of barley water. This was a gentle food for those who could not take solids and certainly could not tolerate the thick humours that wheat produced in the body.

There is much ancient literature on cakes. For an accessible survey of the main cakes, see Dalby (2003: 68–71). Many of them appear in a list in Athenaeus 14. Many were mixtures of milk (Dalby 2003: 91), honey or sesame with the cereal flour. Galen tells us (1.3) how a pancake (or cake in the *teganon*) is cooked. Olive oil is put in the frying pan and the pan heated. A wheat and water mixture is poured into the pan. The mixture sets and thickens, resembling, says Galen, a soft cheese solidifying in a basket (hence quite thick). It is turned over several times to ensure even cooking.

There was great variety in the 'cakes' offered in religious rituals. Burkert (1985: 68) notes, 'in addition to the unground groats of barley which were taken and thrown at the beginning [of the sacrifice], there is also ground barley, *psaista*, in various forms, as flour, broth, pancakes and cakes; here a rich variety is found from place to place'. *Pelanos* and *popanon* are the main terms used for 'poured offerings' and 'cakes' in Greek sources. There was also possibly much variation between communities over what was meant by terms such as *plakous* ('flat-cake', *placenta* in Latin) and *libum* (in Latin). Editors of Cato's work *On Agriculture* are perplexed by the inclusion of cake recipes in this famously austere author. Some have attempted to show that these must be religious cakes and therefore acceptably austere. Others have suggested their commercial value, as an alternative source of income for the farm akin to the tavern suggested to farmers in Varro's work on agriculture. A third explanation would be that cakes covered so wide a range of eating in antiquity that the same name might be applied to a rustic confection as a rich man's titbit, and the same name to 'luxurious' Persian desserts as to a religious offering. We should accept the principles of diversity and the blurring of boundaries between sacred and secular, and – because of this diverse variation – judge discussions and descriptions by their context.

Breads, biscuits and cakes vary in place of origin, shape, ingredients and texture. Athenaeus in book 3 discusses breads, in book 14 cakes. In the latter he introduces as a great authority the book of Chrysippus of Tyana entitled *On Breadmaking*, but later calls Chrysippus 'learned in cakes'. Chrysippus probably wrote on both bread and cakes. The many names that Athenaeus derives from his work indicate sources in Greek and Latin, with many different ingredients, and a greater range than other books known to us. Ancient names for cakes, as with breads, often reflected different cooking methods and ingredients. Galen mentions two sorts of honey-cake, the poured and the wafer cakes (1.4). There were probably more varieties than two. Then there was the flat cake, *plakous*. The plakous is found in many texts, in both religious and secular uses. Galen remarks (1.3) that there are many different kinds of *plakous* in country areas and among the urban poor, made from improvised ingredients. Dalby (2003: 70) notes that a standard list of ingredients includes cheese, honey and flour. He observes, too, that the *plakous* is found in the most elevated company, at the second tables in the *deipnon* of Archestratus (fr. 60 Olson & Sens), and in a flowery comic description in the comedy *Aphrodisios* (fragment 55) of Antiphanes, also written in the fourth century BC.

Among breads used in a religious context, Athenaeus mentions the *thargelos*, used for the Thargelia festival in Athens, the *anastatos*, used for the Arrephoria festival in Athens, and the 'Health', a form of *maza* distributed at sacrifices for people to taste. (3.115a). Many such are described, Athenaeus tells us (3.115b), in book 3 of a book by Aristomenes of Athens, *Items related to Liturgy*.

Cakes were used for many religious purposes, and some seem to have had uses in religious and non-religious contexts. Under cakes, for example, Athenaeus lists the *amphiphon* (14.645a), a flat cake with little torches lit around it in a circle, and used in offerings to Artemis and Hecate. There is the *basynias* which the Delians sacrifice to Iris. It is made of boiled wheat dough with honey, dried figs and walnuts (14.645b). There is the *kreion* (a flat cake or a loaf, according to Athenaeus) which in Argos is carried from the bride to the groom. It is served with honey. There is the *elaphos*, or deer cake, made in the shape of the deer for the festival of *elaphebolia*, and made from dough, honey and sesame (14.646e). There are *mulloi* in Syracuse (14.647a) made for the Panteleioi at the Thesmophoria. They are made from sesame and honey in the shape of a woman's genital organs, and are carried around for the goddesses Demeter and Persephone. (Compare the cakes in the shape of male organs at the Athenian Thesmophoria.) There are *kribanai*, a kind of *plakous* or flat cake, which, says Athenaeus (14.646a), citing Sosibius, a scholarly source on ancient Sparta, were shaped like breasts. 'The Spartans,' Sosibius says, 'use them at women's feasts, and the attendants in the chorus parade them when they are about to sing the encomium prepared for the bride.' The breast shape is reminiscent of the Sicilian cakes made by nuns in the modern period. The breast also implies abundance, and is used in similar contexts elsewhere to suggest plentiful cereal production. Archestratus fragment 5, for examples, refers to the 'wave-girt breast of Eresos', a breast-shaped hill on Lesbos, before introducing a series of specialist loaves (see above). A fragmentary poem of Solon (38 West 1974) also refers to a range of breads and cakes as an expression of abundance:

> They drink and some nibble honey and sesame cakes (*itria*), others their bread, others *gouroi* mixed with lentils. In that place, not one cake was unavailable of all those that the black earth bears for human beings, and all were present unstintingly.

A *gouros* is a cake that Athenaeus could not identify, beyond calling it a *plakous*. We may wonder how flat these 'flat cakes' were if they could also be 'breast-shaped'. Athenaeus also fails to identify the place to which Solon attached this abundance of cakes and breads. It may have been a distant paradise; it may have been Persia (given the comment of Herodotus cited above); it may have been slightly excessive praise for a Greek city state. Something like this *gouros* appears in an elaborate poetic description written in about 400 BC by Philoxenus of Cythera (see Dalby 1996, Wilkins 2000). The poet writes in the dithyrambic style, which was ornate and originally designed for sacred hymns to Dionysus. The style is used by Philoxenus to describe an elaborate dinner. Cakes are brought in for the diners, described as 'mixed with safflower, toasted, wheat-oat-white-chickpea-little thistle-little-sesame-honey-mouthful of everything, with a honeyed rim' (trans. Wilkins). Another is made of 'dough, lentil?, pod, oil, boiled yellow, parched on every side' (trans. Gulick). There may be more poetry than cooking technique in this description. But we may be prepared to believe that poets who gave this much attention to cakes thought of them as an important part of a meal, along with the meat and fish dishes. Cakes do not seem to have been a mere afterthought in the Greek or Roman mind, even if they seemed to be that, comparatively, to the Persians.

The bottom line for our study is that cereals and beans were the basis of the diet for all members of society, with very few exceptions. Flour made from these crops was mixed with water, milk and other liquids, and flavours and such additives as honey and yeast were often important components. There were many names, as there were for fish and plants in the myriad cities of the Greco-Roman world. The names almost certainly exceeded the number of breads and cakes, given local colour and cultural applications such as religious festivals. A standard flat cake or honey-cake might be given a special name to attach it to a particular ceremony. Nevertheless, there was much variation on the theme. The poets give us perhaps some inkling. Chrysippus of Tyana does so as well. The practicalities too are a major factor.

It is difficult to distinguish between religious and secular cakes. Unless we are explicitly told as in the examples above, then religious and secular uses may have overlapped. At the same time, Herodotus reports (1.133) that the Persians considered the Greek meal insubstantial because few cakes were eaten, implying that these were the high point of the Persian meal. These nuances are explored in Dalby (2003: 70) and Wilkins (2000: 304–11). Some cakes such as perhaps the *amphiphon* and the *mulloi* may have been confined to specific religious rituals. Others have names that are often found in religious ritual (*pelanos* and *popanon* in particular). Others again are omnipresent, such as the *plakous* and the *libum*. Three points should be borne in mind. If a person wished to make an offering to a god, there was nothing to stop him or her offering a cake made in the home for human consumption. Many cake names are generic, like sesame or flat cake. If we cannot distinguish a sesame cake destined for a wedding from an ordinary secular sesame cake, that is not to say that the distinction was not very clear to particular people in a particular city at a particular period. We are after all dealing with an enormous time scale, compared with most histories of food. Thirdly, the distinction between sacred and secular does not work well in antiquity. Take the example of the *charisios*, which Athenaeus says was eaten at the all-night festival or *pannychis* (15.668c, discussed by Wilkins 2000: 309–10). The *pannychis* might be a part of a formal festival (see Chapter 3) or, apparently, the equivalent of a symposium (see p. 84). The 'religious' part of the occasion is as imprecise as the *charisios* cake itself and the extent over the Greek world to which this usage applied.

While cereal grains were the staple and received a place of honour in praises of nature's bounty in authors such as Pliny (*Natural History* 18), they could also be subjected to specialist refinement. Those able to afford better flours could choose not just the better cereal but also the more refined and graded flour. Authors alert to the dangers of commercialization (discussed in full in Chapter 7) also record the development of commercial bakeries in Athens and Rome. Plato in *Gorgias* refers to Thearion the baker, Sarambus the vintner and Mithaecus the cook as novelties in Athens who sold goods that could be made at home. Home production in Plato's mind, as in many modern minds, was far preferable to commercial production. Pliny records (*Natural History* 18.28) a similar phenomenon in Rome, the arrival of commercial bakeries during the Macedonian wars in about 170 BC. Mithaecus came from Sicily and the new Roman bakers from Macedonia: commercial production in both cities was, according to these sources at least, stimulated by foreign influence, whether the court culture of fifth-century Sicily or the rich way of life that Rome absorbed from Macedonia. Commercial baking, which in Rome and Italy became an extensive undertaking, with trade associations and milling plants – these are particularly evident in Pompeii – was a technological advance and was a benefit presumably to consumers as well as those freed from the toil of milling with querns. For the argument between simplicity and development (or 'luxury') in Plato and elsewhere, see Chapter 7.

In a discussion of cereals, a note is needed on the drinking of beer. Poseidonius in Athenaeus identifies beer-drinking as a 'barbarian' activity, found largely in such countries as Egypt and France. The political elites drank wine, imported or locally grown, while those who could not afford to connect themselves to the world power of Rome, or did not want to, drank beer made from barley. As in the case of milk (considered in Chapter 5), there is a (lesser) possibility that people in mountainous areas of Greece and Italy drank their own beer or equivalent rather than transporting wine from wine-growing areas.

There are telling passages in Strabo and Poseidonius. These geographical surveys with strong ethnological colouring identify beer-drinking in southern France. Beer is the beverage of the ordinary people, while imported wine is consumed by the elites, who are more influenced by the power of Greco-Roman culture in the broader Mediterranean world. This claim may reflect actual practice. Equally, it may be an ideological construction in the mind of the author, to sit beside the 'simplicity' of the British and the 'purity' of the Germans. These are two peoples at the fringes of the Empire who are imagined to be less tainted by the corruption at the centre but also more remote from the civilized life which radiates from the centre of the Empire. But when Strabo turns his attention to the Ligurian Alps (4.6.2), he describes mountain dwellers who live on sheep, milk and a 'barley drink' and practise transhumance between mountain and pastures near to the sea. When they come to market in Genoa, they trade sheep, fleeces and honey for olive oil and Italian wine, because their own wine is produced in small quantities and is resinated. Since much ancient wine may have been flavoured by pitch, Strabo presumably means that Ligurian wine was so flavoured to a pronounced degree. In Strabo's world, the Ligurians may have been as much part of Gaul as Provence or Lyon. But we should note that here we have evidence for drinkers of barley beverages in the Italian peninsula in the first century BC. Strabo, a writer in Rome, identifies the main factor in cultural difference as being between the city on the plain and the mountains, rather than a crude notion of barbarity in a different culture. Indeed, Strabo notes at the end of his chapter on the Ligurians that some people attest to their being a Greek people, because they use bronze shields. Garnsey (1999) has a different perspective on this passage.

The only archaeological evidence for beer known to me from the Greek world comes from Minoan Crete (see Chapter 1). This would appear to support the hypothesis. In the Classical period, the Greeks identified beer with other peoples, to contrast with their own consumption of wine. Athenaeus (10.447b–d) provides our evidence. The ethnographic writers Hellanicus and Hecataeus noted beer made from rye (*briza*) and (in Thrace) from barley. In Egypt, in connection with bread-eating they make barley beer. The Paeonians (in Macedonia) make barley beer and millet beer. Beer was also an issue for the tragic poets. Aeschylus showed how the god of wine Dionysus punished king Lycurgus of Thrace who foolishly fought against the god and 'drank beer aged over time and made proud boasts, claiming this was a brave thing to do'. Sophocles, meanwhile, in his *Triptolemus* showed how that culture hero brought agricultural technology through Asia Minor to Greece, and along with other cereals mentioned, such as rice, there was also mention of 'beer from the mainland which we are not accustomed to drink'. The mainland may well be Asia Minor. This sharp distinction between wine-drinking Greeks and beer-drinking barbarian neighbours seems to prevail, but stands up less well in the Roman period. By that time, Asia Minor was fully absorbed into the Empire. Any beer-drinking that continued there became part of a complex cultural mix, though traditional Greek thought might have prevailed. Mitchell (forthcoming) has shown that the production of olive oil in the cities of Asia Minor reflected a stronger Greco-Roman cultural presence in a city. Beer-drinking appears to have continued in Egypt, where expertise in wheat and in yeasts and in bread production may have strengthened the practice. In the Near East, too, there is evidence of beer-drinking over a long period in Babylon and in the Persian Empire. Beer-drinking in Greece and more widely in the Roman Empire is reviewed by Curtis (2001: 294 and 370–1). He notes evidence from Spain, Gaul, Germany and Vindolanda in Britain. The evidence, both literary and archaeological, with the exception of Minoan Crete, argues strongly for the making of beer in the countries around the Greek and Italian mainland. The closest most Greeks and Italians came to beer-drinking was probably the addition of barley flour sprinkled on wine preparations. This *cyceon* is found as a restorative in Homer and in a number of religious contexts, including the mysteries at Eleusis.

Cereals were the staple, the basis of the diet. With beans, they provided much of the daily requirement of calories and nutriment. Like cereals, beans and lesser crops are given a full examination in Galen's treatise *On the Powers of Foods*. They are a widely used but often low-status crop, with some medical qualities but also disadvantages, such as the production of flatulence. Flour is made from chickpeas and broad beans; slave-masters use bean flour; gladiators eat broad beans to build up their flesh. Garnsey (1998) gives an excellent review of the use of, and beliefs associated with, the broad bean. Use is extensive but enthusiasm muted. Galen (1.25) recounts with apparent surprise the vegetarian life of a medical student in Alexandria:

> For four years every day [he] used these alone as seasoning [*opsa*] – I mean fenugreek, beans, birds' peas and lupins. Sometimes he also used oils from Memphis, vegetables and a few fruits that are eaten uncooked; for it had been his policy not even to light a fire. So, in all those years this man has stayed healthy and maintained his bodily condition not a whit worse than it was at the outset. He ate them with fish sauce, that is to say, sometimes adding oil alone to it, sometimes also wine, and on occasion also vinegar; but at other times, as with lupins, he ate them with salt alone. (trans. Powell)

This voluntary vegetarianism was close to the diet of many poor people, if not the majority who could not afford meat, except on special occasions. It comes as no surprise to a modern nutritionist that the man stayed healthy for four years with a diet of cereals, legumes and flavourings, since together they probably supplied vital amino acids such as lysine to complement the cereals. Beneficial though this diet might be, meat would always supplant it if it could be afforded, as has happened in recent centuries in Britain and elsewhere. Vegetables are generally dismissed in ancient sources, unless a special point is being made or a comprehensive survey is supplied, as does Galen and Athenaeus. The scornful words of Archestratus are thus not unusual (fragment 60 Olson & Sens): 'all those other dainties are signs of wretched poverty – boiled chickpeas and fava beans and apples and dried figs'. Athenaeus has a lengthy section on lentils, much of which is directed at the claims of fraudulent philosophers.

There was a large range of fruits and vegetables available for ancient eaters. These are reviewed in Athenaeus book 2, Galen *On the Powers of Foods* book 2, and are explored in detail by Dalby (1996). Fruits, and in particular nuts, provide essential proteins and minerals to the

tur, oleum cùm garo iniicere oportebit: si salem pro garo sumas, nihil
diocriter bulliiße videbitur, priore aqua effusa, repentè aliam calente
dum tenera flaccidaque euaserit : quod non facimus, cùm ventris sui

VII. BRASSICA MARINA.   *VI*

Braßicæ ma- *Dioscorides prodiderit marinam braßicam folia ferre rotundæ aristo*

FIGURE 4.3   Seakale, brassica marina, was a wild form of cabbage, according
to ancient thought. The cabbage family was widely believed to have medical
properties, though Galen does not include nutritional value or wholesome
juices among these. Cabbage has an excellent nutritional profile in Wills
(1998: 308–9). Reproduced by permission of the Dean and Chapter of
Exeter Cathedral

staple cereal base, and were important in maintaining good health in the mass of the population that did not have regular access to meat and fish. Fruit and vegetables lacked the status of meat and fish, with the exception of the vine and its grapes, which are discussed in Chapter 6.

Trees and bushes were seen as the providers of human food before the arrival of cereals and agricultural labour in the rift with the gods placed in the myth of Prometheus. Ovid (*Metamorphoses* 1) and Lucretius (*On the Nature of Things* 5) give poetic descriptions of the lives of such hunter-gatherers (see pp. 36–7). We have seen, above, Galen's views on wet-nurses forced to eat wild herbs in the spring and country people forced to eat acorns and other wild plants. In the terms of modern nutrition, such plants might be considered to supply essential minerals and proteins; they were less likely to supply calories, which is often (but not completely) the focus of Galen's nutrition. It is striking that Galen does not rate highly either olive oil or almonds (2.27–9), two foods which are now held in high regard for the unsaturated fat and other health benefits which they appear to offer (Sallares 1991, Wills 1998). Cultivated plants provided a wide range of flavours. Salads, greens, onions and garlic are notable examples. They also provided winter supplies when dried or preserved. And dried fruits such as figs, grapes, raisins and peaches supplied sweetness in the absence of sugar. Galen (2.23) mentions quince cakes boiled with honey and shipped from Syria to Rome.

The fruit which had the greatest importance was the olive, with its distinctive contribution to the landscape, its connection with certain gods – Athena in particular – and its versatility as fruit, cooking medium, and soapy accompaniment to bathing. In the *Odyssey* the olive is the plant of civilization, whose shade covers Odysseus on his return to Ithaca. A stake of wild olive is used to blind the man-eating Cyclops. Olive oil was the prize for victors at the Panathenaic games. Distinctive though the olive was in the Mediterranean landscape, it was not always an easy plant to grow, nor were the trees always to be found in the same locations over the centuries. (See further Sallares 1991, Dalby 1996.)

In some authors, as we have seen, fruit and vegetables do not get a good press. These varied food plants, in the opinion of the doctors, provided varied benefits and the opposite, but in general were of less importance than cereals and pulses because they provided less nourishment (by which they meant energy, the equivalent of our (kilo)calories).

FIGURE 4.4   The mallow was linked with the diet of the poor by Hesiod and
Aristophanes, as it was in many cultures. There are numerous varieties, all
of which 'are totally devoid of unwholesome properties' (Grieve 1931: 506–9).
It was widely praised (by Pliny, Dioscorides and Galen) for its gentle and
laxative properties. Reproduced by permission of the Dean and Chapter of
Exeter Cathedral

Some authors praised mallow and asphodel – Hesiod memorably said that even in mallow and asphodel there is great benefit but Aristophanes perhaps states the matter more accurately. In his *Wealth*, the protagonist Chremylus is arguing with a fearsome personification of Poverty (Penia), who claims that she benefits the citizen. Chremylus describes their lot (543–4): 'instead of bread they feed on mallow shoots, and instead of *maza* on withered radish leaves'. Penia classifies this not as the virtuous life which she promotes, but the life of a beggar. Cereals, then, are the bottom line, with fruit, vegetables and herbs additional material or *opsa*.

Fruits and vegetables are much praised in Roman authors, in Virgil's *Georgics*, and in the agricultural authors. Excellent produce of all kinds was available and new varieties were also brought on. We have seen above the introduction of the cherry into Italy, just as the citron was introduced into Greece, perhaps in the time of Theophrastus. Nor were vegetables too lowly to be linked with luxury. Just as we shall see in the next chapter Pliny's despair at the luxury introduced into Rome by shellfish, so he speaks in similar vein on the cardoon (19.43):

> It might be thought that all the vegetables of value had now been mentioned, did not there still remain an extremely profitable article of trade, which must be mentioned not without a feeling of shame. The fact is it is well known that at Carthage and particularly at Cordova crops of thistles [cardoons] yield a return of 6,000 sesterces from small plots – since we turn even the monstrosities of the earth to purposes of gluttony, and actually grow vegetables which all four-footed beasts without exception shrink from touching. Thistles then we grow in two ways . . . They are also preserved in honey diluted with vinegar, with the addition of laserwort root and cumin, so that there may be no day without thistles for dinner. (trans. Rackham)

He does not object to the Spartan or Cappadocian lettuce, two imports from the East (19.38), or the Greek varieties of beet (40). The lament about the cardoon appears to focus less on its foreign origin than its cost. Earlier in book 19 (19), Pliny praises the cottage garden. He links the garden with the mythical gardens of the Hesperides, Adonis and Alcinous [in *Odyssey* 7]; and with kings: the hanging gardens of the Assyrian kings and the early kings of Rome. The Roman lawcode of the Twelve Tables gave every citizen a garden, whereas nowadays, luxury has invaded the garden, on the model of what 'Epicurus, the *otii magister* or master of leisure, introduced into Athens'. A garden in

Pliny's view predated the gross distinctions of wealth in Rome. It was a poor man's farm and allowed the masses to produce their own food rather than buy food (including imports) in the marketplace. Now that everyone is not supported by the garden, there is better bread for patrons than clients, plants for the rich to buy and not the poor; the water supply is divided up according to wealth, and the rich cool water with ice. Salads, which need no cooking, no fuel, and calmed the appetite, are now less honoured: people want pepper from India and other imports.

This approach to agriculture based on ideology is strong in many Roman texts, and is explored further in Chapters 7 and 9. It reflects anxieties about the success of the Empire and increasing wealth. Suffice for the present to note that these moral dangers can be attached as much to cardoons and the reduction in salad-eating as it can be to meals including fish and imported birds.

Pliny's doctrine on the Republic appears to admit foreign and royal models alongside the model of the citizen-farmer. He also notes imperial support for certain vegetables. Tiberius liked *siser*, skirret, an unidentified root vegetable, and ordered special ones from Germany (19.28: see Dalby 2003: 304–5). Tiberius had opinions also on asparagus (19.42), a plant that grew well in Italy. Cato approved of asparagus, and also hugely of cabbage, which had good eating and medicinal properties. This heavyweight approval for vegetables helps to place them in Roman culture. These are examples to add to the great republican story of Manius Curius eating his turnip tops (see p. 200).

Pliny's ethical views do not preclude foreign plants. Silphium, the giant fennel imported from Libya, is said to be most health-giving and most useful (19.16), even though it was a luxurious import that, according to Pliny (19.15), was, in a consignment of 1,500 pounds, stored by Julius Caesar in the treasury along with gold and silver. Pliny famously tells us that Nero received what appeared to be the last root of silphium growing in Cyrene. Thenceforth its essential quality and flavour were replaced by asaphoetida, another giant fennel which grows in the Afghan area of Ancient Persia. Silphium was one of the classic flavours of Greek and Roman food, found in Greek and Roman recipes and lists of foods. The plant offered the essential flavour of sulphur mixed with garlic, and in addition to its use in cooking also had important qualities as a drug.

Silphium was the valuable import – expressly so certainly in the fifth century BC, if not earlier. It is in the great list of imports into the

Piraeus put together by the comic poet Hermippus (see fragment 63), and is described both botanically and in trade by Theophrastus. There is not complete agreement with Pliny's statement about the plant's demise. Dioscorides mentions silphium from Cyrene in the same period. Arnott (1996: 386–7) cites a number of later sources who mention it, to which we might add Galen, *On Simples*. These texts may simply retain the term silphium for a product that everyone acknowledged no longer came from Cyrene. We may be certain that this plant marked out the sophisticated dinner in a way that locally grown sage, thyme or cumin could not do. It was expensive, but presumably less so than pepper and other imports from the Far East.

The Roman spice trade has been impressively studied by Miller (1969), with useful comments added by Dalby (2000, 2003). Spices ranged from locally grown basil and mint to cumin from the southern Mediterranean, and perfumes and spices from Arabia, Africa, India and the Spice Islands. Again, the more distance the spice had travelled, the more desirable it might appear to be to the rich Roman consumer. As we have seen, the Greeks used incense and myrrh from an early date; pepper is first mentioned in Hippocrates; imports seem to have developed apace after the time of Alexander through to the Roman imperial period. By the time of the cookery book of 'Apicius' a variety of spices both Italian and foreign was expected in many dishes. Pepper appears in more than half the recipes.

Pliny's research is not solely based on stories about iconic figures. He has read the Greek botanists and the Roman agricultural writers. Thus the austere moral perspective that salad is good because it requires little cooking needs to be augmented by questions of variety, regional availability, qualities of taste and nutritional properties.

5
Introduction

Until recently, all meat was seasonal and expensive. Recent changes in breeding and rearing of poultry and livestock mean that it has become cheap and everyday, in the developed world at least. Whether this constitutes an improvement is controversial of course, and the average city dweller will eat chops and burgers without ever having to confront the idea that what he or she is eating was once alive. Such fastidiousness would have been alien in our period, so ideas of ritual sacrifice and preparation of animals may seem a touch barbaric in our squeamish society. In reality they were the reverse, showing respect for the beasts, to the social order and to the gods. Those who confront the reality of slaughter as well as the cost of rearing and feeding livestock will be less inclined to waste the meat, of course. Chinese thinker Lin Yutang said that if a chicken is killed and then badly cooked then that chicken has died in vain – a good thought for our era of fish fingers and chicken nuggets that would have been obvious at any other times.

Thinking in terms of meat currently available to us may confuse the issue rather than clarify. We no longer use oxen to carry our loads so the breeds reared are now solely for the table or milking, much more tender and easily dealt with. The fats from pork and beef that are now considered dangerously laden with cholesterol were highly regarded sources of flavour and nourishment. We still eat these fats, of course, but in disguised form amongst large quantities of starch as sausages or encased in pastry as pies and pudding.

The notion of fish as the centre-piece of a grand meal will strike a chord in Spain and Italy but not in northern Europe where it would never supplant a joint of meat or poultry. Partly this is connected to size and display. A large fish such as salmon or sea bass may have some 'presence' but never the impact of a large, or preferably whole, joint or animal roasted for the occasion. The delicate flesh will not be as satisfying a prospect as roast red meat nor ever have any of its masculine and military associations.

Yet fish was the protein of choice so this is really a cultural as well as practical issue. Britain has always been surrounded by some of the world's finest fishing grounds but the eating of fish has always been as substitute for meat on fast days or as food for the poor. Never has there been the status accorded in the Mediterranean. Possibly this is connected to our damp cool climate, but more likely it is because our diet springs from the Saxon and Germanic taste pattern which had meat, beer and dairy products at its core rather than the grain and olive oil diet which it replaced, in Britain at least, when the Roman Empire disintegrated.

Shared food preferences are not unusual and form part of the glue that bonds people together. Taken a step further, there are the food taboos and dietary laws that are the hallmark of isolated and embattled ethnic groups such as the Jews. Superficially these are held to be part of some hygiene and cleanliness regime but this is not an argument that withstands any scrutiny. Why should ham be more dangerous than chicken? It is more likely that historical and cultural influences have combined to give an agreed style of eating, one that shows solidarity with the other beliefs and principles of the nation.

Meat and Fish

> Of tunnies pickled in the right season, Byzantium is mother, as well as of deep-sea mackerel and well-fed sword-fish, while Parium town is a glorious nurse of Spanish mackerel. And over the Ionian wave a Bruttian or a Campanian will bring as freight from Cadiz or holy Tarentum huge tunny hearts, which are packed tightly in jars and await the beginning of dinner. (pseudo-Hesiod)

Meat and fish were often high-status foods in antiquity. Animals were more expensive to raise than cereals and plants and were never as plentiful in the Mediterranean as in northern Europe. Fish were plentiful, but the arrival of shoals could not be guaranteed at expected times, and large single fish such as turbot and certain breams were difficult to catch and expensive. Farmed animals were often used for other purposes than slaughter, for milk, wool, and from the ox, labour. When they were killed for food, it was normally through the sacrificial process, as discussed in Chapters 1 and 3. Fish, as we have seen, were not normally part of the sacrificial rite, and so were linked with the commercial forces of the marketplace, and in particular with big spenders (see Gallant 1984, Davidson 1997, Wilkins 2000).

Because of the costs of production, meat was expensive, and large-scale consumption of it was an indication of wealth. Hence the meat courses in the wedding of Caranus and in the dinner of Trimalchio. That is not to say that poorer people had no access to meat. This was possible through communal sacrifice, and through dishes like the modern pizza which used a small amount of meat with much cereal and vegetables. The black-pudding or sausage seller in the *Knights* of Aristophanes and the small bars on street corners in Pompeii seem to have sold small amounts of meat (as opposed to whole animals for grand eating) fairly often. There were also many opportunities to preserve meat, whether fish air dried, smoked or in salt, or meat salted and dried. Roman sources suggest many hams and bacons were made (perhaps in small quantities) and salted fish, whether in chunks or fermented into the sauce known as *garum*, are widely referred to in Greek and Roman texts of all periods. Tanks for the processing of *garum* have been found particularly on the northern coast of the Black Sea, in Spain and Morocco, and in Pompeii. Preservation not only extended the life of the food. It also extended the range of its distribution, and modified tastes, so that added flavour was brought to pork meat, and fish juices after fermentation no longer tasted fishy.

Certain processed items were traded under claims of excellence. Strabo says that the finest salted hams came to Rome from France (4.3.2), in much the same way that other sources identified the salt fish of the Pontus and Spain, which was transported in amphorae like that other product of fermentation, wine. All three products illustrate the quality and hence the commercial value of certain preserved foods. Preservation of production surplus to requirement is an essential strategy for peasant farmers and other producers, to protect themselves against times of shortage. But the chemical processes of salting and fermentation also bring new flavours and textures that are desirable in themselves both for taste and other qualities. Galen, for example, has much positive to say about pickled foods, because of the properties of salt and vinegar.

Preserved meat also constitutes an example of meat not eaten at sacrifice. A large amount of the meat consumed in antiquity was the product of slaughter at sacrifice. It is often claimed that all Greek meat was produced in this ritual way. Much Roman meat also came from sacrifice to the gods. It is difficult to be dogmatic in this area, given that some of the evidence is linguistic (religious terms for slaughter do not necessarily imply slaughter on religious premises) and given the myriad cities under consideration in this book. But the general rule is that much less meat was consumed in antiquity than is now consumed in Western Europe and the United States; that the majority of it was in many periods the product of sacrificial ritual; and that the rich certainly ate more meat than the poor. As far as gender is concerned, the Minoan evidence cited in Chapter 1 suggests that some Bronze Age men ate more meat than their female counterparts.

Ancient consumers, in particular Greek consumers, seem to have eaten a much wider range of animals than is now eaten. They were less likely to eat beef, except at big city festivals. The main meat was pork, with some mutton and goat's meat. They relished the different textures of each part of them much more than is the case in modern Britain and the USA. Birds of all kinds were eaten, along with foxes and hedgehogs. There appear to have been few taboos (Garnsey 1999). There were, however, foods that were favoured and those that were not.

The Hippocratic author of *Regimen* II lists meats as (46): beef, which is strong, goat, pork and piglets, lamb, asses, dog and puppies, wild boar, deer, hare, fox and hedgehog. This list progresses from farmed animals to wild animals, and moves to the edge of the human diet in the case of dogs and puppies. Galen has rather more to say on setting the boundaries of the human diet. In book three of *On the Powers of Foods*, he identifies pork as the most nutritious of all foods, then beef and goat-meat, with qualifications about the meat of young animals. Lamb and hares are then considered, followed by wild asses. Old donkeys he finds very unsuitable (3.1), 'like horse and camel meat; which latter meats men who are asinine and camel-like in body and soul also eat!' Bear meat, and the meat of lions and leopards are said to be worse. Galen continues, 'As to dogs, what must I also say? That in some parts very many people eat young plump dogs, especially ones that have been castrated. And as well as these, many eat panther meat, as they also eat that of asses, when they are in good condition, as wild animals are. Indeed, not only do they eat them, but some physicians hold them in high regard. And amongst ourselves, huntsmen often eat the meat of foxes in the autumn, for they are being fattened by grapes.'

The range of meats is wide, but Galen does not specify where, for example, camels are consumed, or panthers. Since elsewhere he notes that camel was eaten in Alexandria, we should ascribe some of these practices to certain parts of the Roman Empire, camel to Egypt and perhaps Mesopotamia, and panther to distant outposts. Camel-eating in the Persian empire is noted by Herodotus (1.133, quoted by Athenaeus (4.143f) in his discussion of Persian meals) in the context of birthday celebrations: 'on the day, the well-off serve ox, donkey, horse, and camel, roasted whole in ovens. The poor among them serve small herd animals'. Herodotus picks up both the choice of special day, which is unusual from a Greek perspective, the unusual animals and the Persian mode of cooking which cooks the animal whole (however big), in contrast with the Greek dismemberment of the animal's body in sacrifice, prior to cooking. Herodotus characteristically notes difference without pejorative comment. Aristophanes, in line with expectations of Athenian comedy, pokes fun at the Persian practice of cooking animals whole in his *Acharnians*, while Galen, in trying to delimit the boundaries of the Greco-Roman diet, dismisses camel-meat without specifying the eaters. He thus characteristically presents a perspective from the centre of the empire, geographically speaking. Roman territories now included parts of the Egyptian and Mesopotamian deserts, and so camel-eating was to be expected and included in an imperial text, even if it might not be commended by a physician writing either in Rome or in his native Pergamum (which had been fully part of the Greek world and the Roman world for hundreds of years). We can identify a similar imperial interest in camels in the description of the procession of Ptolemy Philadelphus quoted by Athenaeus (5.200f) from the *Alexandreia* of Callixeinus of Rhodes (cf. p. 103). The camels carrying loads of spices from the east were part of a royal display of wealth and Dionysiac festivity, which the Egyptian kings were able to import from the east.

How close to home dog-eating came is not specified, but it is only fox-eating that Galen ties to his native Mysia in western Turkey.

Similarly, the eating of wood bugs and snakes is dismissed as an Egyptian, non-Greek practice (3.2). The Greeks and Romans ate certain insects, locusts in particular (see pp. 54–6). We saw in the last chapter that the diet was further defined in terms of edible cereals and plants, with the boundaries being carefully tested through the diet of peasants in the hungry months of the Mediterranean spring.

Meat is a particularly important subject of study for a number of reasons. It derives from sentient animals (an issue discussed further in Chapter 7). It has considerable religious importance, which was discussed in Chapter 3. It is connected in many cultures with status, in particular with men. It is rare in the Mediterranean in comparison with the countries of northern Europe and North America. Fish, as we shall see, was associated with luxurious eating in many ancient texts, but meat too was a luxury for most, albeit a luxury sanctioned by religious ritual. Meat served as a symbol of power and wealth. Greek cities such as Athens which were placed in comparatively dry and rocky terrain were not suited to the production of cattle, yet in the fifth and fourth

FIGURE 5.1 The camel, though a beast of burden, was eaten in Egypt and parts of the Persian empire. It is a sacrificial animal in Islam but outlawed to the Jews in *Deuteronomy*. Galen dismisses camel meat, apparently by mentioning it indicating an Empire-wide range that includes the Middle East but at the same time drawing a distinction between what is edible and what is actually eaten in the heartlands of Italy, Greece and Western Asia Minor. We might contrast Galen's treatment of the dolphin which in much ancient thought is the marine mammal most friendly to human beings (and therefore perhaps only eaten by remote peoples) but for Galen is listed as fish suitable for salting. Harding-King Collection EUL MS11. Courtesy of Exeter University Library (Special Collections)

centuries the citizens slaughtered hundreds of cattle at city festivals in order to demonstrate the wealth and power of the democratic regime. Cattle were imported from regions more favourable to the rearing of animals, two of which, Euboea and Boeotia, reflect a connection with cattle in their names. Similarly, Homer's heroes famously dined on roast beef for the ten years that they besieged Troy, strengthened by this high-protein and very expensive diet which few attained outside epic poetry. Wealthy citizens in Macedonia served a number of meat courses, as is exemplified in the wedding of Caranus described in Chapter 2. In Rome, meat courses proliferate in descriptions of meals. The many meat courses served by Petronius' comic hero Trimalchio, for example, may be compared with the archaeological evidence provided by the Schola Praeconum in Rome which attests massive meat production (*Barnish 1987*). It may be that Italy should be identified as the Texas of the ancient world. To some extent the early Greek historian Hellanicus does this (fragment FGrH 111) in his derivation of the name Italy (a more restricted area in the fifth century BC than Italy as now imagined) from the Italic/Latin word *vitulus*, or calf. Varro mentions the derivation also in his *On Agriculture*. Meat seems to have been a significant element in the Roman military diet (Davies 1971). More meat is also revealed, interestingly, in idealized descriptions of simple eating imagined to have taken place in earlier periods, in which the sturdy Republican peasant exists on simple fare which includes bacon or other forms of preserved pork. Greek idealizations of the past and of innocent rural life often, in contrast, identify a vegetarian life. Plato's *Republic* provides such an example.

The extent of meat-eating is hard to gauge. We may be reasonably certain that the majority of the population did not eat meat often; that they were most likely to eat it on religious occasions; and that the animal most likely to be consumed was the comparatively prolific and comparatively cheap pig. In a powerful study of animal husbandry, Jameson (1988) concludes that the most common sacrificial animal was the pig, that the suckling was the commonest of that category, and that the amount of meat available per person was small when compared with the United States or Western Europe. Jameson's evidence is from Greece in the Classical and Roman periods. For Italy, meanwhile, Varro claims that 'all of our people' keep a pig in Italy at the end of the Republican period. It is not clear precisely how far down the social scale 'our people' might extend. It is not well attested that pigs which were kept during the spring and summer were then killed in late summer, which is a widespread model of pig-rearing in Europe in later periods. This may have been the practice, which may be supported by Roman literary references to preserved hams hanging in the rafters of Italian houses. But it is also possible that in the Greco-Roman world pigs were normally destined for religious occasions and were killed at other times of year. In Greek cities, certainly, large numbers of pigs were killed at certain fertility festivals, in particular those of Demeter

FIGURE 5.2   A hero, perhaps Herakles, reclines on a couch beside a table of meat, which conventionally hangs over the edge in strips. The image is painted on a mixing bowl. Gods and demi-gods were shown in the same dining posture as their human counterparts, as were the dead. The divine images, again, aided refection among the diners and drinkers. Reproduced by permission of the Staatliche Antikensammlungen und Glyptothek, Munchen

such as the Eleusinian Mysteries and the Thesmophoria festival. Jameson (1988) comments on the broad concurrence between the main pig-killing times of year and the major festivals. The religious calendar appears to coincide with the annual cycle of animals to be culled from the herd.

Galen has some evidence for a different model of pig-rearing from that European model. In a discussion of acorns (*On the Powers of Foods* 2.38), which is quoted on pp. 120–2, he notes that famine caused country people (in his native Mysia in Asia Minor) to give up their normal practice of keeping pigs through the winter. They were forced to slaughter them and eat them in autumn. Pliny also (*Natural History* 8.205) mentions the birth of pigs in the month *bruma*, in the middle of winter.

We considered the religious importance of meat sacrifice in Chapter 3. Meat appears here also because of its role as a dietary supplement to the cereal staple, and as a food of much higher status than its contribution to the diet as a whole would appear to warrant (see Fiddes 1991). It is first-class protein, so a most desirable supplement, but in a Mediterranean climate it is not available in quantity to any but the privileged. A city state such as Athens could display the strength of its resources by slaughtering hundreds of cattle at some festivals, as could Hellenistic rulers and Roman emperors. Italy probably did support a higher animal population than the Greek mainland. It is difficult to estimate the extent to which this affected the mass of the population. The distribution of meat certainly was not included in imperial largess until the third century AD. The main conclusions that we should probably draw are these. Comparatively more meat (but not much) was eaten in Italy. Consumption by the rich accounted for the most significant meat-eating. The general paucity of meat is indicated by the contrasting descriptions of the Celts as great meat-eaters in the northern parts of Europe.

The inclusion of pork in sumptuary laws would indicate its importance in the display of the rich. Pliny tells us (*Natural History* 8.209) that pig products offered great variety at the *ganea* or eating house, which links it with the poorer classes. But he moves then to the formal dinner or *cena*: 'Hence there are pages of laws from the censors, and items banned from formal meals (*cenae*): bellies, sweetbreads, testicles, wombs, testicles and halves of pig's head.' Literary descriptions of meals such as Trimalchio's *cena* in Petronius seem to be linked with extravagance, where pork and pork products are included in a series of courses. Here is the rich and vulgar freedman who treats his poorer guests to a surfeit of pork. This is a mark of his wealth, but it may also be a mark of his vulgarity, for he seems to include very little fish in his meal, which elsewhere in Roman culture was seen as a true food of the elite. Fish distinguished those with access to international styles of eating from the traditional citizen of the republic who subsisted on emmer wheat and bacon (Ovid *Fasti* 6, cited on p. 88). There is a possibility that Trimalchio's emphasis on pork is not so much a mark of elegant display as a sign of his servile origins.

Meat invariably appears at the great dinners of antiquity. In certain places – Athens in particular – expensive fish are also in evidence. But meat retains its premium status. It is the major offering that a human being or community could offer to a god. It is the food of the heroes in the *Iliad*. It is the food, too, of Heracles. The gluttonous demi-god is the divine equivalent of Milo the meat-eating athlete (see Chapters 1 and 2). Fragment 6 of the comic poet Eubulus has Heracles express his contempt for vegetables and anything that is not meat:

> Be it hotter or crisper or something between, this is more important for any man than capturing Troy. As for me, I have not come here to browse on kale or silphium or sacrilegious bitter dishes or bulbs. But on what counts first as real food, promoting health and the full vigour of physical strength, I have always been wont to feed – beef boiled and unspoiled, in huge quantity, with a generous portion of foot and snout, and three slices of young pork sprinkled with salt. (trans. Gulick)

His formula of rejection is very similar to the words with which Archestratus rejects vegetables (fragment 9 Olson & Sens 2000), though in his poem, it is fish rather than meat which is the preferred protein.

Rich and poor citizens also had access to wild animals. Wild boar, says Pliny (*Natural History* 8.210), also found great favour. Wild boar feature in a number of literary accounts which derive from the aristocratic sport of big-game hunting. (See Odyssey 19, Juvenal 1 and Petronius.) Deer-hunting should also be mentioned, along with hares and other smaller mammals, not least the famous dormouse. Galen speaks in summary of a range of such mammals *On the Powers of Foods* 3.1, quoted on p. 13. These include the rabbit, the fieldmouse and the dormouse.

The most common meats available to poorer citizens were almost certainly birds. A wide range of birds were eaten, and chickens were not the pre-eminent bird for the table that they now are. A number of birds were kept in captivity, as were dormice and fish. Varro has extensive advice on the rearing of captive birds and fish (3.9), while Galen *On the Powers of Food* 2.18 comments that in his day 'chicken' were simply called 'birds', implying that they were the usual bird for the table. Birds could also form part of the display desired by the wealthy. Guinea fowl are widely attested, flamingos are mentioned by Apicius and others, and pheasants and francolins were imported from the Greek world. Athenaeus reviews a wide variety of animal meats in Book 9.

Meat provided both essential proteins to the ancient eater, and also texture. Both Greek and Roman texts attest an interest in different parts of the body. In animals these might be the head and ears, the trotters, and many of the internal organs. In Rome the womb and

udder were particularly favoured. Apicius concentrates on sterile and
other special aspects of the pig that provided the womb. The delight in
texture links the Greeks and Romans with French and Spanish eating
in the modern world, and Chinese in particular. Texture is much less
sought after in the Anglo-Saxon countries of Britain and the USA.
Here, the burger and sausage take over as the vehicle for the lesser
cuts of the animal. Greek and Roman diners had the textured parts of
the animal, and rissoles and sausages in addition. Apicius devotes a
whole book to the glory of the rissole, and the word for rissole, *isicia*
in Latin, comes up as an item for discussion among the Deipnosophists
of Athenaeus. Texture was also provided by the different parts of the
fish, the head of a conger eel, the belly or tail flesh of a tuna, the cheeks
of members of the cod family. This interest is seen in some fragments
of Archestratus and also in a number of fragments from Athenian
comedies which are parts of speeches where characters enumerate
either their favourite foods or (more often) items in a meal which they
are preparing for someone else. Here many parts of fish and animal are
found, including vital organs and parts of the animal that are linked
with the sacrificial process described in the previous chapter but which
appear also to have made their way to the marketplace for purchase in
the commercial sector. Galen tells us in *On the Powers of Foods* of the
properties of feet, snouts and ears (3.3), tongues (3.4), glands such as
saliva glands, breast glands and testes (3.4), brains (3.7), bone marrow
and spinal marrow, intestines, stomach and uterus (3.12). This medical
evidence is supported by lists of foods from Athenian comedies, such
as fragment 63 of Eubulus:

> Besides this you shall be served with a slice of tunny, pork-chops, kids'
> entrails, boar's liver, lamb-fries, beef guts, lambs' heads, a kid's appendix,
> breast of hare, a sausage, black-pudding, lung, and salami. (trans. Gulick)

The interest in the anatomy of animals is scarcely less than in the
human equivalent. For a review of the animal body, see Durand (1989);
for the human body, Chapter 8 below. Galen's list of body parts is not
confined to quadrupeds. In 3.20 he reviews bird intestines, wings of
hens and geese, cock's testicles, bird's brains. The feet of all birds, he
says, are not really edible, while he cannot comment on the wattles
and combs of cocks. Only at the very end of this list of body parts does
Galen fall short of the range of an enthusiastic Chinese cook.

There is a hierarchy of meats in many sources, which is related to the cost of production. The swineherd in *Odyssey* 14 (a book with many details of animal husbandry, unusual sacrifice and the consumption of meat) describes to his disguised master the wealth of Odysseus as expressed in cattle, sheep and pigs. He offers his guest a small animal because the wicked suitors are devouring the fattest hogs. Athenaeus (4.148d–e) cites a passage from the *History of Alexander* by Cleitarchus, in which the Thebans are said to be mean spirited and stingy as far as food was concerned because the foods they prepared were, 'mince-meat rolled in leaves (*thria*), boiled <fish>, two kinds of whitebait, sausages, ribs and pea soup'. Cleitarchus interprets these foods as meagre offerings (in the place presumably of meat and large fish) which do not reflect what the Thebans could afford.

Similarly, at sacrifice, a rich person or group might perhaps afford an ox (compare the *Orgeones* in Chapter 3). Most would offer a sheep, pig or the young of the animal. The offering of piglets, for example, was widespread. If the worshippers could not afford animal sacrifice at all, or if the cult demanded non-blood sacrifice, then cakes of cereals and other plants were offered. Outside the sacrificial context, meat and meat products were available for sale. Thus the father of Aeschines the follower of Socrates was, we are told, a sausage-seller or black-pudding seller (Diogenes Laertius 2.60). Aristophanes made a sausage-seller the central figure in his *Knights*. It is clear in the play that the sausage-seller is imagined to trade in a number of animal products, all of which may well derive from sacrifice before they were sold to the sausage-seller for retail sale in the Athenian marketplace. Aristophanes comically presents the sausage-seller as the lowest of the low, and it may well be that this was a lowly trade. But nearly all market traders appear to be presented in a bad light in literary texts: this is part of the curious relationships that ancient texts had with the production, distribution and exchange of food (Wilkins 2000, ch. 4). It would be unwise to conclude from the ancient presentation of sausage-sellers that sausages and other animal products were not favoured as food. Since texture was valued, as noted above, eaters of all ranks tucked into heart and kidney and black pudding, independently of the symbolic role of these foods in the sacrifice (which was described in Chapter 3). The strong flavours and textures these foods offer appear to have been favoured by all classes: they are found in luxurious banquets and a book of Apicius (who, however, must be read with care: see Chapter 7), as well as on the market stalls of satirized characters.

It appears to be the case that in Greek culture, the eating of any kind of meat was rarely separated from animal sacrifice. It is fine for the market stall to intervene between sacrifice and dinner and symposium (that is, for the commercial transaction to separate the consumer of the animal from the group who sacrificed it), but sacrifice will normally have taken place, as far as we can tell. This seems to hold true when Eumaeus the swineherd feeds the disguised Odysseus in *Odyssey* 14; true too in the fourth-century Athens of Theophrastus' *Characters:*

> The shameless man is one who after sacrificing to the gods will himself go out to dinner with someone else, and then salt down the meat and store it. At his host's table he calls his slave, then picks up meat and bread from the table and gives it to him, saying so that everyone can hear, 'Make a good meal, Tibeios!' When he goes shopping he reminds the butcher of any small service he may have done him; and he stands near the scale and slips on to it some meat if possible, otherwise a bone to make some soup; and if he gets away with it he's happy, and if not, he whips a bit of tripe off the table and chuckles as he hurries away with it. (trans. Vellacott)

This wonderful profile of low life in the Athenian home and street, which, if on stage or in a literary text, would illustrate the unsavoury 'bomolochus' character described by Aristotle, shows the ethically inadequate man failing to link sacrifice with a shared meal, failing (by implication) to eat reciprocally with others, and failing to buy honestly from the butcher. The social order is as firmly encoded in these scenes as in Menander's *Dyscolus*.

St Paul famously advised the Christians in Corinth, who were concerned that they might be eating meat from pagan sacrifice (Corinthians 1.8). The advice is to eat the meat notwithstanding, because Christ is a stronger deity than pagan gods (I *Corinthians* 8). It appears that meat could be acquired in Corinth by people who did not wish to participate in the sacrificial ritual. Other sources in the Roman period, as we have seen, imply mass production of meat. It is difficult to estimate the extent to which such development really separates sacrifice from meat production. Varro, writing about a century before St Paul, (*On Agriculture* 2.5.11) certainly gives the impression that there was meat raised 'for the knife' – for the butcher that is – and conversely meat raised for sacrifice, *ad altaria* (Frayn 1993: 156, Dalby 2003: 213).

Meat (of undetermined origin) seems to have been available in commercial outlets. Taverns and cook shops in Italy appear to have served cheap cuts of meat and sausages (subject to restrictive legislation from various emperors). We should probably assume that small amounts of meat were consumed by a fair proportion of the population, but not with great frequency. It is worth comparing the Neapolitan evidence from the nineteenth century quoted on pp. 59–60. Some customers ate pasta with a sauce. The very poor had no sauce, and the poorest did not even have the pasta, but only the water it was cooked in as a flavouring. Frost (who brings together some of the passages above) argues for widespread familiarity with meat. Varro claims (2.4.11, on the authority of a lost work of Cato) that the Insubrians in northern Italy salt down 3,000 to 4,000 sides of bacon. Curtis (2001) reviews the extent of meat-eating in Roman Italy.

Fish-eating differed from meat-eating in antiquity. Fish eating, as we have seen, was generally not part of the sacrificial system for either the Greeks or the Romans. Some of their neighbours, the Lydians, the Syrians and the Egyptians, had some sacred fish, the Greeks and Romans far fewer. Athenaeus notes some sacred fish in book 7, and some exceptions to the rule were explored on pp. 107–8. Because they were generally not part of the religious order, fish could be bought at market by anyone who could afford them. Fish supplies are notoriously subject to fluctuation, and antiquity was no different (Gallant 1984, Purcell 1995). For people who lived in easy reach of the coast, fish was at times plentiful and at least sometimes available at low cost, provided the species were shoal species such as anchovies and sardines that could be caught in large numbers. The pessimistic account of Gallant has not generally found favour, though see Purcell (1995) and Hordern and Purcell (2000). I have argued (Wilkins 2005) that much of Gallant's evidence can be accepted, provided fish is seen as a dietary supplement and not a staple provider of calories.

Fish-eating is famously absent from Homer. This is discussed in Chapter 9, but deserves mention too here. The Homeric heroes eat a surprising amount of beef and very little fish. They only eat it in fact when driven by hunger to do so. Fishing, hooks and fish are mentioned in the poems; the Homeric king is said to preside over well-stocked seas if he is a good king. But fish is not eaten. The poet evidently follows a code that promotes meat at the expense of fish. We can be reasonably certain that Bronze Age Greeks did eat fish, to judge from the archaeological evidence cited on p. 7, and the evidence from a number of other Minoan sites, some of which are listed by Curtis (2001: 274–5). The sacrificial cattle belong to the heroic world and perhaps reflect the closeness between the heroes and their gods, together with their wealth in being able to eat meat every day. The codes of later literature identify fish as a great luxury. This is to take the opposite extreme, and is an equally special reading of the role of fish in the ancient diet.

As elsewhere in this book, so with the eating of fish, there is much regional detail to add to the broad picture. It is this variation which is the basis for the poem of Archestratus. Fish such as the red mullet were more common in Greek than in Italian waters, and so commanded higher prices in Roman markets. For many Greco-Roman communities the dolphin was sacred, or at least not eaten. Literature from Herodotus to Pliny the Younger abounds with stories of the proximity of dolphins and human beings. Xenophon, however, came across a very different practice, in his march through Asia Minor *Anabasis*:

> In looking for booty in these positions, the Greeks found in the houses stores of loaves piled up and, according to the Mossynoeci, made of last year's flour, with the new corn, stalk and all, set aside. It was extremely coarse wheat. Slices of dolphin, pickled in jars, were also found, and dolphin fat in containers. The Mossynoeci used this fat just as the Greeks use olive oil. In the attics there were quantities of chestnuts – the broad kind with a continuous surface. They used these in large quantities for eating, boiling them and then baking loaves of them. Wine was found there too. When mixed it tasted sour because of its roughness, but it smelt and tasted good if mixed with water.

The essential points about fish are three. First, as Purcell (1995) has pointed out, the supply of fish is unpredictable. A shoal of fish may be caught, and the price be very low for a short period. The supply may be such that it is converted into animal food, as happens in the modern world. Fish of this kind, such as sardines and tuna, are therefore possibly available to all, to those who have access to the sea, at least. This is with the provision that only occasional generous supplies are envisaged. The supply of singletons, fish which do not move in shoals and are caught individually, is much more problematic and therefore the sale of such fish is at a higher price. These are the fish studied by Davidson (1997), and these are the type of fish taken to the king or emperor when an extraordinary specimen is caught. Stories attached to Polycrates and Domitian provide examples of the phenomenon of the special fish

FIGURE 5.3 This tetradrachm from Syracuse exemplifies the frequent use of fish on the coinage of ancient cities. Fish were one of many images used by local mints to reflect their identity and wealth. Copyright of the Trustees of the British Museum

that must be taken straight to the most powerful member of the community (Herodotus 3.41–3, Juvenal Satire 4, Wilkins 1993: 195–6).

Comparison with sources from the modern period suggests that fish were available to the poor. On p. 59 I quoted the evidence of Heltosky 2004 on nineteenth-century Naples. Camporesi (1993) notes the availability of fish to the poorest inhabitants of town and countryside in twentieth-century Italy. The fish is a pilchard or sardine. This confirms the evidence of our ancient sources.

Secondly, there are many different species of fish, which allow for much elaboration. This great variety of names and appearance allowed certain genres of literature to list and describe great numbers of fish. In Greek culture, the enumeration of fish in the comic theatre was an expected part of the play in the fourth century BC, including varieties beyond the pocket of the majority of the audience on all but the rarest

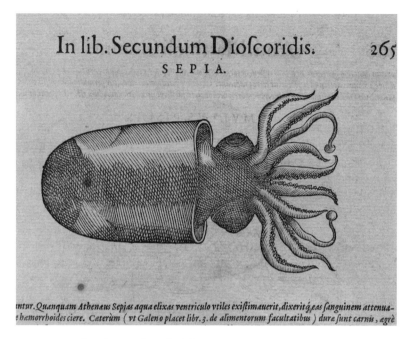

In lib. Secundum Diofcoridis.   265

S E P I A.

ntur. Quanquam Athenæus Sepias aqua elixas ventriculo vtiles exiftimauerit, dixeritq̄,eas fanguinem attenua-
e hæmorrhoides ciere. Cæterùm (vt Galeno placet libr. 3. de alimentorum facultatibus) duræ funt carnis, ægrè

FIGURE 5.4   Fried and stewed cuttle-fish appear in many ancient dishes (Olson & Sens 2000: 206). Galen and Dioscorides note medical applications: for Galen they are nutritious but productive of much (and potentially dangerous) raw humour. The cunning intelligence of the fish was highlighted by Aristotle and perhaps led to a connection with Thetis the sea-goddess. Reproduced by permission of the Dean and Chapter of Exeter Cathedral

occasions (Davidson 1997, Wilkins 2000). Like the beef in Homer, literary fish could thus please the listener, who did not need necessarily to taste the fish in order to enjoy it.

The third point concerns the tastiness of fish. Eating fish was most desirable for those who could do so, as many texts show, Archestratus in particular. Fish consumption was popular also in Rome, despite the Roman construction of her history as a people with a livelihood based on agriculture and a diet of emmer bread and pork. Ovid suggests in the *Fasti* (6.169) that the goddess of door hinges, Carna, a goddess of the old days, expects offerings of pork and bacon, and scorns modern foods such as fish and birds imported from North Africa and Greece. We have noted this passage before. This is an extreme formulation of Rome's republican identity which does appear to have been based on an agricultural economy of citizen farmers. Counter examples need to be remembered in order to balance the picture. Columella, whose work on agriculture has a strong ideological basis in the land and tradition, has no hesitation in describing fish farms and indeed the location of marine species in particular parts of the Mediterranean. Cato the Elder, the republican Roman par excellence, in Plutarch's and many other writers' formulation, used to buy fish as well as meat (Plutarch *Cato the Elder* 4), simply ensuring that he did not spend too much on extravagant cuts. And in the *Life of Augustus*, Suetonius tells us (76) that the emperor in private followed the diet of the common man, which included fish.

We may consider three further points of reference. Pliny exclaims (*Natural History* 9.53), after a review of shellfish: 'why do I mention these trifles when moral corruption and luxury (*populatio morum atque luxuria*) spring from no other source in greater abundance that from the genus of shell fish? It is true that of the whole of nature the sea is most detrimental to the stomach in a multitude of ways, with its multitude of dishes and of appetizing kinds of fish.' He then moves in horror to consider the wearing of pearls as an even worse form of corruption. Pliny's horror is perhaps corroborated by Archestratus who includes a number of recommendations for seafood in his *Life of Luxury*. For example, in fragment 7 Olson & Sens 2000, we are told:

> Ainos has large mussels, Abydos oysters, Parion bear-crabs, and Mytilene scallops . . . you shall buy Peloriac clams in Messene . . .

The host who wanted to make an impression would certainly include shell fish. Juvenal mentions imports of oysters from Richborough in Britain to Rome. All this is not to say that small shell fish were not available to poor communities who lived by the sea. The Sicilian comic poet Epicharmus of the fifth century BC gives an example (fragment 42): 'landsnails and *amathitides*, which are little valued and cheap'. Karali (2000) reviews the range of species of shellfish and considers classes of consumers.

Certain texts clearly distinguish the meat of sacrifice from the fish sold in the market-place. But there is much evidence that the two were available in the market-place and could be bought by all but the poorest. The texture of meat was as varied as the texture of fish; there was much variety of species and cost. And either could be bought for a special occasion. It was just that every day was a special occasion in this sense for the richest citizens. It is thus extremely misleading for Gallant to calculate the annual calorific contribution of fish to the diet of the average Greek citizen, and to conclude that the calorific value of fish was small in comparison with the contribution of beans and cereals. A similar calculation could be done for meat and for vegetables and fruits. All of these non-cereal and non-pulse foods are supplements to the cereal base, and contribute valuable nutrients and taste to the bland staple.

Fish, like meat, could be preserved in times of plenty in order to support times of shortage. Fish is more perishable than meat, but each takes well to drying and in particular to salting. The salting of hams and bacon, as we have seen, is the classic example, which was frequently practised in Italy and Greece, while ham might also be imported from France. Preservation of this kind might be seen as the prudent strategy of the peasant farmer storing food to one side, as he might dry fruits, store grain and keep olives in brine. Such a storage strategy is indeed at work. But preservation has other benefits also. It modifies taste and texture. So, for pork, the textures of bacon, Serrano, Bayonne or Parma ham, and cooked ham are completely different from each other and from the many cuts of fresh pork from the pig. Taste is also differentiated according to the curing processes used. Ham is therefore by no means second best to a pork chop. So too with fish. The salting of fish was a major enterprise in areas of the ancient Mediterranean, as can be seen, for example, in locations in Spain, the Black Sea, the Bay of Naples. The Carthaginians had also used similar techniques at an earlier period (see, for example, Curtis 1991 and 2005, Bekker-Nielsen 2005).

Fish, as we have seen, were less easily managed than pigs could be. An exception to this is the fish farms of Italy which the agricultural writers refer to freely. These were often to be found on the estates of the well-to-do. As far as marine species were concerned, shoals of oily fish might be broadly predictable from year to year, but at any point they may fail to materialize or alternatively arrive in greater numbers than expected. In the Black Sea, in the fourth century BC through into the Roman period, extensive facilities were developed for salting small fish, slices of larger fish (*temache*, slices, are often referred to, as are *temache* of meat) or the production of *garum*. Salted fish had a variety of textures and was also transported comparatively easily in amphorae, the ceramic vessels also used for containing wine. The desirability of salted fish is commented upon by Archestratus in *The Life of Luxury*.

As we saw in Chapter 1, he had no interest in downmarket goods, and even dismissed whitebait as 'shit' (fragment 11, Olson & Sens), evidence if any were needed that poor people had access to small shoaling fish such as anchovies.

In fragment 39 Olson & Sens, Archestratus advises:

> a slice of Sicilian tuna, cut at the time when it would be preserved in storage jars (*bikoi*). The *saperdes*, that tasty Pontic fish, can go to hell I say, along with its supporters. Few there are who know it is a poor and feeble food. Take though a mackerel, three days out of the sea, before it goes into the salt solution and is newly introduced to the amphora – a 'semi-salted' that is. But if you come to the holy city of famous Byzantium, eat again I beg you a slice of *horaion*, for it is good and tender.

And in fragment 40 Olson & Sens, we read, in reference to preserved fish from the Bosporus, 'the whitest that set sail from the Bosporus; but let there be no addition of the hard flesh of the fish that grows in the Maeotic Lake, the fish that it is not lawful to mention in verse'. The fish that will not fit into epic hexameters is the *antakaios* or sturgeon.

Archestratus is operating at the top end of the market. He advises the discerning lover of fish to travel around the Mediterranean in search of the finest fish. For him the *saperdes* is not good enough, a judgement shared by other authorities, as Olson and Sens note in their remarks on this passage. Tuna salts well, but Archestratus appears to counsel using it before salting if Sicilian or as *horaion*, the best preserved fish, if from Byzantium. Lightly salted mackerel is approved, but salted sturgeon is not. Comments on salted fish are available from a number of authors quoted by Athenaeus (3.116a–121e). Galen approves of preserved fish because the salt and other preservatives counteracted accumulations of thick humours such as phlegm in the body. *On the Powers of Foods* 3.40.

Animal Products

Honey

Honey was the main sweetener in antiquity, supported by wine and fruit products, especially dried fruits, which concentrated the sugars. Botanists were aware of sugar cane but it was not used significantly in the Mediterranean area. Ancient writers had much to say about bees, both on the production of honey and on the organization of the hive. There are detailed discussions in Varro and Columella, and famously in Vergil's fourth *Georgic*. These authors embed their practical advice in the rich poetic and mythical traditions about bees. Honey was particularly important in cakes for religious offerings (see pages 127–8) and for the dessert part of the meal, the 'second tables' of the Greek world, which were brought in during the symposium. From a medical perspective, honey was complex. It had many virtues, and was unusual in being a sweet food but with a thinning effect on the humours. It was, however, also liable to provoke disorders. Galen discusses this ambiguity in *On the Powers of Foods* 1.1, though he himself has some strange ideas about the production of honey (3.38). Dalby (1996: 47 and 2003: 179–80) discusses honey and gives a full bibliography. I dissent from his claim (1996: 47) that honey was 'essentially a luxury', since this implies that few had access to it in antiquity. Rather, many had access to it, though probably in no great abundance.

Milk

Consideration of Davidson 1999 and *Larousse gastronomique* might lead us to expect limited use of milk and cheese in the less fertile lands of the Mediterranean in antiquity. Some texts, indeed, might lead us to suppose that the Greeks and Romans were not milk drinkers. Athenaeus tells us, for example (2.46d–e),

> That water is agreed by all to be nourishing is shown from the fact that certain animals such as cicadas are nourished by water alone. Many other liquids are nourishing also, such as milk, barley water and wine. Children at the breast, at least, manage on milk, and many tribes of people live as milk-drinkers.

Greek has the term *galaktopotein*, 'to drink milk', which identifies it as a distinctive activity, of a different kind from wine-drinking or water-drinking. It is noted of the Cyclops in *Odyssey* 9 that he drinks milk and does not know wine. It is said too of the Scythians and Libyans, the pastoral peoples at the northern and southern limits of the Classical world, as also of the French and the British. In many ways milk-drinking identifies the shepherd, the nomad, the pastoralist, to the extent that milk-drinkers are identified as different from the civilized Greek or Roman (Shaw 1982–3; Garnsey 1999). It was possible then, in ethnographic and other writing, to identify the milk-drinker as different from 'us', the civilized people.

We should, however, place beside this feature another, namely that there were many pastoralists in the Greco-Roman world. Sheep and goats, and to a limited extent cows, were kept for milk and wool production at least as much if not more so than for meat. Pastoralists belonged to the Classical world. That said, Euripides still uses the term 'milk drinker' for a peasant who comes to the royal palace in his *Electra*. What we should probably conclude from this evidence is that the consumption of milk was often not an urban but a countryside activity. It is prescribed by doctors, but probably the milk product most available in the cities was cheese. We must distinguish, too, the people who drank milk and not wine from those who consumed both.

There is much discussion of milk in Galen. This may be found in his *On Maintaining Good Health (Hygieina)* 5.7, in *On the Powers of Foods* and in *On the Thinning Diet*. He clearly expects doctors to have to deal with the effects of milk on the body. The doctors were interested in milk from different kinds of animal and found them to have, as in the modern world, very different properties. As we have seen, he often describes mixtures of milk or water, in *On Powers of Foods*, with acorns and many flours. It is an ingredient for mixing into porridge, and a means by which peasants can store and preserve milk. Foxhall and Forbes (1982) describe how, in the twentieth century in Crete, such milk and flour mixtures can be made into bricks and dried in the sun for winter use. Peasants were not the only consumers of milk. Pliny the Younger, the owner of huge villas in Tuscany and Latium, notes that milk is readily available to him.

There is some evidence for butter production in antiquity. Like milk-drinking and beer-making, it may have been more widespread than it appears. Parts of Greece and Italy may well have used significant amounts of butter and other animal fats, and the use of olive oil is unlikely to have been universal. A Greek comedy refers pejoratively to butter-eating in Thrace (Anaxandrides, cited p. 45). Italian evidence is more forthcoming. Pliny describes butter-making, but much of the evidence for the use of butter in Italy concerns medical applications where it acts as a soft medium (Curtis 2001: 399–400).

Cheese was the great dairy product of the Greco-Roman Mediterranean. It was widely produced, varied according to location, and, since it was readily transportable, could be obtained in great varieties in cities. Like wines and fish, therefore, cheeses could be selected by the connoisseur. Pliny gives some idea of the cheeses available. Cheese was also widely used in cakes (as apparently was milk). Cheese might also be used to flavour other dishes, even fish, as Archestratus notes with disapproval. Other milk products were also to be found in antiquity: see Dalby (1996, 2003).

6
Introduction

The modern wine trade is riddled with snobbery and plagued by absurdities of description when trying to compare and assess different wines. This is partly the fault of a vocabulary that is inadequate to describe any nuances of flavour coupled with a massive divide in the cost of sought-after and rare wines in comparison to mass-produced offerings. However, the relative merits of one wine or vintage versus the next fills a library of books and magazines.

In our period of antiquity there are occasional references to better or worse vintages, occasional musings over the superior quality of wine from say, Lesbos, and as time went by a premium for wines from specific districts. But in general the wine seems to be local rather than imported, at least in places that were able to produce their own wine. Archestratus may have pontificated on the best place and time of year to find sea bass but there was no equivalent to Robert Parker guiding the drinking classes as now. Comparisons may be drawn with wine-producing regions today. It can be difficult to find a burgundy to drink in Bordeaux and vice versa. It is much easier to make the choice in cosmopolitan Paris, which lies too far north to produce anything locally in competition.

It is difficult to assess any differences in style between wine then and now. Many Greek grape varieties lay claim to a direct link with antiquity but two thousand years of cultivation will certainly have altered both yields and types of vine grown. Wine was stored and transported in amphorae and these were rendered waterproof by an internal coating of resin which would have affected flavour in the same way as retsina flavours wines from Greece today. This benign tainting is common to much alcoholic refreshment, of course, and the oak flavour imparted by traditional barrel storage is part of the attraction of many wines, whiskies and brandies.

Diluting wines or even sweetening them with grape syrup would similarly reduce any differences between batches of wine. The effects rather than the finer points seem to be the main concern.

6

Wine and Drinking

> Come to dinner quickly and bring your box and your jug. The priest of Dionysus has sent for you. Hurry up! You've been holding up the dinner for some time. Everything else is ready, the couches, the tables, the pillows, the covers, the garlands, the perfume, the desserts; the prostitutes are present. The fine cakes are there, the flat cakes, the sesame cakes, the honey cakes, the dancing girls – Harmodius' favourites – beauties too.

This comic invitation from the *Acharnians* of Aristophanes (1086–93) locates dinner and symposium all within the same occasion of the 'dinner' or *deipnon*. It is a special occasion, a celebratory meal at the house of a religious official, to which the winner of the drinking contest at the festival of the Anthesteria is invited. I discuss the festival below. As noted in Chapter 2, there is a division of gender at the Greek *deipnon*, with the only women present being of very low status.

This chapter concerns wine, alcohol, and the social functions, not least entertainments, that accompanied the consumption of wine. The first point to establish is that wine-drinking, normally with the wine diluted by water, was widespread throughout the Greco-Roman world, to such as extent that the term 'water-drinker' could be used rhetorically as an insult. Wine was one of the few addictive substances available in antiquity, and so on occasion its use was controlled by law. There are at least claims to such legislation in regard to women under the Roman Republic. The drinking of wine was linked with a large number of religious rituals, both at formal festivals and in the home. The production

FIGURE 6.1   The Drinking Contest of Dionysus (the god of wine) and Heracles
(the demi-god with a limitless appetite), found at Antioch in Syria, *c.*100 AD
(mosaic) © Worcester Art Museum, Massachusetts. The demi-god and god
compete in a drinking competition. Drinking vessels are set out in the
foreground. The reclining god retains his composure and is the clear victor.
Diners were often given representations on the floors, walls and tableware of
themselves or of mythological versions of themselves in order to aid reflection
on the civilised world of the dining room. Photo: www.bridgeman.co.uk

of, and trade in, wine was of considerable economic importance. Wine
was also linked, through its social manifestation the symposium, with
inspired writing and song. The archaic symposium was the occasion
for much poetic performance, and the poetry reflected this (Bowie
1986). Examples from Xenophanes, Sappho, Theognis and Anacreon

are quoted below. The classical symposium generated philosophical reflection. The games and activities associated with the symposium generated a vast literature, which may best be seen in its Latin forms in the poetry of Horace, and in its Greek in the pages of Athenaeus.

The Anthesteria was a festival of Dionysus. The Greeks believed that Dionysus was a god of ambiguity. In Euripides' phrasing, he was both most terrible and most gentle. He crossed boundaries, blending male with female, Greek with foreign, civic with the natural world. He was a god linked with the dead as well as the living. He also introduced the vine to Greece. This god of the natural world had the power to produce foods such as milk and honey spontaneously from rocks and plants, as Euripides describes in his *Bacchae*. He could also cause rivers to flow with wine rather than water. Philostratus describes a wall painting imagined to be found in a house in Naples (*Imagines* 1.25):

> The stream of wine which is on the island of Andros, and the Andrians who have become drunken from the river, are the subject of this paint-ing. For by act of Dionysus the earth of the Andrians is so charged with wine that it bursts forth and sends up for them a river; if you have water in mind it is not great, but if wine it is a great river – yes, divine! For he who draws from it may well disdain both Nile and Ister and may say of them that they also would be more highly esteemed if they were small, provided their streams were like this one.

Philostratus reflects the luxury villas of Campania and Tuscany, which were as much at home in Greek as in Roman culture (if they could be separated). Similar images of Dionysus are to be found in villas at Pompeii and other cities in the Bay of Naples. The Romans worshipped Dionysus as Liber, or Bacchus, one of the cult titles of Dionysus. Bacchus was one of the Greek divinities introduced into Rome in the third century BC in order to preserve the city from the Carthaginians and other outside threats. But the god might also become a threat, and in 186 BC the Senate suppressed the female cult of the Bacchanalia in fear of anti-state conspiracy. These ambiguities are reflected in cult. The Anthesteria (or flower) festival in Athens and the Ionian cities of Asia Minor celebrated the opening of the new wine – in early spring rather than in the autumn like Beaujolais nouveau. Burkert (1985: 237) sets the scene:

> At the sanctuary of Dionysos *en limnais* the Athenians used to mix the wine for the god from the jars which they transported along there, and

then taste it themselves . . . Delighted with the mixture, they celebrated Dionysos with songs, danced, and invoked him as the Fair-flowering, the Dithyrambos, the Reveller and the Stormer.

This is how an Attic local historian [Phanodemus FGrHist 325 F 12, quoted by Athenaeus 11.465a] describes the beginning of the festival on the 11th Anthesterion:

> The beginning of the new vintage, the first fruit offering, is set in the sanctuary which is only opened at sunset. The day is filled with prepara-tions; the clay vessels are carted in from the small vineyards scattered throughout the countryside, small-holders, day-labourers, and slaves come into the city, and friends and strangers wait for nightfall outside the sanctuary. Then, as the jars are broken open, the god is honoured with the first libations.

On the second day, *Choes*, the wine jars were opened and men drank competitively from large jugs. Slaves and children also joined in, this being one of the rituals of incorporation for the young child into the family. There were also dark aspects to the second day, for the house and city were subject to invasion by the dead. There was also a further form of drinking, in which at a trumpet sound everyone drank an equal measure simultaneously, but in silence and each at an individual table. This was said to be in memory of the arrival in Athens of Orestes, with hands still polluted by the blood of his mother Clytemnestra. Also on this day, the king archon, one of the chief magistrates of the city, who had organized the solitary drinking, gave his wife in sacred marriage to Dionysus at the god's temple in the marshes, somewhere to the south of the acropolis. On the third day of the festival, *Chutroi*, or Pots, mixed grains were boiled with honey in the pots. Burkert (1985: 240) comments, 'this is the most primitive cereal dish of the early farmers, older than the discovery of flour-milling and bread-baking; in funeral customs it has survived down to the present day'. Modern Greek *kolyva* offers an example of Burkert's funerary mixture. The myth of the flood, according to Burkert, lies behind the primitive porridge. At the end of the day, the dead are invited to leave.

The festival combines new wine with death, the individual household with the polis, the integration of new wine and new members of the family with deceased members. The connection between wine and death is well established, and can be seen in the myth of Icarius, in the

Odes of Horace (1.9), and in the drunken ramblings of Petronius' Trimalchio. Icarius lived in the village of Icaria, on the northern slopes of Mount Penteli in Attica. When Dionysus brought his wine to Attica, Icarius accepted it and shared it with his neighbours. Becoming drunk, they feared (like Theban Pentheus in the *Bacchae*) that a bad element rather than a benefit had been brought into the community. They killed Icarius, and his daughter, Erigone, hanged herself from a pine tree. This sad tale was incorporated into the Anthesteria (along with the solitary drinking in memory of the matricidal Orestes). Pots were produced whose paintings showed girls on a swing, in connection with Erigone. The beautiful site of Icaria still has its pine trees. A sixth-century statue of Dionysus has also been found there, along with a theatre where the fierce myths of the wine-god (among others, probably) were portrayed. A monument from the fourth century also survives, recording the victory of a sponsor of a performance at the theatre. We might also note the ambiguities in the *Acharnians* of Aristophanes. Here, the protagonist, Dicaeopolis, restores the Dionysiac festival to his deme, and wins the drinking competition at the Anthesteria – two virtues. Yet in the eyes of many commentators (Bowie 1993; Fisher 1993) he acts selfishly, against the interests of his fellow citizens (this is discussed in Wilkins 2000: ch. 3) and recalls the solitary drinkers who imitate Orestes. Dark themes in comedy are important, otherwise we might believe (with Henrichs 1990) that the terrible Dionysus was portrayed exclusively in tragedy and the merry wine god exclusively in comedy.

The difficulties of dealing with alcohol are reflected in many forms: in poetry which urges balance and restraint; in drinking rituals which again balance communal intoxication with dexterity and wit; and in warning stories of drinking that got out of hand. Despite the dangers, wine and its consumption were held in the highest regard in antiquity, and the symposium, the part of the meal where wine was consumed in Greek and often in Roman culture, was always seen as the moment for wisdom and cultural reflection. The *deipnon*, or part of the meal where much of the dining took place, rarely attained that status. (The diners in Athenaeus achieve it, but the *Deipnosophistae* is a special case.)

It is not certain that wine originated in the Near East and was brought either mythically by Dionysus or by technology transfer to the Greco-Roman world. The cultivation of the vine, as with other cultivated plants, may have developed independently in a number of locations. However, McGovern (2003) claims, on the basis of the latest DNA

<figure>FIGURE 6.2   The journey of Dionysus over the sea; his turning the ship's mast into a vine and his pirate captors into dolphins expresses the mobility of the god and the plant sacred to him. In ancient thought, the vine was an essential part of the civilized Greco-Roman world, but it was acknowledged to have travelled, like other plants, from lands to the East. Reproduced by permission of the Staatliche Antikensammlungen und Glyptothek, Munchen</figure>

evidence available, that the cultivated grape appears to have originated in communities in Eastern Turkey before 5000 BC. The present state of evidence and knowledge seems to indicate the diffusion of the plant from there to Mesopotamia and Europe. McGovern also reviews the evidence for mixtures of wine with beer and many other flavourings in the Near East, a number of which (with the exception of beer) are reflected in Roman authors.

Many of the rituals of drinking and dining post-date Homer. We have seen that reclining rather than sitting at the table was one such major development. Archaeological evidence indicates much acquaintance with wine in the Minoan and Mycenaean Bronze Age, in the form of drinking cups, amphorae for transport, and chemical residues. These show use both of resinated wines and of wine flavoured with plants such as bay and rue. McGovern (2003) has evidence for resinated wines in the Near East some millennia earlier. Such flavouring is found also in the historical period. In the Homeric poems, there is no formal symposium as such, as far as can be gleaned. But there are many features of drinking which relate to the later form of the symposium. Heroes in Homer who arrive at the home of a host are normally given food and drink on arrival (in *Odyssey* 4, for example). There is normally no great differentiation between eating and drinking. Rather, Homer uses the formulaic phrase, 'when they had put away from them the desire for food and drink . . .'. The eating and drinking are bundled up together. The mealtime is then complete, and it is time to turn to other activities, such as sleep, negotiation, story telling, singing and dancing, accompanied by wine mixed in a bowl or crater.

In the later, archaic, period, the story telling, singing and dancing and other aspects of entertainment seem to have been contained within the symposium part of the occasion. By the imperial Roman period, however, the drinking is closer to the Homeric model. Drinking starts at an early stage, in Petronius and Athenaeus at any rate, with the guests receiving wine at the very beginning. Entertainments too come during the meal in Trimalchio's household, and for the Deipnosophistae, the philosophical diners of Athenaeus, the conversation that is at the centre of their activities continues unabated from the outset, though entertainments are said to be provided in the symposium part of the meal. The evidence of Athenaeus, once again, is particularly important for our purposes since he is writing towards the end of our period and is summing up earlier practice. He is also describing a Greek-style meal in Rome and so in many ways is fusing the two cultures.

By comparison with later modes of drinking, heroic drinking in Homer can be said to be a model of good practice, and this is precisely the claim in Athenaeus book 5. It is also worth noting that details of eating and drinking are not normally provided in the Homeric poems. 'The desire for eating and drinking' covers much of the detail in many passages, and in others 'all kinds of foods' (unspecified) are provided. The preparation of meat is a concern for detailed treatment; the preparation of wine is less so. This is in marked contrast with later periods.

The diners and drinkers also sit on chairs in Homer. Later in the Greek archaic period, significant changes seem to have been introduced into the institution of the symposium, as was described in Chapter 2. The most striking of these is the *kline*, or couch, on which the diner and drinker reclined. This seems to have come to the Greek world from the Near East, and to have spread its way westwards to the Etruscans and Romans. Then too came ceramic wares to grace the tables of the drinkers: drinking cups, mixing bowls, ladles for scooping out wine, strainers and coolers. All of these could be decorated elaborately, as could vessels in gold and silver, which became increasingly common from the fourth century BC, and possibly much earlier (Vickers and Gill 1994). Of particular interest was the incorporation of drinking into an ethical social code, which guided the drinker between the extremes of drunkenness and of not participating fully. Balance in various ways was sought, and this included social balance – proper conduct between equals, politically appropriate behaviour, proper behaviour among peers. An aristocratic code that reinforced the political order of the evolving city-state speaks very strongly from much archaic Greek poetry.

Songs, new forms of poetry to complement Homeric epic, and sympotic entertainments were all developed in the archaic period. Elegiac and iambic poetry in particular had strong links with the symposium.

> Now at last the floor is swept, and clean are the hands of all the guests, and their cups as well; one slave puts plaited wreaths on their heads, another offers sweet-smelling perfume in a saucer; the mixing-bowl stands full of good cheer; and other wine is ready, which promises never to give out – mellow wine in jars, redolent of its bouquet; and in the midst the frankincense sends forth its sacred fragrance; and there is water cool and fresh and pure. The yellow loaves lie ready at hand, and a lordly table groans with the weight of cheese and luscious honey; an altar in the middle is banked all around with flowers, and singing and dancing and bounty pervade the house. But men of good cheer should first of all praise the god with pious stories and pure words; they should pour libations and pray for power to do the right (for that is the duty closer to hand); 'tis no sin to drink as much as you can hold and still get home without an attendant, unless you be very old. Praise that man that even in his cups can show forth goodly thoughts, according as memory serves

him and his zeal for virtue is at full stretch. In no wise is it good to relate the fights of Titans and Giants nor of Centaurs, the fictions of men aforetime, or their violent factions, in which there is nought that is wholesome; but it is good ever to have regard for the gods. (Xenophanes fragment 1 West, trans. Gulick, 11.462c–f)

I love him not who, when drinking his wine beside the brimming bowl, speaks of strifes and tearful battle, but rather him who, mingling the bright gifts of the Muses and of Aphrodite together, is ever mindful of welcome good cheer. (Anacreon, trans. Gulick, 11.463a)

Come goddess of love, and daintily, from golden cups pour out mingled nectar for our merry-making. (Sappho, trans. Gulick 11.463e)

Much archaic lyric and elegy concentrates on the balance required at the drinking feast between intoxication and relaxation in the group. There is emphasis too on group solidarity, sharing the same ethical framework, and avoiding strife and tales of disruption. There is much emphasis on purity, both ritual and psychological in the Xenophanes poem. The occasion of this poetry has also been the subject of much debate. Sometimes the setting is overtly religious, as in the fragment of Sappho, which invokes a deity. Often it is a group of comrades at a symposium, as in Xenophanes and in the elegies of Theognis, which are addressed to a certain Cyrnus. This young man is urged to follow the 'right' path and to avoid the political dissension of the lower orders in the city.

Among one's fellow diners let a man have his wits about him, let everything seem to escape his notice as if he were not there, and let him contribute jokes, but when he's outside let him be firm, recognizing the temperament which each one has. (Theognis 309–12, trans. Gerber)

The term for fellow diners is *sussitioi*, the same as for Spartan diners. The group attempts to maintain social cohesion through shared eating and drinking rituals and thereby implicitly a shared ideology. The advice specific to drinking is this (473–96):

Let a slave stand by and pour wine for him who wants to drink; it's not possible to have a good time every night. But I'll go home – I've had my limit of honey-sweet wine – and I'll take thought for sleep that brings release from ills. I've reached the stage where the consumption of wine is most pleasant for a man, since I am neither sober nor too drunk.

Whoever exceeds his limit of drink is no longer in command of his tongue or his mind; he says wild things which are disgraceful in the eyes of the sober, and he's not ashamed of anything he says when he's drunk. Formerly he was sensible but then he's a fool. Aware of this, don't drink wine to excess, but either rise before you're drunk – don't let your belly overpower you as if you were a wretched hired help for the day – or stay without drinking. But you say 'fill it up!' This is always your idle chatter; that's why you get drunk. One cup is a toast to friendship, another is set before you, another you offer as a libation to the gods, another you have as a penalty, and you don't know how to say no. That man is truly the champion who after drinking many cups will say nothing foolish. If you stay by the mixing bowl, make good conversation, long avoiding quarrels with one another and speaking openly to one and all alike. In this way a symposium turns out to be not half bad. (trans. Gerber)

The ethical dimension to these words recalls the passage of Xenophanes quoted above, and anticipates many later passages in comedy and elsewhere that reflect on the dangers of drinking too much and missing the delicate balance between friendly drinking and unwise intoxication (Athenaeus, Wilkins 2000).

The occasions of this poetry varied. It was normally designed for recitation among a group, often of an aristocratic background. The martial elegy of Tyrtaeus, we are told (Aristoxenus, quoted by Athenaeus 14.630f), was recited in times of war. Philochorus of Athens, meanwhile (Athenaeus 630f), says that the poetry of Tyrtaeus had been so effective in gaining the Spartans victory that

> they instituted the custom in their military campaigns, when they had finished their dinner and sung the hymn of thanksgiving, of having each one sing something by Tyrtaeus; their commander-in-chief acts as judge and awards a piece of meat to the victor. (trans. Gulick)

On the circumstances of performance see further West (1974), Bowie (1986), Gentili (1988). Many of these poems reflected upon the shared life of citizens, such as war, civil strife and the dangers of the sea. An early poem of Archilochus, for example, fragment 4 West, combines the rituals of drawing and drinking wine with a night watch on board ship (Bowie 1986: 16).

A further element is the theme of competition, and the need for the group to develop excellence among itself by games and sympotic practices as well as athletic and physical feats.

A long sympotic tradition developed on the nautical theme of being all at sea when drunk (Slater 1976, Wilkins 2000: 238–41).

A number of sources tell us of varying drinking practices in the Greek cities. Critias in his *Constitution of the Spartans* (quoted by Athenaeus 11.463e–f) says, 'The Chian and the Thasian drink a health out of large cups from left to right, the Athenian from small cups from left to right, while the Thessalian pledges in large cups to whomsoever he wishes. But the Lacedaemonians drink each his own cup separately, and the slave who pours the wine (fills up again) with the quantity he has drunk off' (trans. Gulick).

Alongside the literary tradition came the celebrated wine cups and mixing bowls showing scenes of life and myth in the black figure and red figure styles, among others. One preoccupation of the cups is to reflect the act of drinking, and the delicate line the drinker treads between inspiration and intoxication. Lissarague (1990) draws the parallels between images and cups with the help of archaic and comic poetry and the commentary of Athenaeus. Particularly striking in this field is the list of cups in Athenaeus' eleventh book. The symposium was thus a time for reflection, with friends and equals. People became drunk together. They shared the wine and water mixed in the bowl or crater, to a strength dictated by the symposiarch or chief drinker. They might have to perform feats of balance, based on mental or physical agility; they might reflect on images for drunkenness, such as nautical images, or images of disorder such as battles between the Greeks and their gods and primitive peoples and their gods. They might also perform games, such as the wine-flicking game of cottabos, and other entertainments (see below). The vase (and sometimes tomb) paintings reflect many aspects of the eating, drinking and entertainment put on at the symposium.

All of this activity was ordered by ritual. At the end of the dinner section of the occasion, the tables were replaced, hands washed, garlands replaced, and libations of neat wine were offered to various gods, including the 'Good Spirit', Dionysus, and Hygieia or Good Health, the divine acolyte of Asclepius. The neat wine offered at this stage contrasted with the watered wine of the symposiasts. At the end of the evening, they might sing a hymn (a ritual hymn to Hygieia is sung at the end of the *Deipnosophistae*: see Wilkins 2005a). Then they might disperse home, as they do at the end of Plato's and Xenophon's *Symposium*, or set out on a revel, or *komos*, like the maenads and satyrs of Dionysus. There are records of such *komoi* getting out of

FIGURE 6.3   Symposium showing three men playing cottabos with a female musician and servant. Detail from a red figured amphora, Greek, British Museum. Evidence from vase paintings and from Athenaeus reveals two versions. Diners flicked the wine dregs from their cups at targets, either sinking little ceramic boats that floated on water in a large vessel, or trying to dislodge a disk balanced on the top of a pole. The disk should fall on the head of an image of a slave placed halfway up the pole. The game indicates an interest in the tension between skills of concentration and intoxication. Photo: www.bridgeman.co.uk

hand. Alcibiades arrives as a drunk but relatively well-behaved *komast* in the middle of Plato's *Symposium*; Philocleon behaves with wanton violence after a symposium in the *Wasps* of Aristophanes.

It has sometimes been thought that the symposium belonged to oligarchic elites throughout the Greek classical period (roughly the fifth and fourth centuries BC). This has been implied in some remarks in Murray (1990) and elsewhere, and is explicitly stated in Davidson (1997). It seems to me that it is a mistake to contrast the symposium, a generally private affair celebrated in the homes of members of the elites of the city states, with the festivals and other public and communal activities of the city community as a whole. Archaic and aristocratic traditions certainly appear to have been strong in the classical city, even democratically ruled cities such as Athens and Argos. But the symposium appears to have been open to all, to have been celebrated on public and private occasions, and in civic contexts as well as private homes. The evidence is discussed in Wilkins (2000) and Fisher (2000). The distribution and drinking of wine, like the distribution of meat, seems to have operated across the classes and through ritual and commercial outlets. Thus a poor citizen might expect to eat most meat at public festivals and to drink wine among peers and friends on more limited occasions than the rich. But the *kapeleion* or wine shop/grocer should not be seen as the poor man's equivalent of the symposium. It was an additional, non-ritualized place for drinking. The poor man drank at festivals, weddings and other occasions. The wine might be less good, the furniture less expensive, the entertainment less subject to international competitive pressures. But the institution was the same. It would be extremely misleading, I believe, to suggest that the poor drank in a commercial context, while the ritualized symposium was the preserve of the rich. Aristophanes' *Wasps* has been seen as a test case for Murray's and Davidson's view. I have tried to argue (Wilkins 2000) that the symposium is so pervasive in Greek comedy, and is accepted as a social institution, where the activities of the elite are generally attacked, that we should conclude that the symposium was familiar and available to all.

This is not to deny that drinking in bars and wine shops was important for poorer members of society in the Greek and Roman worlds. There is plentiful evidence for such establishments, particularly in the Campanian cities, and considerable evidence for a wide range of such outlets, some of which provided food, others entertainments, and others sexual services.

Sympotic drinking was so much part of Greek identity that it was seen as strictly a male activity, which others were unable to perform. Thus women of status were not admitted to the symposium, and were considered particularly susceptible to wine. Much of the evidence is comic, and potentially misleading, but women were thought to drink excessively and to drink neat rather than mixed wine. Foreigners too, such as the Scythians and Persians, were thought to drink their wine neat. They failed to follow the sophisticated Greek practice of mixing wine with water, just as they performed other rituals, such as animal sacrifice, differently. Slaves also were, in the Greek imagination at least, excessively affected by wine.

There were women at the Greek symposium, but these were *hetaerae* or courtesans, who contributed to the sexual stimuli of the occasion and emphasized the pleasurable element of the occasion. Thus strictly ordered symposia, such as Plato's fictional symposium and those of Athenaeus' diners do not have *hetaerae* present. Women attended *cenae* and *convivia* in Rome, as was discussed in Chapter 2. There appear, however, to have been restrictions on women drinking in the Republican period (Valerius Maximus 2.1). There was legislation relating to kissing, for a husband to test whether his wife had been drinking. And exemplary anecdotes attached to supposed female drinkers. This was an area for unease, and ideological reflection in the Roman mind, akin perhaps to the need for sumptuary legislation to restrict women's spending on clothes and other items. There was a republican fear, as in the Greek world, that women were in need of restraint.

The symposium, as we have seen, flirted with imbalance and with disorder. Athenaeus quotes passages from comedy where the drinking goes too far. There are incidents in the historians and orators of drinking getting out of hand (Timaeus at Athenaeus 2.37b–e, Demosthenes 54). Plato is clear on the subject in his *Laws*. In the first book, where the communal dining in Sparta and Crete is contrasted with less controlled consumption of food and drink in other Greek cities, it is the symposium which is identified as the most dangerous example of insufficient regulation, and the giving up of the self to pleasure. This is the view of the Spartan and Cretan speakers, whose societies do not apparently include the symposium. The Athenian stranger, meanwhile, has much to say on the symposium.

The archaeological evidence for the symposium is particularly rich. It includes mixing bowls, drinking cups and other ceramic tableware, and some of the metalwork produced. There is also good evidence for the special drinking rooms in the Greek and Roman house, drinking rooms in public buildings, and the wine shops found in Greek cities and in Pompeii, Herculaneum and Ostia (see Chapter 2).

Many kinds of eating and entertainment are linked with the symposium. This was the stage in the meal where the second tables were served. Archestratus shows us how in fragment 60 Olson & Sens (trans. Wilkins):

Always festoon the head with all kinds of garland at the feast, and with whatever the fruitful floor of the earth brings into flower. Dress your hair with fine distilled perfumes and all day long throw on the soft ashes

FIGURE 6.4 A wild follower of Dionysus, or satyr, attempts to balance a wine cup on his penis. This sketch by Francois Lissarrague of a vase painting illustrates both the sexual content which may be found in an ancient symposium, and the importance of balance while drinking. A delicate line must be trod den between civilized inebriation among friends and drunken loss of control. For many other artistic examples, see Lissarrague 1990.

> myrrh and incense, the fragrant fruit of Syria. And while you are drinking, let these tasty dishes be brought to you: the belly and boiled womb of a sow in cumin and sharp vinegar and silphium; the tender race of roasted birds, whatever may be in season. Have nothing to do with those Syracusans who drink only in the manner of frogs and eat nothing. No, do not be taken in by them, but eat the foods I set forth. All those other *tragemata* are a sign of wretched poverty, boiled chickpeas, broad beans, apples and dried figs. I do though applaud the flat-cake born in Athens. If you cannot get one there, go and get one elsewhere and seek out some Attic honey, for that is what makes it flaunt itself proudly. That is how a free man should live: the alternative is to go beneath the earth and the bottomless pit and Tartarus to destruction and be dug down countless stades deep.

Different kinds of second table can be seen, for example, in comic descriptions and in Athenaeus (see Wilkins 2000), and others, including shellfish at Trimalchio's *cena*.

The Greeks of the fifth and fourth centuries BC seem to have expected the entertainment (whether poetry, riddles, dancing girls or philosophy) at the symposium stage of the proceedings. Some of the great meals of the Hellenistic period seem to depart from this pattern (see Caranus (p. 44 above) and the symphony of Antiochus Epiphanes p. 49 above and Athenaeus 5.194e–f). By the Roman period, there seems to be drinking and entertainment throughout the meal. Trimalchio offers everything from recitals of Homer to symphony music and acrobats, while Pliny the Younger describes elegant entertainments at some meals and lascivious dancing at others. Philosophy was available at some great meals in the Roman period, as Athenaeus observes (9.381f). The whole meal might also be themed, as the Emperor Domitian exemplifies after his supposed victories over the Dacians. The ordinary people were given public dinners and grotesque games in the arena. Something special was served to the senators and knights, which recalls the link discussed above between Dionysus and the dead (Cassius Dio 67.9, trans. Cary).

He prepared a room that was pitch black on every side, ceiling, walls and floor, and had made ready bare couches of the same colour resting on the uncovered floor; then he invited in his guests alone at night without their attendants. And first he set beside each of them a slab shaped like a gravestone, bearing the guest's name and also a small lamp, such as hang at tombs. Next comely naked boys, likewise painted black, entered like phantoms, and after encircling the guests in an awe-inspiring dance took up their stations at their feet. After all this the things that are commonly offered at the sacrifices to departed spirits were likewise set before the guests, all of them black and in dishes of a similar colour. Consequently, every single one of the guests feared and trembled and was kept in constant expectation of having his throat cut the next moment, the more so as on the part of everybody but Domitian there was dead silence, as if they were already in the realms of the dead, and the emperor himself conversed only upon topics relating to death and slaughter.

There is furthermore much evidence for entertainments combined with meals and drinking for less exalted members of society, whether at public banquets, as Dio mentions, or at inns and bars. The evidence for Pompeii and other Italian cities for dice, dancers, sexual partners, musicians and other entertainment is collected in Kleberg (1957).

Athenaeus is the best literary source for the symposium, recording, as he does, many aspects of garlands, singing and dancing, as well as poetry, that might not immediately be associated with formal drinking. He also gives the extensive catalogue of types of drinking cups, which can be tied reasonably closely to the archaeological record. Writing in the sympotic tradition, with all its self-consciousness and self-reflexivity, Athenaeus bases the drinking of his Deipnosophists on the model set in the archaic period by Xenophanes. Thus the Deipnosophist Plutarch introduces the poem (quoted above), 'since I myself can see that your symposium, on the model of Xenophanes of Colophon, is full of delight.' The sympotic tradition ran through both a poetic form and, after Plato's *Symposium*, a prose form in which sympotic activity or philosophical discussion might be the focus of attention. The *Symposia* of Plato and of Xenophanes became the model for many successors. This tradition is explored by Romeri (2002), who demonstrates that Athenaeus differs from much of this tradition in giving food equal weight with the wine. Many of the earlier *Symposia* – and Plato is a prime example – get the eating out of the way as rapidly as possible in order to move to the philosophical discussion during a session of moderate drinking. Where there is not moderate eating and drinking, as among the philosophers at the *Symposium* and *Lexiphanes* of Lucian, gross disorder invades the occasion. Athenaeus of course signals in his title *The Philosophers at Dinner* that his focus is different from his predecessors. Since he is writing in the imperial Roman period, it is not completely clear to what extent he reflects on Greek practice, or has been influenced by the Roman pattern of more integrated eating and drinking.

Wine production, wine festivals in the calendar and social ritual gave wine a powerful place in the Greco-Roman world. Much drinking was of local wine. As with other foods discussed in earlier chapters, poorer citizens consumed cheaper versions of what was accessible to the rich. (There appear to have been exceptions to this rule in parts of the Empire which had earlier been on the borders of Greco-Roman influence. France and Egypt, we are told, imported and then produced wine for the consumption of the rich, while poorer citizens drank beer. It is not clear that the distinction was quite that stark in, say, 200 AD after more than a century of integration into the Roman system. Beer was still drunk, but wine was less foreign in France than it had been when Poseidonius (quoted by Athenaeus 4.152c) was writing in about 100 BC.)

There appear to have been clear differences between Greek and Roman wines. The former produced vintages that were praised and much enjoyed. Lambert Gocs (1990) reviews modern Greek equivalents, which again do not rival the great wines of Italy and France, in the imagination of the public at least. Ancient Greek wines are not normally identified by year, nor narrowly by place. Rather, they are said to be Thasian or Chian or Lesbian. Archestratus fragment 59

Olson & Sens provides an example (Athenaeus offers many more, most drawn from comic texts).

> When you have drawn a full measure for Zeus the Saviour, you must drink an old wine with a really grey old head, its moist locks festooned with white flowers, born in Lesbos with the sea all around. I praise Bybline wine from Phoenicia, though it does not equal Lesbian. If you take a quick taste of it and are previously unacquainted, it will seem to you to be more fragrant than Lesbian, for this lasts for a very long time. When tasted, though, it is very inferior, and the Lesbian will take on a rank not like wine but like ambrosia . . . Thasos also produces a noble wine to drink, provided it is aged over many good seasons down the years. I know too of the shoots dripping with grape clusters in other cities. I could cite them, praise them, and indeed their names are well known to me. But the others are simply worthless beside the Lesbian wine. Some people of course like to praise products from their own locality. (trans. Wilkins)

Clearly, if such a wine was imported into, say, Athens or Corinth, it was different in character but also more expensive than a locally produced equivalent. The enjoyment of such wines in Athens is attested both in poetry and in the archaeological record, where buildings apparently for the sale of wine have remains of amphorae from overseas. Greek wines also appealed to the Roman palate. Cato, of all people, has recipes for making Greek-style wines in his treatise on agriculture. The Romans meanwhile set about the creation of a very different wine trade. In addition to cheap local wines – the Sabine wine enjoyed by Horace on his farm is a famous example – vintage wines were produced, especially on the fertile hillsides of Latium and Campania, between Rome and Naples. Here small areas came to have brand names similar to 'appellation controllée', and vintages such as Falernian, Fundian, and Caecuban were marketed at great price. The wine business, because great profits were available, but also great risk if the weather was bad, brought high returns to investors. Purcell (1985) and Tchernia (1986) have demonstrated the economics and cultural resonances of the Roman wine industry. A good overview is set out by Dalby (2003: 350–60) and by articles in Robinson (1994). There has been much research on the movement of Roman wines, based on amphora stamps and discoveries of amphorae in shipwrecks.

Wine was important too in medicine. We have seen that Hygieia or Good Health might be invoked at the beginning and end of the symposium. The hymn to her at the end of the *Deipnosophistae*, in fact, is the same as the hymn inscribed on stone at the medical complex at Epidaurus. Doctors were linked with the symposium, and in literary versions from Plato to Athenaeus, a doctor is often present. Medical literature, too, has much to say on the effects of wine on the body. Doctors with wide geographical interests, such as Galen, also name wine from less familiar areas, such as parts of Asia Minor. (See further Jouanna 1996.)

7
Introduction

The importance of meat and fish in the daily diet is partly one of affluence and partly of preference. In all cases there is the idea that it is more macho to eat meat and to care little about its preparation, the notion that it is rather effete to take too much interest in the spicing and finer points of your red mullet or sea bass and much more rugged to shovel down whatever is put in front of you regardless. Ancient Greeks may have loved fish but the heroes of battle still ate meat.

Even today, intricate cooking and its appreciation seem, in the United States for instance, more associated with Californians and immigrants from the Mediterranean and the Atlantic coast than the descendants of settlers in the Midwest. Perhaps memories of Stewpot's cooking in *Rawhide* have coloured the view but there is the thought that large swathes of middle America are content with steak and fries, possibly with a little salad, coke or beer. Conversely, the urban coasts are hot spots of cookery interest, the starting point of Asian fusion cooking and powerhouse of new culinary ideas; also the focal point of a renaissance in top-quality winemaking and its appreciation.

In Britain the fascination for refined cooking is largely confined to metropolitan London, with the countryside seen as the supplier of traditional produce that needs the sophistication of imported exotica such as spices and rare fruits to blossom into something more sophisticated. Londoners are regarded as having less backbone, to be less properly English, whatever that may be. Like all assumptions, all these have elements of truth alongside much envy and misconception.

Perhaps there are mental links for us between the connoisseur's ability to distinguish intricate nuances of flavour and texture, a skill that comes with practice as well as the possession of a good palate, and the idea of self-indulgence and excess, personal weakness and lack of self-control. The appreciation of fine eating is in good company, along-side poetry, literature and much art, in that it flourishes as something with mass appeal only once wealth, stability and security can be taken for granted.

Interestingly, those who cook the food are regularly male and macho. A tour of Britain's kitchens will produce cooks who look like tired footballers more than hairdressers, and the more dainty and fiddled with the food, the more likely you are to meet some tough guy in the kitchen. Our top chefs from recent years, Gordon Ramsay and Marco Pierre White, have reputations for hard, disciplined and aggressive kitchens.

Then as now, of course, fine dining was largely the province of the comfortably off. Those with street food and basic carbohydrates to eat will have been able to despise the idea of such indulgence as well, of course, as feeling a touch envious. Restraint with fish and meat, the *opson* of the meal, amongst the wealthier classes was considered model behaviour; those who ate more than expected were considered greedy and unrefined. This best demonstrates the resolution of the conflicting pressures, showing that one is wealthy enough to understand and appreciate good food but self-controlled enough to limit the extent to which you indulge.

Food in Ancient Thought

The first in our fourth decade of convivial questions shall be the discussion we had concerning variety in diet on the occasion of a banquet during the festival of the Elaphebolia, for which we had gone to Hyampolis. On our arrival there we were entertained at dinner by Philo the physician, who, as we saw, had provided a mighty feast for us. Our host, having noticed that one of the young boys who came with Philinus took bread and wanted nothing else . . . rushed out to get them something that they could eat. After a long time he came back with a few dried figs and some cheese for them. 'This', I remarked, 'is what happens when people provide elaborate and costly fare.'

Plutarch and his friends consider the question whether a varied diet is easier on the digestion than a simple diet. It is a medical question, set in a social occasion on a feast day of Artemis in the central Greek region of Phocis. This chapter explores ancient thought on animals and plants, and the philosophical debates on food and mealtimes, which were, too often for some, pleasurable and therefore problematic occasions.

We have seen many examples of the way in which food was thought to fit into the civilized order, and into the greater worlds of the whole earth and the universe. In Chapter 1, a Hippocratic doctor showed how human society had evolved from prehistoric barbarity, in which early human beings had to eat raw foods like wild animals do, to its present good order with cooked foods that were suited to the human body. The cooking skills of advanced human civilizations were thus able to prepare food in the way best suited for the human digestive system, which was itself thought to be a natural process of cooking. A second example can be seen in the myth of Prometheus which expressed the vulnerable position of humanity in the universe, as the pawn between the Titan Prometheus and the Olympian Zeus. Eventually, a place for humanity was established that was well below the level of gods but above that of animals (see also Chapter 3). This was enshrined, so to speak, in the sacrificing of a lower form of life, the animal, to the higher, the god.

In this chapter I explore the place of food and animals in the cosmic order, taking as examples Plato's *Timaeus* and the Hippocratic *Regimen* I. Then, within the civilized order I consider the taxonomy or ordering of plants and animals in relation to human beings. Finally, I consider the main concern attached to food in ancient thought, the dangers of pleasure and luxury. We have seen such examples already as Pliny the Elder's exclamations on shellfish and cardoons.

Regimen I, the first of a group of four Hippocratic treatises on food and diet, places the human animal within the cosmic forces of fire and water. In a theory based on Heraclitus and other Presocratic philosophers, the author shows these principles constantly at tension in the universe and on earth. At the human level, the soul is likewise a blend of fire and water (7) and the body is nourished and augmented by food. The stomach in fact (10) is a major organ that nurtures what is good for the body and destroys what is bad by adjusting the proportions of fire and water. This remarkable document then moves on to show how fire and water lie behind the human social and cultural system in *Regimens* II to IV (see further Chapter 8).

Plato's views on how human beings fit into the cosmos are set out strikingly in *Timaeus*. Here the four elements of earth, air, fire and water are interrelated and underlie the universe, which was created according to mathematical principles. Combinations of elements account for the structures of bodies, of vital fluids and sensation. The human soul is tripartite, with the intellect in the head, and the emotions in the heart. 'The appetite for food and drink and other natural needs of the body they located between the midriff and the region of the navel, building in the area a kind of manger for the body's food; and they secured appetite there like a wild beast, which must be fed with the rest of us if mortals were to exist at all. And they put it in this position in order that it might continue to feed at its stall, but be as far as

FIGURE 7.1   The Jersey cow is a much more regular sight in southern England than in Mediterranean lands. Poseidonius and other ancient ethnographers identified the Celts as notable meat-eaters in comparison with Greek and Roman practice. Ancient meat-eaters witnessed the life and death of cattle and other animals much more intimately than their modern counterparts. At the same time, voluntary abstinence from eating meat seems to have been restricted to special ascetic and religious groups in antiquity. Courtesy of Malcolm Huxtable.

possible from the seat of deliberation' (70–1, trans. Lee). This idea that the stomach is necessary but dangerous I will return to shortly.

Towards the end of the dialogue Plato describes the creation of women from lesser men, and the creation of animals. Birds grew from flighty men, land animals from men not interested in philosophy, and fish, from the most unintelligent and ignorant of all. 'That is the origin of fish, shellfish and everything else that lives in water. They live in the depths as a punishment for the depth of their stupidity' (trans. Lee).

Plato's account establishes a clear hierarchy of god, man, woman, animal, fish and also borrows much from physics to explain the components of the universe, and medicine to explain the functioning of the body. There are similarities with the myth of Prometheus. There is also a common relationship between living things, which resembles the transmigration of souls of Pythagoras. He and his followers abstained from eating animals for this reason (see Chapter 5). The case for vegetarianism also arose in the works of Empedocles the Presocratic philosopher, Plutarch and Porphyry the Neoplatonic.

The relationship between human beings and animals has implications beyond the vegetarian issue. For people who do eat meat at least occasionally (in most cultures the majority), the question arises of how to care for the animal, how to kill it for food, and how to take responsibility for that killing. In some countries in the West in recent years, abbatoirs have been placed away from urban centres so that consumers do not witness the death of animals, meat is sold in neat chunks which do not resemble animal shapes, and government regulation is partial and fluctuating. As a result the individual citizen is often not in possession of the facts of slaughter. Citizens in antiquity who witnessed the victim's death – who heard it and smelt it and watched it and witnessed the throwing of blood over the altar – were very clear about what constituted the death of an animal before they ate its meat. They also seem to have taken responsibility for its death.

Comparison with the modern world can be instructive. Does the removal of the deaths of animals from most people's experience make us more or less humane, more or less responsible? Then there is the prioritizing of issues. One can become politicized above another. Thus in Britain in 2004, apparent cruelty to thousands of foxes took political precedence over cruelty to millions of chickens. Far more citizens eat chickens than hunt foxes, but humane farming of chickens is kept away from the political agenda. At the same time, millions of other animals lead comparatively luxurious lives as pets. Definitions of what constitutes cruelty to animals, which animals count and which do not, and what responsibilities human beings have towards animals all require debate.

The relationship between human beings and animals was explored both in philosophy and in a number of other areas in antiquity, such as fable, comedy and verse. The best comic example is to be found in the *Birds* of Aristophanes, in which a human being takes control of the universe from the gods and restores it to the earlier cosmic power, the birds. This is a utopia in which many analogies between human experience and the life of birds are drawn. The basic relationship between human and bird worlds, however, remains unchanged in the crucial areas of who eats whom and who sacrifices what to whom: birds continue to be eaten (if they have the wrong kind of belief) and human beings continue to sacrifice to the gods (Wilkins 2000). A similar play, *The Fishes*, was written by a contemporary of Aristophanes, Archippus. Here too, links and analogies seem to have been drawn between the world of fish and the world of human beings.

In didactic epic poetry, the world of fish is explored in the *Halieutica* of Oppian, which was written at about the same time as the *Deipnosophistae*. Here the marine world is described in considerable detail. The relationship between human beings and fish is seen as a kind of warfare, akin to the relationship between humans and wild animals, which Oppian also wrote about in epic verse (Purcell 1995). The sea is too deep and too vast to be charted or understood fully: there are many marvels, such as Pliny in his *Natural History* found on earth. At the same time, the fish are often portrayed in terms that belong to human families and societies. Thus 'than the tuna,' says Oppian (1.756–64),

I deem there is no fish that dwells in the brine more lawless (*athemisteron*) or which exceeds it in wickedness of heart; for when she has laid her eggs and escaped from the grievous travail of birth, the very mother that bare them devours all that she can overtake: pitiless mother who devours her own children while yet they are ignorant of flight and hath no compassion to her brood. There are also those which are not produced by bridal (*gamoisi*) or birth – races self-created and self-made: even all the shellfish, which are produced by the slime itself. (trans. Mair)

In book 2, we read (43–5),

Among fishes neither justice is of any account nor is there any mercy or love; for all the fish that swim are bitter foes to one another.

And later (2.642–8), the *kestreus* or grey mullet is said to nurse the gentlest and most righteous mind. For only the kindly grey mullets harm neither one of their own kind nor any of another race. Nor do they touch with their lips fleshly food nor drink blood, but feed harmlessly, unstained of blood and doing no hurt, a holy race. (trans. Mair)

What is to be the relationship between human being and fish? To eat the lawless or the gentle fish? Outside imaginative literature, there were many attempts to classify and catalogue the natural world. The lists of animal and plant names that appear in Athenaeus derive ultimately from the pioneering works of Aristotle on zoology and Theophrastus on plants. These treatises are philosophically complicated and raise large issues of classification. But they also allow eating to be an interest – in Aristotle's discussion of the locust, for example, or Theophrastus on silphium.

From humanity's relationship with animals and plants, we move to ancient texts which address big issues connected with food. These will largely concern pleasure and luxury. First, however, the big picture of the Greco-Roman or 'civilized' world.

A world view was much in the minds of the two authors who contribute so much to this book, namely Galen and Athenaeus. Galen in his treatise *On Maintaining Good Health* helps to locate himself and his readers in the world of Greek culture within the Roman Empire. German children, he says (1.10), 'are not well brought up. But we are not writing these things for Germans or other savage or barbarian peoples; nor indeed for bears, boars or lions, or any other animals, but for Greeks and for those who were racially born as barbarians but pursue the cultural formation of the Greeks'. Galen does not conceive of Greek culture as an exclusive club, and takes on the huge complexity of the Roman Empire to which people can be assimilated. This can be illustrated later in the same treatise where Galen discusses wine (5.5). Galen's world includes the great Italian vintages such as Falernian, established Greek favourites such as Lesbian, and wines from his own part of Asia Minor such as Mysia and Bithynia. Cilician and Galatian wines are also mentioned. When it comes to old men with kidney disorders, then additions of betony or the Celtic herb *kestron*, or nard or pepper (both from Asia) might be in order.

Galen's geographical terms of reference cover the whole Roman Empire and beyond. This feature is equally evident in the treatise *On the Powers of Foods*, in which Galen ranges from the Spanish rabbit to

Syrian pistachio, from Thracian rye to Alexandrian camel. That spatial range is complemented too with a social range rarely achieved in ancient authors. In his discussion of naked wheats (*On the Powers of Foods* 1.2), Galen observes two groups of people, country folk on feast days and athletes, both of whom are different from 'us', the members of the elite writing and presumed to be reading this treatise. The country people, as we saw on p. 57, add cheese to their bread at festival times, and this combination does harm even to the strongest constitution. Reapers and ditch-diggers are given as examples, who are seen as more able to concoct unleavened bread than athletes, the archetypal strong men of the ancient imagination. Galen explains that labour makes the peasants so hungry that their stomachs seize half-digested food. 'This is why these people later suffer very troublesome illnesses and die before they reach old age. Ignorant of this, most people who see them eating and concocting what *none of us can tackle and concoct* congratulate them on their bodily strength' (trans. Powell). The peasants, the athletes and us. Galen, the imperial physician, who also attended gladiators and the emperor on campaign, ranges widely in coming to his world view. He ranges widely, also, through medical textbooks and literature, drawing on not only Hippocrates and medical authors and other relevant technical authors such as Dioscorides, but also Plato, Aristotle and Aristophanes. Thus, for example, in the short treatise *On Habits (peri ethon)*, Galen reflects on advice from Plato's *Timaeus* as well as the precepts of Hippocrates and the Hellenistic doctor Erasistratus. Thus doctors were influenced by philosophy and the philosophers by doctors. We saw Plato's interest in the human body in *Timaeus* above, and in the *Republic* he draws on ideas of Hippocrates and a regime proposed by the somewhat shadowy figure Herodicus of Selymbria.

This world view, which Galen put together over a range of treatises, incorporates the natural and cultured world, the cosmos and civilization. Many of Galen's predecessors had described the natural and moral world in relation to food, and such beliefs and explanations of natural phenomena are the subject of this chapter.

Throughout much of the ancient thought on food runs a strong theme of contrast, between sufficiency and excess, simplicity and complexity, usefulness and pleasure. We shall see this reflected in Chapter 9, on literature, and elsewhere in the book we will return to the strong theme of excess that needs to be suppressed. It was widely held in antiquity that human beings were subject to desires in particular areas that relate to the basic human needs to eat, to reproduce and to clothe themselves. Elaborate systems of thought emerged to define and help to identify these. Luxury was often thought to reside in certain parts of humanity, in particular those in other cultures, women, slaves, and those male citizens who might be tempted from traditional codes of behaviour. These ideas are prevalent in many different sources, particularly those comparing traditional belief with outside influence. Thus below we will see Cato's comments on Greek influence in Italy in the second century BC, and similar Greek comments on Persian influences at an earlier date on Greece. We shall also see Seneca's commentary on the extravagance of the Roman elite in the first century AD. Much of the debate was set out by Plato in a series of discussions surrounding this issue of desire.

The most striking philosophical ideas to emerge, however, and those most frequently expressed, concern luxury and pleasure. In authors of nearly all periods, there are warnings about luxury (often perceived as a threat to the citizen body posed by foreigners and other external groups) and about pleasure. Very few authors totally reject pleasure, but pleasure was thought always to have the potential for more insistent forms of itself and general insatiability. Even authors widely thought to believe in pleasure, such as Epicurus, write in very circumspect terms about it, as we shall see. The interest in pleasure in this chapter will often be contrasted with notions of need or utility. A typical example of the contrast is to be found in Plutarch's *Table-Talk* 2 (629c):

> Some of the preparations which are made for dinners and drinking parties rank as necessities, my dear Sosius Senecio; such as the wine, the food, and of course the couches and the tables. Others are diversions introduced for pleasure's sake, and no essential function attaches to them; such are music, spectacles and the laughter-maker Philip at the house of Callias. [In Xenophon's *Symposium*]

We shall see that authors differ in their classification of what comes under the heading of pleasure and what counts as utility. But for Plato, Galen and Athenaeus, this contrast is conceptually vital in order to ground their world view in an acceptable ethical and intellectual framework.

This feature is particularly prominent when social and religious aspects of food are played down and the demands of the body and the dangers of pleasure are at issue. In the works of Plato, we can see food identified as potentially damaging in *Gorgias*; as accepted in the social and festive fabric of *Laws* and the *Symposium*; and in an ambivalent light in the *Republic*. At the other end of our period, in the *de abstinentia* of the neo-Platonist Porphyry, we shall see food treated as the enemy of the philosopher, or ascetic sage, who should not be subject to the pleasures of the flesh that are enjoyed by ordinary mortals. Cato the Elder and Musonius Rufus will be trenchant opponents of certain aspects of eating in a Roman context, as will Seneca and the Stoics.

As we have seen elsewhere, the fourth century BC was an important period for the development of thought in this area. Plato played an influential role in his analysis of pleasure. We shall begin with the *Republic*. Socrates, Adeimantus and Glaucon are establishing what will be needed to sustain life in the ideal republic. The basic necessities are established (371a–c) as cereals, wine, clothes and shoes. They will need houses as well, and will be largely naked and barefoot in summer, clothed and shod in winter. They will be nourished by barley meal, which they will make into *maza*, and by wheat flour which they will put on reeds or leaves and bake into bread. They will recline on rustic couches spread with yew and myrtle and will feast with their children, going on to drink wine, wear garlands and sing hymns to the gods, 'living pleasantly together, having no more children than they can afford and taking careful watch of both poverty and war'. These details are important, for the discussion will shortly get on to what counts as luxuries. The details so far cover the basic essentials mentioned above of food, reproduction and warmth for the body. They identify barley and, surprisingly, wheat as essential foods; they provide for rituals of consumption, including reclining and garlanding the head; and economic considerations of adequate supplies and the dangers of threats from outside (presumably if stronger neighbours envied what these people had). Note in particular that an agricultural model is envisaged, with no foods provided that do not grow in Attica. Thus trade is not proposed. Glaucon reminds Socrates that so far his citizens are dining without any *opsa*, or meat and vegetable supplements to the cereal base. This word triggers certain implications of indulgence and uncontrolled desire, as discussed in Davidson (1997).

Socrates is able to incorporate *opsa*, the tasty dietary supplements to the bland cereals, which are essential to human health, as we now understand nutrition, and adds salt, olives, cheese, the bulbs of the tassel-hyacinth and green vegetables, 'the kind that they boil in the

herbæ, quam itaphidem agriam vocant.

I. PIPER.   * II. M

FIGURE 7.2   Pepper appears in medical and literary writers from the fourth century BC to the cookery book of Apicius in late antiquity. The spice was valued both as a flavour and for its heating qualities in medicine. See Dalby 2003: 254–5. Miller 1969: 80 identifies pepper as 'the staple commodity of the Roman imperial trade with India'. Reproduced by permission of the Dean and Chapter of Exeter Cathedral

countryside'. There will also be dates, chick-peas and beans to nibble, myrtle berries and acorns to roast in the fire, and moderate drinking. 'In this way they will lead their life in peace and in good health, and will be likely to grow old and pass on this kind of life to their children.' Glaucon says this is a life fit only for pigs. What are needed are couches to recline on, tables to eat from and tasty and crunchy foods 'such as people currently enjoy'. Socrates' response is striking: 'it seems', he says, 'that we are considering not so much how to set up a city as how to set up a luxurious city'. This is a city which is not necessarily 'healthy', that may have injustice within it, and may have to fight wars. The items he identifies in such a luxurious city are these: couches, tables and other dining materials, tasty food, myrrh, incense, courtesans, cakes, painting, gold, and ivory. There will be a large number of trades, huntsmen, artists in sculpture, painting and music, poets and their assistants, rhapsodes, actors, dancers, undertakers of work, craftsmen of all kinds of articles including women's adornment, a host of servants, tutors, wet nurses, nurses, hairdressers, barbers, makers of *opsa* and cooks. 'We will also need swineherds.'

Plato also has an important point to press in *Gorgias*, which is an extended dialogue on rhetoric, pleasure and aspects of society which might be useful or not for the individual and the body politic. The mind and soul are considered higher parts of the person than the body. But when it comes to care of the body, there are good and bad people to turn to for advice. The doctor will advise what the body needs, while the cook will advise on what will give pleasure. This division between medicine and cooking played a powerful role in ancient thought (though in this book we have also seen many examples of cooking and medicine working together harmoniously). Plato names certain tradesmen (518) who were prominent in Athens, Thearion the baker, Mithaecus the cook and Sarambus the vintner.

Comedy, meanwhile, also in the fourth century BC, developed certain figures associated with good eating: one of these was the chef who prepared the food, and had a great deal to say about it. Another was the parasite who scrounged food and drink from a base not of right like the other participants, but of poverty and inequity, like the beggars in the *Odyssey*. The third was the *hetaera* or courtesan who relieved men of their money at the symposium, the drinking part of the evening. All of these stock characters – and their recurrence indicates a continual anxiety about the problem – illustrated for the audience the dangers associated with pleasure. These dangers beset young men in particular. Athenaeus notes, for example (4.165e), that comedies mocked a certain Ctesippus, son of Chabrias, who was so devoted to prodigality (*asotia*) that he sold his father's tomb (a gift from the city of Athens) to support his luxurious life (*hedupatheia*). This last is an interesting term, which first appears in the works of Xenophon, and is the title of the parodic poem of recipes from the fourth-century poet Archestratus (see p. 47).

A more positive evaluation of food and eating emerges in other systems of thought in antiquity. One interesting area is in medicine, where, as described in Chapter 8, food and cooking are at the heart of the civilizing process and at the heart of the digestive system. Food in moderation, that is. This is made very clear in medical texts from Hippocrates to Galen. Galen strikes a very Platonic note, for example, in *On the Powers of Foods*, when commenting on cooks' use of herbs to enhance taste (2.51, quoted on p. 11). He also comments (3.26) with puzzlement on the enthusiasm in Rome for the livers of red mullet, which are mashed up in *garum* and olive oil:

> Gourmets have marvelled at red-mullet liver on account of its tastiness ... I do not think it has either the taste or the benefit to the body to justify such esteem ... Nor again can I understand why very many people buy the largest red mullet, which has flesh that is neither tasty like the smaller ones, nor easily concocted since it is quite firm. Consequently I enquired of one of those who were buying red mullet at a high price whatever was the reason for his eagerness for them. He answered that while he bought old ones like those particularly because of the liver, he did so because of the head as well. (trans. Powell)

In much of his work, Galen concerns himself only marginally with the food habits of the rich. These were a greater concern to many authors, such as Pliny and Columella, at the beginning of his *On Agriculture*, where contemporaries are portrayed as deviating from traditional values (especially those enshrined in agriculture) in favour of smart, rhetorical, urban-based display. Along with ancestral acres go the part-time soldiering of the citizen-farmer. Athenaeus, in his review of luxury in book 12, follows a model for state development which begins with a community full of vigour and martial courage; it then becomes successful, grand, and, crucially, 'soft', and finally is shipwrecked on the shoals of luxury. Athenaeus has examples of both states and individuals suffering from such softness. These are contained in ethical anecdotes with a clear protreptic purpose.

Food is often an integral part of such social and cultural development. Hence twice in Herodotus, an invading general is asked why he invaded an agriculturally poorer country, only to meet with defeat. The argument seems to be that Egypt and Persia respectively are richer than their neighbours in food and agriculture and so the desire to invade them is amazing. The discourse of luxury also contrasts current extravagant eating with an earlier, more restrained version. This is seen in Greek authors, Roman authors, and indeed in Persia where, for all the splendour at court, the traditional foods on which Persian identity is built are the terebinth and a kind of cress (Sancisi-Weerdenburg 1995). Galen comments on contemporary idleness (which contrasts with earlier virtue) (quoted in Chapter 8). Pliny, as we have seen before, regrets modern decadence (*Natural History* 8.210):

> the boar was divided into three parts and the middle one was called the loin of the boar. The first Roman to serve a whole boar at his banquets (*epulis*) was Publius Servilius Rullus . . . [early first century BC] That is how close the beginning of this now daily event was. It is noted in historical texts, presumably for the improvement of these customs, by which two or three boars are eaten at once, not indeed as the whole meal, but just as a starter.

Greek and Roman writers saw many examples of this kind of development, and generated contrasting centres of simplicity in the past or in non-urban areas. Athenaeus places such simplicity in the poems of Homer, for example. The question for us is whether developments of this kind were significant for the history of food and eating, or were different from the development of food in culture – such as that set out in Chapter 1. These luxurious phenomena might, for example, have been isolated occurrences, which elicited similar reactions in very different centuries and have more to do with philosophical literature than the development of eating practices. Pliny notes changes in the consumption of wild boar, as does his fellow moralizing author Juvenal in *Satire* 1. But Pliny in the same passage also reports that Cato the Censor at the beginning of the second century BC had written speeches that denounced *callum*, or the 'hard fat' of the wild boar. Cato on the evils of bacon was probably well worth the hearing.

Cato is often held up as the stern Republican figure who tried to maintain traditional Roman values in the face of Greek influence. He opposed the expansion of Roman interests in the Greek world; he opposed the Scipionic family who were influential in expansion in Spain, Carthage and Greece. And he famously complained of the import of pretty young men into Italy and of salted fish from the Black Sea which at 300 drachmae an amphora was more expensive than the price of land (Polybius 31 and Athenaeus). Plutarch in his *Life of Cato* sets out Cato's own eccentric dining habits, such as his habit of eating bread and wine with his slaves.

We need to see this picture for what it is, an image specially composed for maximum political and rhetorical impact. The triumphant philhellene general Aemilius Paullus with his Greek interests and Greek books, was not the diametrical opposite of Cato, for Cato studied Greek, used Greek treatises in his work on agriculture, and was the patron of the young Oscan poet Ennius. This trilingual speaker became another icon of austerity in Republican Rome, but one of his works was a Latin version of none other than the *Life of Luxury* of Archestratus. This is not to accuse Cato and Ennius of hypocrisy, but to note that these were complex times, with complex international exchanges and ideologies. It was not too much for a protégé from the Greek south to make available to Latin readers a poem from an earlier century in Greek Sicily. Luxury was one of these ideological discourses. Plutarch compares Cato's eating with that of two of his neighbours, Manius Curius Dentatus and Valerius Flaccus. The former famously defeated Pyrrhus, the Macedonian invader of Italy, and after this great victory and three triumphs went back to digging on his farm. Plutarch reports (2.1):

> the Samnite ambassadors found him on his farm sitting at the hearth boiling turnips. They wanted to give him a great deal of gold but he sent them away with the message that a man for whom such a dinner sufficed had no need of gold, and that for himself it was a much finer thing than gold to conquer people who had it.

Valerius, meanwhile, admired the dining habits of Cato, which consisted in sitting at table with his slaves and eating and drinking the same wine as they had, and invited him to dinner (*deipnon*). It would be surprising if this *deipnon* that Cato attended was a non-hierarchical affair with slaves sharing the aristocratic wine and bread, for this was Cato's entrée to political influence in Rome. Nevertheless, once Cato was a powerful man at Rome, Plutarch reports that among other aspects of the simple life, (4.2), 'he was happy with a simple dinner [*deipnon*], a cold breakfast/lunch [*ariston*] . . .' and he continued as a politician and as Censor to oppose excess. He thought [4.2] that 'the Republic was not guarding its purity because of its great size and that by ruling so many areas and peoples, it was becoming involved with many ethical systems and accepting examples of very varied ways of life.' Plutarch's words echo those of Polybius. This is an ideological battle for the soul of the traditional Republic that is in competition with the expansionist Republic of the second century BC. At 16.4, Plutarch reports that Cato's candidature for the office of Censor was based on the need 'to cut out and cauterize luxury and softness [*truphen kai malakian*] like a hydra' (see Astin 1978: 173).

This ideological debate set on the figure of Cato the Elder is crucial for the thought of this chapter. It shows perfectly the tension between the claims of traditional rural life and the demands of the growing city with its outside influences. There are fears in some quarters that an expanding empire may be in danger of sinking beneath a flood of foreign luxuries. Food and dining have a role to play in this process. It is also a process and way of looking at the world that is not exclusive to Rome, but is mirrored in Athens and probably many other Greek cities. I discuss this in Wilkins (2000: chapter 6). There are echoes in Greek and Roman comedy, where such tensions could be played out to large and varied audiences. It is a common feature above all in the Roman literature that is explored in Chapter 9, the *Satires* of Horace and Juvenal (in Satire 11, the latter explicitly refers to Manius Curius), the letters, speeches and essays of Cicero and Seneca, the *Fasti* of Ovid (see above) and the myth-making histories of Sallust and Tacitus. Our concern is the history of food, which derives from very varied sources. The reception of that history, however, depends heavily on this morally loaded literature of the early Roman Empire.

Cato in later life ran a harsh regime for his domestic slaves, which, according to Plutarch (*Life of Cato* 21.4), included regulation of their sex lives and summary execution where judged necessary. Of dining arrangements, Plutarch reports:

> early in life when he was still poor and serving in the army he was not bad tempered about anything to do with diet but said that it was shameful to argue with a servant over what to put in his stomach. Later on, when he was a more important man of affairs, and gave formal meals [*hestiaseis*] to friends and fellow magistrates, he punished with a whip immediately after dinner anyone who had been negligent in serving or preparing the meal.

There were, however, also unusual benefits for slaves, for, Plutarch reports (20.4), Cato's wife breast-fed not only Cato's son (which an aristocratic wife might be expected not to do) but also some slave children in order to make them well disposed to Cato through this shared nurture.

Cato's attempts to regulate the rituals of dining and the impact of foreign practices find many echoes in the comedies of Plautus and Terence, which were written in the late third century and early second century BC. When these plays were translated from the Greek originals of Menander and others and adapted into Latin versions, they were put on at different festivals from their Greek predecessors (see Chapter 3) and made a significant adjustment to the presentation of the lavish meals cooked up by the boastful chefs. To take the festivals first, a number (The Games of Apollo, The Games of Ceres, The Games of the Great Mother) were introduced to bolster divine support to the city of Rome through the Hannibalic crisis that threatened Rome's survival. (They were added to the very ancient Roman Games and to the production of comedies at the funerals of major aristocrats.) Feasting and entertainments were important elements in these festivals, and one of these elements was comedy. These interesting developments echo our earlier remarks on Rome's dependence on aspects of Greek culture at the same time as certain citizens were declaring their hostility to Greece, at least in certain contexts.

The plays of Plautus and Terence are overtly translations from the Greek and often say as much in their prologues. The characters and settings are Greek. But it is also clearly the case that the playwrights are also writing about Rome and Romans. There are explicit references to Roman institutions, such as sumptuary laws against luxury (see Fraenkel 1960 and Leigh 2004). One way in which the plays are angled, however, is to contrast the countryside (with simple and traditional virtues) with the city to which lavish meals belong. The cities are the focus of Greekness, and sometimes the verb *pergraecari* 'to go round like a Greek' is used to denote lavish dining by young men (Gruen 1984). Astin 1978: 173, 179 lists the following plays of Plautus: *Poen.* 603, *Bacch.* 813, *Truc.* 87, *Most.* 22, 64, 960. These are precisely the foreign influences that Cato and indeed Polybius were worried about (31.25.2–8):

> The first direction taken by Scipio's ambition to lead a virtuous life, was to attain a reputation for temperance [*sophrosune*] and excel in this

respect all the other young men of the same age. This is a high prize indeed and difficult to gain, but it was at this time easy to pursue at Rome owing to the vicious tendencies of most of the youths. For some of them had abandoned themselves to amours with boys and others to the society of courtesans, and many to musical entertainments [*akroamata*] and banquets [*potous*], and the extravagance [*poluteleia*] they involve, having in the course of the war with Perseus been speedily infected [*herpakotes*] by the Greek laxity in these respects. So great in fact was the incontinence [*akrasia*] that had broken out among the young men in such matters, that many paid a talent for a male favourite and many three hundred drachmas for a jar of salt fish. This aroused the indignation of Cato, who said once in a public speech that it was the surest sign of deterioration in the republic when pretty boys fetch more than fields and jars of caviar [sic] more than ploughmen. It was just at the period we are treating of that this present tendency to extravagance declared itself, first of all because they thought that now after the fall of the Macedonian kingdom their universal dominion was undisputed, and next because after the riches of Macedonia had been transported to Rome there was a great display of wealth both in public and in private. (trans. Paton)

The imperial period brought to Rome many new problems, which had only been a distant threat at the time of Cato the Elder. With greatly increased national wealth and the ability to acquire land in other countries, luxurious lives could be led both in Italy and in the provinces, such as Sicily, North Africa and in the Greek East. The fertility of Sicily and Africa were proverbial. Of Emporia, Polybius (31.21.1) notes that Massanissa cast envious eyes and tried to wrest the fertile terrain from the Carthaginians. By the Imperial period, there were luxurious villas in North Africa, many of which have supplied the mosaics in the collections of the Bardo Museum in Tunis and the museum at Sousse.

People lived well. Successful and rich families had large incomes and were able to spend them on luxurious foods as well as large houses, complements of slaves and all the elements of the good life. Members of the elite competed between each other to display their success and status; they also used such areas of spending to establish their place in the social and political hierarchy. Eating and drinking provided social occasions on which such displays could be made. Social and economic demands ensured that people took advantage of the many fruits of empire available in the markets of Rome (Aelius Aristeides 26.1–29; Dalby 2000). They had access to variety, quality and quantity, depending on taste. This is an area on which literary and philosophical texts have much to say. It is important to note the starting point of such texts and their relation to social and economic concerns. Plato and the comic poets of Athens in the fourth century BC shared many concerns but also had very different perspectives in this area, as was discussed above. By the imperial period in Rome, a rich commentary was available on the dangers of eating. This came from a number of directions, which were interlinked. Philosophers continued to rail against appetite and luxury, as Plato's Socrates had done. We shall explore the views of Musonius Rufus and Seneca, both of whom were Stoic philosophers writing in the first century AD. We shall also consider the impact of the rival beliefs of Epicurus. Then there were literary commentaries discussed in Chapter 9. In many ways, these literary and philosophical forms saw food as an enemy that was always capable of transforming itself from useful nourishment into something much more seductive and dangerous, pleasant tastes that appealed to the appetite. We therefore need to refer elsewhere in the period to texts which put food into a broader perspective, to Pliny, Athenaeus and Galen, each of whom integrates eating into a social and intellectual framework.

The major elements that Musonius Rufus emphasizes in his remarks on food are *sophronein* (soundness of mind) and *enkrateia* (control). The views of Musonius are reported in summary form, and he is said to have repeated them often and emphatically, as a matter of no small importance. Acceptable objectives are inexpensive as opposed to expensive foods, readily available rather than rare foods, 'appropriate' foods (*sumphulon*, 'of the same category', an example of which is food produced by plants) which include plants, cereals and animal products. Most are foods which need no cooking, such as seasonal fruits, milk, cheese and honey. If the effort of cooking is required, as for cereals, that too is acceptable. Meat, however, is a more bestial food (*trophen theriodesteran*) and more suited to wild animals. It is heavy and an impediment to reason. Musonius (in summary) continues:

> for this reason, also the people who make larger use of it seem slower in intellect. Furthermore, as man of all creatures on earth is the nearest of kin to the gods, so he should be nourished in a manner most like the gods. Now the vapours rising from the earth and water are sufficient for them, and so, he said, we ought to be nourished on food most like that, the lightest and the purest; for thus our souls would be pure and dry, and being so would be finest and wisest, as it seemed to Heraclitus when he said, 'The clear dry soul is wisest and best'. (trans. Lutz)

Musonius is further reported to have been opposed to ingenious cooking methods, the arts of cooking, cookery books and the threats to health posed by elaborate food. The greatest danger is the pleasure of eating, the satisfaction of which is insatiable, and reduces human beings to the level of dogs and pigs, which lack reason. The pleasures of eating attack men several times a day; people may eat too much or too quickly; they may eat the wrong sort of food, at the wrong time. They may abuse hospitality by not serving the same kind or amount of foods to friends as to themselves. The throat and stomach are designed to be not organs of pleasure but processors of food. Failure to control appetite leads to the demand for variety, for ships to sail the seas, for cooks to be valued more than farmers and for estates to be squandered. The philosopher believes that cheaper diets make for stronger people, noting the diet of a slave, of countrymen over city-dwellers, of the poor compared with the rich. (As we shall see in the next chapter, Galen's medical opinion of the diet of the poor man and the countryman is much less rosy than the philosopher's.) On tables and sympotic furniture, Rufus decries gold and other expensive ornamentation in favour of earthenware and cheap but useful metalware. Final proofs come from the austerity of the Spartans, which was more desirable than all the riches of the King of Persia, and lead to a summative declaration on luxury:

> I would choose sickness rather than luxury, for sickness harms only the body, but luxury destroys both body and soul, causing weakness and impotence in the body and lack of self-control and cowardice in the soul. Furthermore, luxury begets injustice because it also begets covetousness. For no man of extravagant tastes can avoid being lavish in expenditure, nor being lavish can he wish to spend little; but in his desire for many things he cannot refrain from acquiring them, nor again in his effort to acquire can he fail to be grasping and unjust; for no man would succeed in acquiring much by just methods. In still another way the man of luxurious habits would be unjust, for he would hesitate to undertake the necessary burdens for his city without abandoning his extravagant life, and if it seemed necessary to suffer deprivation on behalf of his friends or relatives he would not submit to it, for his love of luxury would not permit it. Nay more, there are times when duties to the gods must be undertaken by the man who would be just toward them, by performing sacrifices, initiatory rites, or some other such service. Here too, the wastrel would be found wanting. Thus he would in all ways be unjust toward his city, toward his friends, and toward the gods, in failing to do what it is his duty to do. (trans. Lutz)

It is clear that several positions are being made here which are very different from those seen elsewhere in this book. We shall see similarly polarized beliefs in Porphyry. This essay on food resembles Seneca's views and those of many other philosophers. It offers a totalizing overview of Roman society which is internally consistent but depends on special readings of religious, social and economic codes. Seneca's *Epistles* reflect similar Stoic beliefs of self-control and constraint of bodily desires, but from within upper class life. Thus *Epistle* 114, for example, reflects:

> Where prosperity has spread luxury over a wide area of society, people start paying closer attention to their personal turnout. The next thing that engages people's energies is furniture. Then pains are devoted to the houses themselves, so as to have them running out over broad expanses of territory, to have the walls glowing with marble shipped from overseas and the ceilings picked out in gold, to have the floors shining with a lustre matching the panels overhead. Splendour then moves on to the table, where praise is courted through the medium of novelty and variations in the accustomed order of dishes.

As for the food itself, Seneca in *Epistle* 78 summarizes views we have seen many times:

> 'How very unfortunate he is,' people say, 'to be sick like that!' Why? Because he isn't melting snow in his wine? Because he isn't breaking ice into a bumper goblet to keep the drink he has mixed in it chilled? Because Lucrine oysters aren't being opened for him at his table? Because there isn't any bustling of cooks about the dining room, bringing in not just the viands themselves but the actual cooking apparatus along with them? For this is the latest innovation in luxurious living, having the kitchen accompany the dinner in to the table so as to prevent any of the food losing its heat and avoid anything being at a temperature insufficiently scalding for palates which are nowadays like leather.

Seneca's social commentary follows a broadly Stoic pattern. Many authors suggest that the Epicureans took a very different approach to food, since pleasure was the goal, rather than the enemy as set out in Plato and the Stoics. Despite misrepresentation in popular literature and thought, in Athenaeus (3.101f–104c, 5.186e, 7.278d–280b) and elsewhere, Epicurus and his followers in fact seem to have taught restraint in eating, in order not to disturb personal well-being. Thus in his letter to Menoeceus, Epicurus advises a simple life:

The pleasurable life is not continuous drinking, dancing and sex; nor the enjoyment of fish or other delicacies of an extravagant table. It is sober reasoning which searches out the motives for all choice and avoidance, and rejects those beliefs which lay open the mind to the greatest disturbance. (trans. Gaskin)

Musonius Rufus is the latest of a long line of philosophers who took exception to cookery books. Plato in *Gorgias* contrasted the cookery book of Mithaecus of Sicily unfavourably with medical works (see p. 197).

Archestratus played up to this by naming his poem the *Hedupatheia* or *Experience of Pleasure (Life of Luxury)*. The dangers of the cookery book do not need to be spelled out. They advise the cook or the household slave or householder how to make food more pleasant or refined to the taste. While this may alarm the moralist, to the social anthropologist and food historian, the cookery book marks an advance in sophistication and in the preparation of the products of agriculture for the table. Such books are only produced under certain cultural conditions (see p. 47), some of which Goody has set out (1982: 97–9). An agricultural surplus is required. It is no surprise that the cookery book appears to have originated in Sicily, the land of the rich tyrant's court, rather than on the less fertile Greek mainland. A central authority is required, which can gather resources and also a large group of discriminating palates who are able and interested enough to prefer one taste over another. A literary culture is required, such that the recipes will be written down for interested readers rather than passed by word of mouth from professional to professional. The Greek cookery book, then, reflects a mature stage of cultural development. In some ways it is artificially divided from medicine by Plato since many doctors wrote cookery books (*Opsartutika*: see Athenaeus 516, Galen *On the Powers of Foods* 2.27), which may have resembled the recipes doctors assembled in treatises on drugs and pharmacology. Just as the doctor needed to prescribe the amount of cooking required for a certain food, so he set out combinations of drugs. This medical role is close to the advice on cooking and complex spicing of many recipes in the cookery book of 'Apicius'.

The cookery book may also draw on raw materials from outside the locality. They may incite the reader, the consumer or indeed the author to travel to foreign parts in search of particular delicacies. They may add to the demand for foreign imports to a city.

The number of cookery books that have survived is few. There are only a few fragments of the works of Mithaecus, of the recipe books of the doctors and of Paxamus (who is mentioned by Columella). The principal survivors are Archestratus and Apicius. They well illustrate Shaun Hill's categories of the manual (Apicius) and of the aspirational (pp. 245–6). Archestratus does instruct how to cook certain fish, but much of the poem is taken up with ingenious tricks with Homeric verse, cheeky incitements to pleasure, and various amusements to please the apparently sympotic audience – if the poem was composed for performance after a *deipnon*. The main effect is to give the reader or listener a virtual tour round the Mediterranean, to urge travel in pursuit of pleasure, and to describe the delights of fish in considerable detail. It is thus a work of literature which aims at several objectives. Thus it is possible for Athenaeus both to quote it for its wit, its commentary on fish and its range of places, while denouncing it for its incitements to pleasure. For Athenaeus, Archestratus is as much a threat to good living as is Epicurus, or at least Epicurus in popular thought. As part of the humour, speakers in Athenaeus sometimes quote Archestratus through the medium of the Stoic philosopher Chrysippus. The incitement to pleasure is thus safely wrapped up in the disapproving words of a leading Stoic.

The book of Apicius, by contrast, is a late compilation of a number of different works which combine medical interests, rare foods and adaptation of cheap foods to make equivalents of expensive foods. Unlike the poem of Archestratus, which survives only in quoted fragments, the book of Apicius survives in its own manuscript tradition. It is rich and varied in both linguistic and culinary terms, and for its heavy spicing heralds a later age that extended to the Mediaeval period. It is not easy to see how the work as compiled relates to anything that Apicius might have written. Anecdotes told by Athenaeus and others indicate a connoisseur rather than a cook. The cookery book certainly indicates use of imported ingredients, such as pepper and parrots. The cook at the forefront of innovation and unusual flavouring can certainly benefit from this book. The cook with very few resources may also find much of value, such is the range of materials.

Defining moments in this process of movement seem to be provided by the cookery book of Archestratus and the *Deipnosophistae* of Athenaeus. The former explicitly lines up his poem in the ranks of luxurious living, while Athenaeus, for all his ironic comment on Archestratus, presents all his sympotic evidence for the diversity of mealtimes in the

Greek world and beyond in terms of variety from city to city and text to text. Everything it expresses is luxurious in the sense that it is not simple, traditional and ritually enshrined. Luxury is presented in a negative light in book 12, to be sure. But the embedding of luxury in the Roman world of the second and third century AD is nowhere made more strongly than in the pages of Athenaeus. The Roman magistrate Larensis puts on dinners whose lavishness knows no equal, and whose raw materials most decidedly do not come from the traditional hillsides of ancient Latium.

Imperial Rome was in the position of being able to command the best products of all the countries in the empire, and to assemble them and enjoy them in Rome. Some, like Musonius, rejected them altogether. Others, like Seneca and followers of Epicurus, enjoyed them with care. So Pliny tried to survey the whole empire, with an emphasis on the excellence of Italy and a warm regard for traditional values. Others, like Athenaeus, celebrated the diversity and tempered the dangers of excess by adopting a broadly Stoic restraint, and by emphasizing not so much the material foods and drinks themselves as literary representations of them. The Deipnosophists have all kinds of luxurious foods spread out before them, but they eat little (to the disgust of the Cynic philosophers amongst them) and quote literary descriptions of and comments on the foods. Many of these discussions, but not all, present ancient thought from the perspective of the elites who enjoy the benefits of empire. They even dismiss the opinions of the mass of the population as insufficiently reflective and too close to bodily (sometimes 'animal') pleasures. Galen is one of the exceptions to this rule in his work on food, since he seems to base his thought on the evidence of the whole population. The diet of the peasant has a contribution to make to the debate. It must be considered alongside Galen's reading of a Platonic dialogue or any other seminal work.

Finally, I consider the remarkable work of the Neoplatonist philosopher, Porphyry, *On Abstinence*. Porphyry's aim is to return his reader to the vegetarian life, after a lapse. It is an ascetic work, since it makes clear that only the philosopher and not the mass of the population (rich or poor) can tolerate a life without meat, but it is not as extreme as Musonius Rufus. Its main virtues for this book are three. It is an impressive record of vegetarian beliefs in antiquity. It preserves parts of many works that are now lost, such as Theophrastus' work *On Piety*, and is an impressive review of ancient debates about gods, animals, and plants, and their relationship with the world of human beings. He has much to say about Pythagoreans, and Epicureans, for example, and also about the dietary rules of the Jews and Egyptians. And he pays much attention to social institutions. The philosopher who wants to devote himself to god and to purity can separate himself from many aspects of human society; most people cannot. So, for example, the needs of the athlete are considered (2.3), and not just rejected out of hand.

8
Introduction

It is easy to smile at the medical beliefs of the past. Just as those in centuries to come will fall about laughing at the idea of people starving themselves in the midst of plenty to achieve thinness in the twenty-first century, so we shake our heads at the belief that a balance between coolness and warmth, or moistness and dryness, in foods was the major factor in a healthy diet or that blood-letting helped combat infection. The Romans used lead vessels to boil down grape syrup in order to sweeten wine, a practice that has poisoning as the sure final result, but we had the combination of lead pipes and soft water to give us village idiots for centuries thereafter and are presently suffering widespread childhood asthma and sensitivity to allergens which researchers are beginning to link to powerful chemicals now used in cleaning agents. The only real change is in the areas of our ignorance.

Two things remain constant. Top medical men will specialize in diseases of the rich rather than problems of the poor. The relief of effects of obesity and overindulgence are researched and treated, not those of malnutrition and poor diet.

The second and more interesting aspect is that we all subscribe without question to whatever theories on food and nutrition are current and that these colour our choice of food and its preparation. A post-war shopping list would have centred on milk and butter for healthy teeth and bones, lard and beef dripping for strength, and sugary drinks for energy. All suppositions were basically correct and reflected beliefs of a time when industrial quantities of salt, cheap fat and saccharine were not yet part of the national eating plan and before cooking had largely withdrawn into the reheating of prepared products. Recently de-rationed items like sugar and sweets accounted for plenty of tooth decay but little obesity. Yoghurt and low fat or low sugar foods were rare and there was little perceived need for them.

The salts and hidden fats of large-scale commercially manufactured ready meals that took over in the seventies and beyond have had much darker effects despite much greater awareness of health and nutrition, whilst dietary fads involving carbohydrates or food-combining diets have become widespread.

What is interesting is not that we accept such advice without hesitation but that major changes in how and what we eat spring from this. Animals are bred to be leaner, vegetables are held to be healthier options despite chemical residues from spraying, and carbohydrates, the cereals upon which the Mediterranean diet is based, are currently the villains of the mealtime piece.

The medical and nutritional advice of Greek and Roman times would have coloured the choices made and the dishes created in much the same way, so an inkling of what was commonly believed will help in understanding why certain foods may have been overlooked whilst others were highly prized.

Most of our culinary herbs and spices will have started in the medicine cupboard; coriander, for instance, was supposed to clear out bed bugs, and a sophisticated knowledge of the effects of powerful plants and mushrooms was well known and used. The trade in grain would have provided the infrastructure for trade in much more exotic items such as spices and medicinal plants as well as the ideas and knowledge that came from the east with them.

8

Medical Approaches to Food

Many physicians prefer this vegetable [lettuce] to all the others, just as they do figs among the autumn fruits . . . If it were really true, lettuce would be second to none, not only of vegetables but of all the most wholesome and nutritious foodstuffs. For they say that it generates blood. And some do not simply say blood, but they add 'much', asserting that lettuce generates much blood. But these people . . . are further from the truth.

With characteristic vigour Galen (*On the Powers of Foods* 2.40) criticizes the errors of other doctors. Operating at the cutting edge of science in the material world of the body where the best indications of its condition were the outer appearance, the properties of the urine and faeces excreted, and the properties of food and drink ingested, doctors often disagreed on the evidence. Disagreement extended to the effects of a particular food on the body.

This chapter addresses medicine and diet. Before moving to strictly 'medical' matters, however, I repeat the point made in Chapter 1, that the medical system of Hippocrates and Galen was based on 'cooking', that is, on the assimilation of the natural raw material into the civilized human world. Then a second stage of cooking begins when food is eaten and the heat of the body assimilates the food into the bloodstream and into the building of tissue. Cooking is thus more integrated into Greek culture, or at least into Hippocratic thought, than into ours. It should be added that divine intervention was a strong element in ancient medicine as far as many patients were concerned. So the cooking of sacrifice also played a part in ancient medicine.

We have many records of sacrifice to the gods of healing. Here is one of about 400 BC from Epidaurus:

> To Asclepius sacrifice a bull, and a bull to the gods who share his temple, and a cow to the goddesses who share his temple. On the altar of Asclepius sacrifice these things and a cock. Let them dedicate to Asclepius as his portion a medimnus of barley, a half medimnus of wheat, one twelfth medimnus of wine. Let them set before the god one leg of the first bull. Let the *hieromnemones* take the other leg. Let them give one leg of the second to members of the choir, and the other to the guards, as well as the entrails. (*Inscriptiones Graecae* IV 2, 1, no 41, trans. Edelstein & Edelstein)

Asclepius, with Apollo the main god of healing, was worshipped like many other gods: the details here resemble those for the Panathenaia quoted in Chapter 3. Asclepius received sacrifices, festivals and even a couch to eat on (in a shrine near Tithorea in Phocis in central Greece, according to Pausanias 10.32.12). The Hippocratic doctors did not deny the influence of the gods in diseases and cures (*Sacred Disease* 1), but they sought to give a scientific account of what they perceived as natural phenomena. Many of the sick went to healing sanctuaries such as the temples of Asclepius at Epidaurus and Athens, as some modern Cretans go to St Antony at Patsos (see Chapter 3). Patients might also be treated by incubation, or sleeping in the god's temple. A comic version of this incubation, which highlights aspects of eating, is discussed in Chapter 9. Aristophanes exaggerates, but eating clearly was part of the ritual because sacrifice was involved and, Pausanias tells us (2.27.1), sacrificial offerings had to be eaten within the boundaries of the shrine (and not taken away).

There are strong links between this chapter and Chapters 7 and 9 on thought and literature, respectively. This will become particularly clear when we look at the wide philosophical interests of Galen at the end of our period and the philosophical underpinning of Hippocratic thought some 600 years earlier. Much of the discussion of medicine implies conceptions of the body which literary authors developed in other ways, in discussions of excess, of an appetite out of control or a body that was too large or too small.

Previous chapters have shown how medical authors imagined civilization to have developed from primitive to cultivated eating (Chapter 1) and how important the apparently modern notions of the raw and the cooked were conceptually for the thought of Hippocratic writers and of Galen. These belong to the progressivist approach to human development. An alternative picture was described by Hesiod and others, who saw a decline from early paradise towards the creation of agriculture, sacrifice and women as a punishment imposed by Zeus. The woman, Pandora, opened her box and out flew, among other things, many harsh diseases. Roy Porter writes in similar vein in his *Blood and Guts* (2002: 1–3): 'Epidemics arose with society, and sickness has been, and will remain, a social product no less than the medicine which opposes it. Civilization brings not just discontents but diseases ... Hunter-gatherers beset by harsh and dangerous environments, our palaeolithic precursors led brief lives.' [The Hippocratic view.] 'Nevertheless, they escaped the plagues that were to besiege later societies ... Infectious diseases (smallpox, measles, flu and the like) must have been virtually unknown, since the micro-organisms responsible for them require high population densities to provide reservoirs of susceptibles. Neither did these isolated hunter-foragers stay put long enough to pollute water sources or deposit the filth which attracts disease-spreading insects. Above all, they lacked the tamed animals which have played so equivocal a role in human history. While domesticated creatures have made civilization possible, they have also proved continual and often devastating sources of sickness.' This latter point is close to the dark Hesiodic vision. Some diseases transmitted by animals are mentioned in Chapter 1; for discussion of the relationship between animals and human beings see Chapter 7.

This chapter is most concerned with ancient theories of nutrition and ideas of what constituted good and bad health. A word is, however, needed at the outset on modern approaches to ancient evidence. The Hippocratic doctors and Galen believed that foods both nourished the body and brought a number of immediate and potential qualities which they called *dunameis* ('powers' or 'properties'). These *dunameis* in particular modified the state of the humours in the body, along with the internal organs and other functions.

Modern approaches to nutrition are also interested in a balanced diet, and emphasize the nourishment needed (hence the cereal base is recognized as the most important nutrient, as is the *sitos* in Hippocrates and Galen). Energy requirements are the first consideration, with a daily average of 2,550 calories needed for men, and some 1,940 for women (Wills 1998). Supplements of fats and proteins are also needed, which may be supplied by animal and plant material (including beans), and then minerals and vitamins. Where a modern nutritionist might say that a particular condition is caused by a zinc or vitamin deficiency, an ancient doctor was likely to attribute the cause to a *dunamis* of the foodstuff. The ancient doctor was more likely to find a cause based on food since a narrower range of causes was known, and there was no viral or microbiological form of explanation.

A second modern approach to ancient nutrition which has produced good results is the analysis of skeletons from ancient cemeteries to establish nutritional evidence from the chemical analysis of bones. This might identify diseases suffered (malnutrition in particular) and also deposits left in bones from the diet experienced. Thus the team in Crete have identified fish, meat and other dietary components in ancient populations (see p. 7), while studies at Pompeii and Herculaneum, for example, have identified certain diseases. Garnsey (1999) summarizes conditions indicative of malnutrition, and draws some striking conclusions on general health and longevity, including some unexpected suggestions on life expectancy between different status groups. Compared with other impacts on life expectancy, in particular childbirth and infancy, dietary constraints were not particularly damaging, though they were chronic. Sallares (1991: 283–6) also discusses malnutrition.

Garnsey's conclusion, it seems to me, is not strikingly different from the impression left on the reader of the first two books of Galen's *On the Powers of Foods*. The third book of the treatise, on meat and fish, is not greatly relevant to a study of malnutrition since much of the population consumed little meat or fish on a regular basis, and as we saw on pp. 54–5, the first step for the peasant in a bad winter was to kill the pig, then eat the meat, followed by the food that was stored for the pig, namely acorns. On many occasions, Galen notes that peasants had to find their food some way down the food chain of normal or desired foodstuffs, because of food shortages, particularly in the spring. Galen addresses the complexity of the issue in 2.39:

Men in my part of the world [Mysia in western Asia Minor], who usually reject the stems and leaves of turnips [*gongylidai*], which they also call *bouniadai*, also eat these when *they lack better foods*; and in this circumstance also eat radishes and what, in our local vernacular, is called *raphys*. One might say that this plant is wild radish. And *under the compulsion of famine*, people often eat pellitory, water-parsnips, alexander and fennel; and wild chervil, pimpernel, gum succory, French carrot, wild carrot, and after boiling them, the tender shoots of most trees and shrubs. But some eat them *even in the absence of famine*, just as some eat the top of the date palm, which some call its brain.

Why must I go on to talk about tender thistles? Because, *famine aside*, these are really a reasonable meal when eaten with vinegar and fish sauce . . .' (trans. Powell)

Galen addresses the issue of food shortage on numerous occasions in his consideration of food plants and cereals. But he also brings out regional variation, and different estimations of certain plants, according to preparation and perhaps time of year. Some of the plants that he considers animal rather than human food – bitter vetch is an example – also appear within the category of a medicine. Thus cattle normally eat bitter vetch; (poor) human beings may do so when compelled by food shortages; and wealthier human beings may do so when ill. There are, as we shall see, many plants and animals which appear both in Galen's book on nutrition, *On the Powers of Foods*, and in his pharmacological work, *On the Powers and Mixtures of Simple Medicines*. Drugs ('simples') are stronger forms of foodstuffs. Galen considers that some items, such as wine, do not strictly qualify as foods, while others, such as onions, are both foods and drugs. The form recommended by the doctor is determined by patient need, whether for the maintenance of good health or for strong intervention.

Ancient medicine offers a fascinating perspective on ancient eating, since medicine was less interventionist than modern clinical medicine and a doctor such as Galen was able to declare that diet was the most useful arm of medical science. Greek medicine developed with the pre-Socratic philosophers in the fifth century BC and continued alongside traditional medicine and religious healing. Food played an important part in Hippocratic medicine; its role was expanded in the fourth century BC by Mnesitheus of Athens and Diocles of Carystus; it was taken further by the Hellenistic doctors such as Diphilus of Siphnos, and was integral to the Hellenistic medical debates over different schools. Of all this, Galen gives a powerful synthesis and critique.

Celsus (*Proemium* 19–22), an encyclopaedic author rather like Pliny, Galen and Athenaeus, gives a useful summary on the different schools. The digestion of food and drink is considered one of the 'natural actions'. Followers of Erasistratus say that food is ground up (*teri*); Plistonicus that it putrifies (*putrescere*); Hippocrates that it is 'cooked thoroughly' (*concoqui*); and followers of Asclepiades (the Methodists) that food is transmitted raw, as swallowed. These views, says Celsus, determine the food prescribed: if the doctor believes in grinding, then he chooses food that grinds easily; if concoction, then food that heats easily; if putrefaction, then again, what is suitable.

We saw in Chapter 1 that the Hippocratic author of *On Ancient Medicine* provided a model of human development in which food played a major role. It is clear, too, in *Airs, Waters, Places*, that environmental factors were seen to play a major role in the formation of the human being and on the state of health to be found in general as it differed from locality to locality, and from season to season. Many other works have comments to make on food and eating, of which *Humours* and *Aphorisms* provide striking examples. Of particular interest for the present enquiry, however, are two bodies of Hippocratic works, the *Epidemics*, and the collection of *Regimens*, four in all, which, with a remarkable intellectual sweep, cover cosmology, foods and bathing, lifestyle (meals, exercise, daily regime) and dreams. Also of interest are the more focused treatises *Regimen in Health* and *Regimen in Acute Diseases*.

Regimen I sets the human organism both in its biological context and also into a much larger cosmic context. Thus in 1.5, the author declares, 'all things, both divine and human, run up and down reciprocally'; in a statement reminiscent of the famous dictum of Heraclitus, 'all is flux'. The author claims that this elemental approach is the only true context for a discussion of regimen (1.1). This is the context too for the growth and nourishment of the human body (1.25), and indeed for the formation of the embryo. Thus if prospective parents want a girl, then they should eat foods that are colder, moister and softer, while for a boy the parental foods should tend to the dry and warm. These bodily elements are affected by season (1.32) and by age, so that warmer foods are needed in the winter, for example, and the old need different food from the young.

Further natural processes, to which the human body is subject, are driven by climate, season and location, according to *Regimen II* (2.37–8): the considerations of *Airs, Waters, Places* are thus relevant to diet in the Hippocratic author's mind, albeit with some variation on the author of the sister treatise.

On food itself, much detail is given (compare pp. 17–20). Foods are listed in the order bread and cereals; beans and pulses; animals, birds and fish; water and wine; vegetables; fruits. I discuss this order below when comparing the Hippocratic text with the updates provided over the next 600 years by Diocles of Carystus, Mnesitheus of Athens, Diphilus of Siphnos and Galen. The Hippocratic author addresses raw foods – wheat and barley, for example – and cooked products such as bread and cakes. He is interested in plants that might be considered bland or pungent, and in the properties of different parts of the plant, such as the leaf or the root. There are raw foods in the sense of wild, uncultivated products such as wild apples, and then of cultivated plants, whose properties might be modified by cooking. Most attention to cooking is given in chapter 56, which considers the various kinds of food preparation undertaken in the kitchen, in the light of the over-arching approach to fire and water:

> the powers of foods severally ought to be diminished or increased in the following way, as it is known that out of fire and water are composed all things, both animal and vegetable, and that through them all things grow and into them they are dissolved. Take away their power from strong foods by boiling and cooling many times; remove moisture from moist things by grilling and roasting them; soak and moisten dry things, soak and boil salt things, bitter and sharp things mix with sweet and astringent things mix with oily . . . Foods grilled or roasted are more binding than raw, because the fire has taken away the moisture, the juice and the fat. So when they fall into the belly, they drag to themselves the moisture from the belly, burning up the mouths of the veins, drying and heating them so as to shut up the passages for liquids. Things coming from waterless, dry and torrid regions are all drier and warmer, and provide the body with more strength, because, bulk for bulk, they are heavier, more compact and more nutritious than those from moist regions that are well watered and cold, the latter foods being moister, lighter and colder. Accordingly, it is necessary to know the property, not only of foods themselves, whether of corn, drink or meat, but also of the country from which they come.

Here the basic procedures of cooking are integrated into the elemental theory of *Regimen I*, the geographical framework of *Airs Waters, Places* and the Hippocratic model of digestion.

Cooking, however, is only part of the Hippocratic dietary regime. The Hippocratic doctor complements advice on food and drink with baths (57), bodily oils, vomiting, sleep, exercise (walking, running, exercise in the dust). These activities produce fatigue, or *kopos*.

Regimen III takes further the lifestyle regimes with different plans for ordinary people and for discerning people of means. It helpfully offers a regime for working people, who are exemplified as people who do not have special foods and drinks; who exercise out of necessity (in the course of their work?); who journey on business and who earn a living at sea. These are not the very poor or the very rich, but 'the many' (3.68) or 'the majority' (3.69). The recommendations highlight seasonal factors (the growth of human beings is compared with tree-growth in 3.68) and include advice on sleep and sexual activity as well as exercise, mealtimes (how many and at what times in the day) and food. Thus barley-cake and vegetables are better than wheat in summer, for example. Rich people's diet, by contrast, has much to say on surfeit (*plesmone*). Problems might be caused (3.75) by coldness in the stomach. Exercises may resolve the problem, as may warm yeasty bread, red wine and pork stock, or fish boiled in sharp brine (compare Archestratus). Neat wine helps, but puppy meat is less good. It is clear from these prescriptions that many items of food in these diets derive from the standard foods of the time. The Hippocratic doctor prescribes fish heads (3.82), or back meat and tail meat (3.79), which also appears in the special recipes of Archestratus for the gourmet seeker of the luxury lifestyle. Other foods, however, are special preparations – if, that is, dogs were eaten rarely, as Galen claims at a later period. Wine was normally diluted, as we discussed above.

The final treatise in the series, *Regimen IV*, discusses dreams. This striking essay ties dreams into disturbances of the soul, which might reveal dreams of natural disorders, the dead, or very positive images of the natural world. The remedy for such disturbance lies in exercises, bathing and modifications to the diet, and in one case, watching comedies. Disturbance can be reduced, for example, by eating less (4.88). If food actually forms part of the dream (4.93), it is likely that the patient lacks food and his soul is expressing a desire for something (the text is disputed).

Much of the material in the *Regimens* concerns the daily diet. Elsewhere, Hippocratic doctors prescribe various foods for specific conditions. So, for example, a number of foods are used for therapeutic purposes in the *Epidemics*. In 7.62, Alcman has a kidney condition. For seven days he took no food, but only a honey and water mixture. Then he could manage progressively lentil water, lentil puree, boiled dog, *maza*, and neck of beef or boiled ham, along with supporting treatments.

Keyser (1997 [Debru vol.] 181–3), with bibliography, points out that since a separate book on Hippocratic pharmacology has not survived, the closest the Hippocratic doctor came to the administration of drugs was to prescribe foods in concentrated form. Galen makes a clear distinction between foods and drugs in his separate treatises *On the Powers of Foodstuffs* and *On the Powers of Simple Medicines*. There is a long history of treatment for the maintenance of good health and the correction of ill health. The distinction is made in the quotation from *On Ancient Medicine* in Chapter 1 and in such Hellenistic treatises as Diphilus' work on *Food for the Sick and for those in Good Health*. Those in ill health (as are the majority of the case studies in *Epidemics*) are in need either of a correction in diet or of a more concentrated form of drug, which would often come from plant or animal sources.

Special diets that survive are to be found in the Hippocratic *Regimen in Acute Diseases*, and in Galen's *On the Thinning Diet*. The latter addresses the problem of humours which have become out of balance, broadly with a predominance of phlegm. The foods recommended in the treatise are almost exactly the same as those in the general list ordered in Galen's *On the Properties of Foods*, but they are ordered very differently. Thus the best foods are the alliums, garlic and onions, since these have a cutting quality that break through thick humours and reduce the danger of conditions associated with thick humours, such as conditions of the liver, kidneys, spleen; problems with the joints; chronic breathing problems (Galen *On the Thinning Diet* 1). Vegetables in this diet are generally better than cereals; meat is worse still, in particular pork, though meat produced from wild animals and mountainous areas is better, as are certain kinds of fish. The worst of all are milk and cheese. The classifying of foods according to this principle of cutting or thinning the humours gives a fascinating contrast with Galen's classification according to nutrition.

It is also notable that even though Galen's humoural system is quite different from the chemical and biological base of modern medicine, modern science identifies among other properties of garlic the ability to prevent blood clotting or thrombosis (Davidson 1999: 331). Similarly, cholesterol which, though vital to life (like phlegm), is dangerous when it builds up to high levels of deposit in the arteries, can be cut back by eating certain vegetables and unsaturated fats derived from plants. Conversely, it is increased by fats derived from animals, most notably those which solidify at room temperature such as cheese and bacon fat. The science is thus different but the dietary correction is not dissimilar.

We saw too, in Chapter 1, that the Hippocratic theory of digestion was based on the idea of cooking. The rawness or otherwise of food was of great importance in this system, as the cooking of food reduced its natural powers, as it were, and pre-cooked it for the digestive system. The Hippocratic author of the *Regimens* has comment to make about this, as indeed about the balance between food intake, exercise and bathing, which form the three pillars of Hippocratic treatment (to which on occasion only were added the risky procedures of surgery and other mechanical intervention).

Galen's treatise entitled *On the Maintenance of Good Health (Hygieina)* offers some striking assumptions about the world in which he exists. The treatise reviews what a good daily regime might be, based on the development of the human body from infancy (books one and two) to old age (book six). It seems to be the male human body which Galen generally has in mind, and the child rather than the nurse or mother even when discussing breast feeding, which is given detailed examination. He also has a Greek body in mind. When considering the ideal body, Galen claims (2.7 = 6.127 K) that a well-ordered body is unachievable in a very hot country or a very cold one since heat produces a skeletal physique, while a cold climate disturbs the mixture of humours and makes the vital organs excessively hot. The standard to follow, declares Galen, is that of the sculptor Polyclitus, like whose images many well-ordered bodies may be seen 'in our country', while among the Celts, Scythians, Egyptians and Arabs, you would not even dream about such bodies. Such cultural specificity is striking, but very much in line with the Hippocratic authors of such treatises as *Airs, Waters, Places*.

It is axiomatic in Galen's discussions of foods that plants and animals differ greatly according to environment, and so, equally, do human beings. Thus wet-nurses who eat wild plants in the hungry period of the Mediterranean spring are liable to develop skin conditions that they pass on to their nurselings (*On the Powers of Foods* 3.14; see p. 59). So too, grey mullet that live in the open sea differ from those living in lakes or polluted rivers (3.24) and wild animals living in the mountains have firmer flesh than a domesticated animal raised on the plains (3.13). Subsequently, when such animals are eaten as food, they modify the humours of the consumer. This is where the properties or 'powers' of food lie, in their potential to trigger a reaction in the bodily mix of a human being. This relationship is a complex one, and is explored in *On the Powers of Foods* and *Mixtures*. Each person has his own bodily characteristics, and each food will have been produced in its own special environment, both of which factors are crucial in pronouncing on what will be the effect on the humours. Galen claims, in this difficult situation, to be pre-eminent in his understanding of general principles and particular circumstances. Others take too much account of fixed rules and ignore the special needs of the patient. What is needed is experience, which Galen claims to have in abundance, but an experience tempered with sound theory (on the concept of 'qualified experience' in Galen see van der Eijk 1997).

It can thus be seen from this evidence and the discussion of Galen at the beginning of Chapter 7 that Galen developed a sophisticated synthesis of natural history and cultural commentary which enabled him to treat the patient within the demands of the natural world and of Greco-Roman culture. For many readers he may be classed as a doctor and technical author. But it is clear that his therapy is rooted in Greek philosophy and the history of his own Greco-Roman culture. As I noted in Chapter 7, he is curing the Greek body in the Greek tradition, and would expect to recommend different remedies for a German or Egyptian patient. Equally characteristic of Greco-Roman culture is the emphasis on exercises and gentle forms of athletics that are described in detail in *On Maintaining Good Health*. Advanced athletics are a different matter, and he draws on the legendary Milo of Croton when discussing that special category of patient. As has frequently been observed in this book, Galen is not oblivious of ordinary working people, any more than the Hippocratic author of *Regimen III*, and lists a considerable number of working activities, which he classifies as 'exercise and work' (2.8). These are: digging, rowing, ploughing, pruning vines, carrying loads, harvesting, horse-riding, fighting in the infantry, walking, hunting with dogs, fishing, and other tasks undertaken by artisans and the unskilled, named as house-builders, bronze smiths, shipbuilders, plough makers, and manufacturers of goods for war and peace. Galen points to the difference between such workers and himself: 'we were once caught in the countryside in winter and were forced to split wood *for exercise*, to throw barley into a mortar to break it and husk it, which country people do *as work* every day.' Galen's prescriptions on diet and lifestyle may thus be read as socially more holistic than most and certainly as holistic from a medical perspective.

The influence of Plato in the history of thought on the subject of food has already been noted on a number of occasions. His concerns in the *Gorgias* about pleasure, and useful doctors and meretricious cooks, for example, have been frequently noted. On diet, Plato notes in the

Republic the figure of Herodicus of Selymbria, who was a citizen and possibly an author who in Plato's view spent too much of his time worrying about food. Here was a rich man who devoted too much of his concern to comparatively trivial matters to do with the body, at the expense of the more important concerns of the soul. Plato did not oppose all pleasure, merely the wrong sort of pleasures, namely those which delight the body at the soul's expense. A number of critics have picked up the comments on Herodicus and linked them with the ancient treatises on diet. The works of the Hippocratic author, of Diocles and Galen, it is suggested, pandered to the hypochondria of the pampered rich who had nothing better to concern themselves with. Edelstein (1967) is a particularly prominent example. No doubt there is some truth in this suggestion. Rich people in many different cultures at many different times were able to buy themselves special cures and attempted to stave off mortality more strongly than their poorer compatriots. Hypochondria is also a widespread phenomenon, not unknown in contemporary societies. Furthermore, there are and were commercial pressures from doctors and allied professions who wish to make money out of people's fears about health, body weight (whether too great or too little) and mortality.

The charge of hypochondria is, however, a second-order issue as far as the Hippocratic *Regimens* and their successors are concerned. As we have just seen, diet was one of the three basic branches of medicine. With its sister art of pharmacology (which generally drew on stronger versions of the same foods, among other things such as metals and rocks), it formed two-thirds of medical intervention. And the third was the dangerously invasive surgery, practised without knowledge of antiseptics and biological infection. Hippocratic thought also built its dietary advice on to a theory of cosmic elements, which placed the human organism within the natural order, alongside stars, other animals and plants. We have seen, too, that the pampered rich man was given much space in *Regimen III*, and was given much more detail, as might happen in a modern practice in Harley Street. But consideration was also given to the majority of people, those who had to work through necessity. We might note that the categories of worker considered were those who travelled, and those who undertook sea voyages. Why these categories, rather than stonemasons or vegetable sellers? The key is probably movement. Workers who travelled were subject to temperature variation ('heated contrary to what is suitable, cooled contrary to what is useful', *Regimen* 3.68), which established a daily regime that was unstable. Diocles also gave advice for travellers (fragment 184 van der Eijk), which focuses on the special demands of walking and the special diet needed, according to season.

Galen provides a different category of patient, the peasants of Asia Minor. His curiosity and range are such that he asks all classes of people what they are eating and why.

He also offers much social commentary in the form of anecdotes, which makes him an engaging writer in the same school as Athenaeus and Suetonius. And in his *Hygieina* or *Maintenance of Health*, Galen sets out his advice for a healthy life, as the Hippocratic author of *Regimen III* had done, and as Diocles of Carystus also did in fragment 182 van der Eijk. The fragment of Diocles concentrates on daily regime, the distribution of meals, sleeping, walking and sexual activity. Galen's long treatise is based on the human life span, starting with the infant and child and finishing with the old man. Galen is interested, for example, in the irresponsible lives of young men: as with cooks, his treatment shares concerns with comedy, and helps us to read those plays in a wider context (see Chapters 7 and 9).

The role of cooks has been discussed elsewhere in this volume. Their very existence is not all that well attested outside comic texts, where they are a stock figure of fun. Plato mentions them, and so do the medical writers. The important point here is whether the doctor follows the Platonic antithesis which contrasts the useful doctor with the cook who aims at providing pleasure to the palate. General aspects of cooking are addressed in *Regimen I*, in which the author supplies a survey of arts, among them (1.18) cooks. These 'mageiroi prepare for people tasty dishes (*opsa*) of things that differ and things that are similar, mixing up all sorts of things, making from things that are the same things that are not the same, as food and drink for a person. If he made everything the same, there would be no delight.' The cook is securely in the doctor's sights in this early fourth-century text, not excluded as Plato might wish, yet in line with his divisions linked with pleasure and delight. There is cooking, by which civilized life is sustained and digestive processes are facilitated; and then there is the fancy cooking of the hired cook, who needs to be kept carefully under control. On the other hand, from the point of view of skills, the cook's activities are not dissimilar to those of the cosmic processes, which cause change by mixing and separation (1.4). [A related idea is also seen in *On Ancient Medicine* (20), where the qualities of cheese are of interest not in absolute terms but in relation to the human body.]

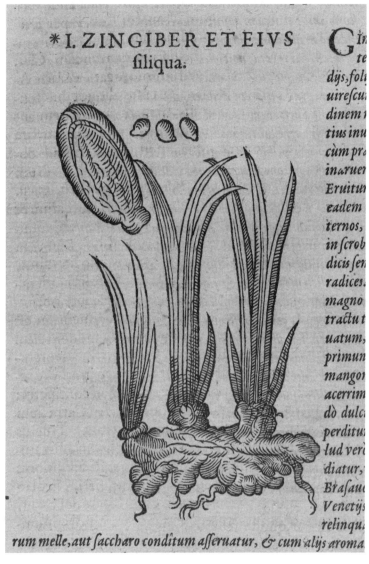

FIGURE 8.1   Ginger was a key import from distant lands. Unlike pepper, which was multi-purpose, the heating qualities of ginger and its potential as an antidote seem to have outweighed its use in cooking: see Miller 1969: 53–7, Dalby 2003: 159. Galen describes a drug made for people who have lost their appetite, from honey, quince juice, pepper, ginger and vinegar. Reproduced by permission of the Dean and Chapter of Exeter Cathedral

Preparations of food are also at the centre of fragment 187 van der Eijk of Diocles of Carystus, who writes:

> Since most foodstuffs require additional preparation of some sort, and some become better if some things are added to them, others when some things are withdrawn from them, and others again when brought into a different state, it is perhaps appropriate to say a little about these. Not least important among such, both for health and for pleasure, is the purging of things that are raw . . . (trans. van der Eijk)

The doctor thus has some ground to concede to the cook, and indeed certain doctors also wrote books on cooking and symposia. Galen was one such, and a number of others are listed by Athenaeus (see p. 207). Doctors would not make many concessions to cooks, however. Galen in his books of *Hygieina* or *Maintenance of Health* identifies the cook as one who provides precisely the wrong kind of food. This might be because the cook aims at pleasure. In 2.11, the cook must be the assistant of the doctor since the cook prepares food without knowing the medical outcome, which is the preserve of the doctor.

The physiology of the human digestive system is complex. This brief summary is based on Pocock and Richards (1999). In broad terms, food and drink are taken into the mouth, ground as necessary by the teeth, lubricated and prepared for digestion by saliva from three glands, and swallowed down the oesophagus to the stomach. There, food is mixed with acids, enzymes and other components of gastric juice and churned, with some absorption of nutrients into the stomach wall. Few compounds are absorbed at this stage, but they include alcohol and aspirin, for example. The stomach temporarily stores food, and passes it, churned and mixed with gastric juice into 'chyme', through the pylorus to the duodenum, or first section of the small intestine. The major absorption of food and nutrients into the body takes place in the small intestine, which receives secretions from the liver and pancreas in addition to its own secretions. The surface area of the small intestine is estimated to be some 200 square metres. Muscular action (or *peristalsis*) transports foods subsequently to the large intestine, and then passes matter unfit or not needed for digestion to the anal canal to be excreted. Pocock and Richards estimate that an adult consumes about one kilogram of food daily and one to two litres of liquid. There is a complex nervous system built into the gut wall, which, together with some twenty peptide hormones, regulate the gut. Connections between

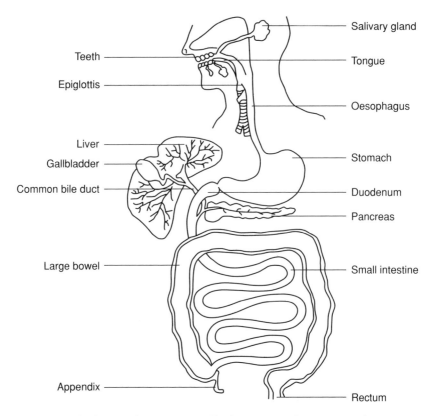

Salivary gland

Teeth

Tongue

Epiglottis

Oesophagus

Liver

Stomach

Gallbladder

Common bile duct

Duodenum

Pancreas

Large bowel

Small intestine

Appendix

Rectum

FIGURE 8.2 The human digestive tract. The human oesophagus, stomach
and digestive tract is a complex and sophisticated series which has a close
relationship with major organs, the liver in particular. In modern thought, the gut
transfers energy, vitamins and minerals to the blood and major organs. Galen's
system is very different, but provides a coherent account of how ingested food is
converted into blood and tissue, and how many processes are in play in addition
to calorific energy

the blood supply and the gut are complex. Seventy per cent of blood
to the liver comes through the portal vein from the stomach, spleen,
pancreas, small intestine and large intestine, and 30 per cent from the
hepatic artery. The portal vein thus delivers nutrition-rich blood to the
liver for distribution and assimilation into the rest of the body. At the
same time, the liver also secretes bile for a number of purposes, among
which is digestion.

Once the chyme is ready for absorption, it is diffused through the cells of the wall of the gut to become capillary blood. Sugars are absorbed in the duodenum and upper jejunum, amino acids and peptides for proteins in the small intestine too, as also fatty acids and vitamins. Fluids are absorbed in both the small and large intestines. Pocock and Richards (1999: 428–9) describe the body's nutritional needs as follows: carbohydrates provide rapidly accessible energy and heat; proteins build enzymes, hormones and also have a structural role; fats support organ tissues, nerve sheaths and cell membranes; vitamins regulate essential bodily functions; and mineral salts are essential for cellular processes.

This rapid review summarizes the modern understanding of digestion, as far at least as conventional medicine is concerned. (I refer to alternative medicine and the Ayurveda below.) The purpose of this summary is to provide a structure for understanding Galen's physiology of the digestive tract and his approach to nutrition.

The broad structure of the gastric tract is described by Galen in *On the Use of Parts* 4.8: the oesophagus (also known as the *stomachos*) is only the pathway for the food; the stomach (*gaster*) is the organ of cooking/heating/digestion; and the intestine is the organ of distribution (*anadosis*). Galen was particularly concerned with the points where the oesophagus joined the stomach and where the stomach joined the duodenum. Cold humours gathered here paralysed the digestive system. Celsus gives a similar summary in *On Medicine* 4.1.6–7. The Hippocratic author of *Fleshes* (13) describes the process of digestion in rather more detail:

> For when food and drink collect in the stomach and intestines, and are heated, the vessels arising there draw off the finest and moistest part, leaving the thickest part behind, which turns to faeces in the lower intestines. As the foods are heated, then, these vessels draw off the finest part from the stomach and the upper intestines – the part above the jejunum (*nestis*) . . . When the nourishment arrives, it gives up the particular quality corresponding to each part, for it is by being watered by this nourishment that every part increases, the hot, the cold, the gluey, the fat, the sweet, the bitter, the bones, and all the other parts that are in a person. (trans. Potter)

The process which Galen calls *anadosis* or distribution seems to correspond to what is now known as absorption and assimilation. Galen explains in *On the Natural Faculties* 1.8–9 that a process of alteration of foods is needed (*alloiosis*) before assimilation or *homoiosis* can take place. Hippocratic doctors and Galen appear to have believed that nutriment passed through the gut walls straight into veins. In *Regimen II* 56, the author comments on acidic foods opening and cleansing the mouths of the veins in the gut, while Galen in *On the Powers of Foods* 1.12 speaks of the mouths of the veins that belong to the stomach and intestines. Galen asked himself, too, how the different organs relate to each other in their acquisition of nourishment (*On the Doctrines of Hippocrates and Plato* 410–1.15–17 de Lacy), and what the purpose for each might be:

> The stomach contracts around the food and draws from it the fluid proper to itself; then when it has had its profit and is completely filled, it pushes all the residue into the jejunum. From there, in turn, the liver draws to itself the fluid that was initially prepared at an earlier time in the stomach, although the stomach certainly does not alter it for the sake of the liver . . . Now just as the residue from the stomach becomes suitable for the liver, in the same way the residue from the liver becomes suitable for all the other parts that follow; the liver too did not alter the nutriment for their sake, but it happens in the way I described, when the nutriment, in being changed and altered by the liver, becomes more suitable for the parts that come after the liver. For as the liver itself drew the nutriment through the veins from the stomach and intestines, so the parts that are placed after it draw the nutriment to themselves through other veins, and then still other parts do so; and this process continues until the nutriment has reached every part of the animal. In every case, each part prepares and predigests the nutriment for the part that comes after it in the continuity of the distribution. (trans. de Lacy)

Galen in this passage is engaged in a complex argument about the relationship of the major organs of the body, the heart and the liver, together with the brain. In book 6 of *On the Opinions of Hippocrates and Plato*, he rejects the Aristotelian theory that the heart is the seat of the mind as well as of the arteries (a cardiocentric view that was developed further by the Stoics), and adopts the Platonic tripartite soul. He quotes from Plato's *Timaeus* but goes further than Plato had done in locating Plato's three aspects of the soul in specific organs. Thus the rational part (*logistike*) of the soul he locates in the brain, the spirited part (*thumoeides*) in the heart and the desiderative part with the appetite in the liver (374–5. 9–19). For our purposes, the liver (the most important organ as far as the absorption of nutriment into the bloodstream is concerned) processes the food for its own purposes before passing it on to the heart, the brain and all the other parts. According to Galen's modified Platonic theory, the liver houses the desiderative part of the soul, but it also has other properties (*dunameis*). He notes (374.14.19) that Aristotle modified the term desire, which Galen attaches to the liver, into such terms as nutritive or vegetative or reproductive (thus locating the aim of the desire). Plato spoke only of desiderative, with reference to the wide range of desires that that part of the soul experienced.

In this philosophical treatise, then, Galen relates Plato's theory of the tripartite soul (as expressed in the *Republic* and *Timaeus*) to his own physiology, locating each part in its own organ, and thereby refuting to his own satisfaction the mistakes of Chrysippus and other Stoics in particular. He links the structure of the body (with its digestive system and dietary needs, that is, with the essential appetite that replaces damaged tissue and makes the young body grow) with the philosophers' interest in desire and morality, as discussed in Chapter 7. As Tieleman (2003) has shown, Galen's system depends on Plato but contains physiological certainties that Plato nowhere affirms. This is partly because, as Galen says, doctors are interested in organs and the philosophers are interested in the activities of the soul. Because of his synthesizing interests and belief that the good doctor is also a good philosopher, Galen comes close to those literary and moralizing texts analysed in Chapter 9 which focus on the power of the tongue and throat in appetite, together with the power of the belly and the liver. All of these body parts, and the liver in particular, drive the body's appetites that are always in need of being brought under control. He thus physiologically, spiritually and ethically locates food and desire in the liver. We might add that the liver was also one of the vital organs or *splankna* that were at the centre of sacrificial ritual and of other religious activities such as divination (see Chapter 3, Vernant 1989 and Durand 1989).

Galen also addresses the difficult question of how blood, once manufactured from food in the liver, can then be turned into other body parts (*On the Natural Faculties* 3.4, trans. Brock): 'How, then, could blood ever turn into bone, without having first become, as far as is possible, thickened and white? And how could bread turn into blood without having gradually parted with its whiteness and gradually acquired redness? Thus it is quite easy for blood to become flesh; for if nature thicken it to such an extent that it acquires a certain consistency and ceases to be fluid, it thus becomes original, newly formed flesh . . .'

In the absence of adequate dissection of the internal organs of the body, many discussions of digestion argue for the effect of an agent on the internal organs of the body by analogy with external properties. In an exception to this line of reasoning, Galen explains the properties of alliums:

> The reason that all these substances [such as mustard, pickles, garlic and onion] which cause injury externally do not do so when taken internally are: that they are changed and transformed by digestion in the stomach and the blood-making process in the veins; that they do not remain in one place, but are divided into small parts which are carried in all different directions; that they are mixed with many humours, as well as with other foods taken at the same time as themselves; that their digestion and excretion are carried out quickly, by which processes that in them which is proper to the nature of the animal is assimilated while the excess sharpness is excreted by stomach, urine and sweat. (*Mixtures* 3.3, trans. Singer)

The division into small parts is a concept Galen uses elsewhere (its pharmacological importance is discussed by Debru (1997). The role of the humours is central to ancient medicine. The humours were to be found in plants, animals and human beings, and for the last might be lodged in various parts of the body, including the digestive tract. Galen shows, in *On the Powers of Foods* (1.1), that the connecting point between oesophagus and stomach might be a location for problems:

> I personally know of someone who complained about the area that is around the mouth of the stomach, and I reckoned from his description that phlegm had collected at this point, and so I advised him to eat his food with mustard, leeks and beets, since phlegm is cut by these foods. He excreted a great deal of phlegm from his stomach and was completely cured of his complaints. But then conversely he suffered from indigestion after eating biting foods and felt biting pains in his stomach. He had eaten mustard with beet, and not only was he taken unawares by the biting, but also was made considerably worse. He was of course amazed that he should be hurt so much by what had before been so beneficial, and he came to me to find out the reason. (trans. Grant)

Phlegm might cause worse problems that that, as Galen explains at the beginning of *The Thinning Diet* 1:

The thinning diet is indicated for the majority of chronic diseases, which can, indeed, frequently be treated by such means alone, without recourse to drugs. It is therefore important to form a clear idea of this diet; for wherever a result can be achieved purely by regimen, it is preferable to refrain from pharmacological prescriptions . . . kidneys and joints, . . . chronic breathing difficulties, . . . enlargement of the spleen and hardening of the liver, . . . epilepsy. (trans. Singer)

This quotation is taken from a treatise on a special diet designed to thin the humours, that is, to reduce the viscosity of certain humours, in particular phlegm. It becomes clear, however, from Galen's later and longer treatise *On the Powers of Foods* that thicker humours were often more problematic than thinner ones even though nourishment most went with thick humour. His comment on beef, the most highly prized protein in many respects, as we have seen, is severe:

Beef furnishes nourishment which is substantial and not easily digested, although it generates thicker blood than is suitable. If anyone more inclined by temperament to melancholy should eat their fill of this food, they will be overtaken by a melancholy disease. These diseases are cancer, elephantiasis, scabies, leprosy, quartan fever and whatever is detailed under the heading of melancholia . . . In the thickness of its substance, beef exceeds pork to the same degree as pork exceeds beef in viscosity. (Galen, *On the Powers of Food* 3.1, trans. Grant)

Galen makes it clear that for him, nutrition comprises the daily diet, which should be adjusted to meet the needs of certain conditions in the body. The body both receives nourishment, *trophe*, and is subject to the qualities or powers (*dunameis*) inherent in the food. The food may be heating or cooling, thickening or thinning, bitter, austere, sweet or sharp. All of these qualities had an effect on the body, in particular on the vital fluids or 'humours' of the body. Good health and many conditions of bad health could be addressed by matching foods to what particular bodies required. The diet was a comparatively mild mechanism for maintaining good health and controlling disease. Stronger remedies were to be found in the pharmacopeia where similar plant and animal materials, but in more concentrated form, were ranked alongside mineral and other supplements.

I will take four examples of foods from Galen's treatise *On the Powers of Foods* to illustrate the versatility of foods as far as the doctor was concerned. Nourishment was one vital consideration, but there were a number of others, as we shall see. The ease with which a food passed through the intestinal tract was important, as was diuretic considerations, and a wide range of attributes of the humours.

Galen describes oats at 1.14:

> This grain occurs in greatest quantity in Asia, especially in the part of Mysia lying beyond Pergamon, where much einkorn and emmer is also produced. It is food for draught animals, not for men, unless perhaps at some time when, being at the extreme of hunger, they are forced to make bread from this grain. Famine aside, when it has been boiled with water it is eaten with sweet wine, boiled must or honeyed wine, the same as einkorn; and it is sufficiently warm, very much like that grain. However, it is not as hard as einkorn. This is why it provides less nutriment for the body, and the bread produced from it is unpleasant in other respects. Not that it checks or stimulates the bowel. Rather, in this respect it is situated at the halfway mark. (trans. Powell)

I comment below on social aspects of this passage. For the moment, I note that Galen addresses raw and processed forms of the oat, that nutritional quality is partly based on the density of the seed; that in terms of humours it is warming, and that in its intestinal passage it neither restricts nor stimulates. Galen's next cereals (1.15) are *kengchros* and *elumos*, broom millet and foxtail millet:

> Sometimes bread is made from these when a lack of the above-mentioned cereal foods supervenes, but it is poorly nourishing and cold, and obviously friable and crumbly, as if containing nothing fatty or glutinous. So, as you might expect, it is drying for a moist stomach. But in the country, after boiling the flour from this grain, they mix in pork fat or olive oil and eat it. Broom millet is superior to foxtail millet in every respect. In fact, it is more pleasant as food, easier to concoct, less constipating and more nourishing. Sometimes country people eat the flour from these grains with milk, after boiling it, as they do with wheaten flour. It is clear that this food is as much superior to the items when they are eaten on their own as milk is superior to the natural qualities of both, in the production of healthy humour and in everything else. By everything else I mean concoction, gastric emptying, distribution (*anadosis*), and sweetness and pleasantness when eaten. For with these grains there is nothing pleasant, particularly with foxtail millet in our part of Asia. In other countries, just as in Italy, it is much better. (trans. Powell)

This passage clearly illustrates the qualities of cereals which are of limited nutritional value. Their coldness is notable; and their friable texture determines their drying powers in the stomach. Their taste is noted, and in this context of foods that are marginal to the human diet, pleasantness of taste is relevant. With it, in this case at least, goes ease of digestion and nourishment. The cereals require combination with milk and can thereby lead to positively healthy humour and to multiple benefits, in digestion, distribution and gastric flow.

The second two foods I have chosen to illustrate Galen's method are juniper and cedar fruits (2.15–16):

> People call the fruit of the juniper 'juniper berry'. It is quite bitter, with little sweetness and still less astringency. It is also rather aromatic. So it is clear that it is also warming because of the pungency (for everything pungent has been shown to be warming), but not least also on account of its smell and taste, which are aromatic; for all aromatics are warm. It also clears out material in the liver and kidneys, and it is plain that it thins thick, viscid humours. This is why it is mixed with drugs that promote health. But it contributes little nutriment to the human body. If one takes a lot of them, they irritate the stomachos and heat the head, and in this connection they sometimes bring about fullness in the head and produce pain there. In the bowel they neither inhibit nor promote excretion. However, they produce urine flow to a moderate extent.
>
> The fruit of the cedar, which they call 'cedar berry', is the same as juniper berries in colour and form – for they are yellowish and round, too – but they differ in terms of pungency. Actually, this fruit runs close to being a drug, since it gives no nutriment to the body unless one has first soaked it in water. For this is a common feature of all pungent foods, that when their pungency has been released they contribute insignificant nutriment to the body. Furthermore, the fruit of cedars is harder and drier than that of junipers, just as it is also without doubt smaller, nor is it to the same extent aromatic. So it is obvious that it is quite irritating to the stomachos and productive of headache, unless one takes it in small amount. (trans. Powell)

These two foods are barely foods at all. As Galen notes, the fruit of the cedar is virtually a drug since it alters the body and provides no nutriment, and the juniper is similar. Interestingly, these two berries are not thereby excluded from this treatise on foods: nutriment is not the only criterion. These foods are on the borderline between foods and drugs, as are, for example, onion and garlic and many aromatics. As we shall see, there is a considerable overlap between the items to be found in this treatise, which are in general sustaining of the body, and those placed in the treatises on drugs, which produce a change in the body. The issue for the present, however, as we saw with the millets above, is that the nutritional value of foods for Galen, as for a modern nutritionist, was not confined to nutriment alone. In addition, he considered *anadosis*, movement through the intestinal tract, and 'powers' or the potential to modify the humours in the body.

Galen deals with drugs in a number of treatises, such as *On the Powers and Mixtures of Simple Drugs [Simples]* and *Complex Drugs according to Place* and *Complex Drugs according to Kind*. Drugs, as I have noted, are often dried or stronger versions of foods which are administered not to nourish or maintain the body but to introduce a change. Much of the scientific methodology of *On the Powers of Foods* is derived from the earlier treatise on *Simples*. Pharmacology was a major stimulus for the medical profession in the Hellenistic period, as a number of the kings who succeeded to the empire of Alexander the Great felt the need to defend themselves from poisoners. Probably the most prominent of these was Mithridates VI of Pontus, but others include Lysimachus and more than one Ptolemy. Antidotes from poison might be gathered from many exotic parts of the expanding Greco-Roman world, and royal patronage provided resources for research work into drugs and nutrition. The fear of assassination is a further aspect of the importance of the court as a centre for developments in foods and drinks, whether for display or curative purposes. The risk of poisoning – and poison is clearly an anti-food which harms rather than nourishes – was ever present, as is illustrated by anecdotes from the Persian court and from the Julio-Claudian dynasty in Rome. Poisons might be administered with food at mealtimes, sometimes in remarkably devious ways which involved the poisoner in eating or drinking a healthy part of the same item which the victim was about to swallow. Galen claims walnuts and rue at the start of the meal counter all poisons.

Ecology

Environment was crucial in Galen's mind. Here is what he says about grey mullet (3.24):

> They are better or worse according to their food. For while some have plenty of weed and valuable roots and so are superior, others eat muddy weed and unwholesome roots. And some of them that dwell in rivers running through a large town, eating human dung and certain other bad foods, are worst of all, as I said. So that even if they remain for a very

short time after death, they straightaway become putrid and smell most unpleasantly. They are all unpleasant to eat and concoct and contain little nutriment but much residue. Accordingly it is not surprising if they produce an accumulation of unhealthy humours in the body of those who eat them on a daily basis. Although these are among the worst, against that is the fact that, as I said, the finest of all grey mullet are the ones in the clearest sea, especially where neither muddy nor smooth beaches surround it, but sandy or rough ones. If the beaches are open to the north wind, so much the better. For while in all animals proper exercises contribute in no small degree to a healthy humoral state, the purity of the wind mingling with the water further augments the excellence of their substance. It is also clear from what has been said that, for this reason too, one sea is better than another so far as it is either completely clear or receives many large rivers like the Pontus. For in such a sea the fish are as superior to those living in pools as they are inferior to those in the open sea. (trans. Powell)

As noted above, the Hippocratic doctor placed his human patient both in the larger natural world of the cosmos and in the natural world of animals and plants. Galen brings out this concept of human life clearly in a number of his works. We saw above that the ideal body was a Greek body and not an Egyptian one that was too hot or a German one that was too cold. In his treatise on foods, the items are clearly placed in environmental and seasonal terms. Plants must be eaten at the right time of year, as must fish and animals. As noted above, a river fish has different qualities from its sea-dwelling relative, and a goat or bird raised in the mountains is quite different from the equivalent raised in the plains. The age of the animal is also relevant, as is the age of the human patient. These points are well illustrated in Galen's companion treatise to *On the Powers of Foods*, namely *On the Maintenance of Good Health* or *Hygieina*. At 5.6, Galen discusses the danger of intestinal blockage in old men:

Now obstructions of wine are moderate, but those from foods which produce thick or viscid juice it is not easy to cure. Wherefore old men must not eat much of starches or cheese or hard-boiled eggs or snails or onions or beans or pig-meat for food, and still more that of snakes or ospreys or all those having hard flesh difficult to digest. On this account, therefore, they should not eat any of the crustacea or mollusca or tunnies or any of the cetacea or the flesh of venison or goats or cattle. These also are not useful for anyone else; but for the young, mutton is not a bad food, but for old men none of these, and still less the flesh of lambs, for this is moist and viscid and glutinous and phlegmatic. But the flesh of fowls is not unsuitable for an old man, and of those birds which do not live in swamps, rivers or pools. And all dried foods are better than fresh.

Galen explains the humoural consequences of location more fully in a passage of *On the Thinning Diet* 8:

> Birds of the marsh meadows, lakes, and plains are wetter and produce more waste. Animals that live in the hills are invariably drier and hotter in mixture, and their flesh is the least sticky or phlegm-producing. In fact, everything that grows in the mountains is far better that what grows on flat land . . . (trans. Singer)

Similar arguments will apply to plants. Galen's interest in the seasonality of plants is mirrored in the botanists. Dioscorides raises the issue in the preface to *Materia medica* (7):

> One should not fail to notice that plants ripen either sooner or later according to the specific character of the country and climate. Some, according to their own particular nature, bear flowers and leaves in the winter, others produce flowers twice a year. Anyone wanting experience in these matters must encounter the plants as shoots, newly emerged from the earth, plants in their prime and plants in decline. (trans. Scarborough & Nutton)

Environmental concerns are prominent in Galen and much other medical writing in the Hippocratic tradition. Alongside these concerns, Galen also provides much geographical comment. He specifies, for example, the emmer wheat of Mysia, the rye of Macedonia, the grapes of Cilicia, the tuna of Sardinia. This locates foods securely in their place. Possible downsides to this might be a loss of universal application: foxtail millet in Asia is not the same as the foxtail millet grown in Italy. But there are enormous rhetorical advantages. Specific examples give confidence, especially if principles are given for wider application. And a system that can take in the vastness of the Roman Empire also gives Galen powerful claims to authority, especially when they are supported both by his personal inspection of a number of plants and by extensive reading of technical authors.

As impressive as Galen's environmental and geographical range in *On the Powers of Foods* is his social commentary. We saw above his comments on the country people of Asia who are forced by hunger to eat oats and millet which are normally considered fit only for animal food. I have commented elsewhere on this in Wilkins (2001, Wilkins in Powell 2003: ix–xxi). Galen was interested in country people because they regularly ate food in their diet which wealthy people only ate if prescribed as a drug. An example of this is bitter vetch (*On the Powers of Foods* 1.29):

> Cattle eat bitter vetch in our area and among many other peoples. It is sweetened in water beforehand. Human beings avoid this seed completely, for it is unpleasant and contains bad juices. However sometimes in a famine, as Hippocrates remarked, they come into their own out of harsh necessity. We ourselves use bitter vetch with honey as a drug for getting rid of thick fluids in the chest and lungs, first preparing it as we do lupins. (trans. Grant 2000 and Powell 2003)

Galen elsewhere is interested in defining the boundaries of the human diet. To the evidence drawn from famished peasants can be added the practices of other peoples. Thus Egyptians who eat wood bugs are not Greek in either their eating or their reading practices (3.2). Galen does not imagine that Egyptians will read his treatise, nor can be visualize Greeks eating insects and snakes as the Egyptians do. And people who eat lions, donkeys and bears are closer in spirit to those animals than a human being should be.

I discussed above Galen's interest in the nutritional requirements of manual workers. The reapers and ditchers at country festivals, he found, had strong enough constitutions to manage the powerful combination of cheese baked with bread, but they died young all the same. Athletes too could eat much more bread and meat than a member of the elite could manage. Soldiers also had special requirements. Galen notes at *On the Powers of Foods* 1.11:

> In some countries they use barley meal for bread-making, as I saw in the countryside in Cyprus, and yet mostly they cultivate wheat. The ancients also used to prepare barley meal for people on military service. But these days the Roman soldiery no longer uses barley meal, having formed a prejudice that it weakened them. For it gives the body a small amount of nutriment, sufficient for the ordinary individual who is not in training. (trans. Powell)

On the Powers of Foods is mainly a treatise aimed at gentle intervention. If stronger medicine is needed, then drugs, or *pharmaka*, were at the doctor's disposal. Galen wrote a number of influential treatises on what he called simple medicines (individual plants, animal products

In lib.Secundùm Dioſcoridis.   323
I. ZEA.   *II. ZEA DICOCCOS.*

diderim, quæ legitimam referat zeam. Verùm enimuero quod zea, Italica ſit Spelta facile ex Dioſcoride coniectari poteſt, quòd ſcripſerit duplicem eſſe zeam, quarum vna ſimplex, altera dicoccos appellatur, eo quòd in geminis putaminibus gra-

FIGURE 8.3   Dioscorides discusses two forms of primitive wheat, perhaps emmer and einkorn. As botanists and doctors tried to list all the plants of the Roman Empire, they found much confusion in the written record, and the use of terms in texts that bore no resemblance to the plants in the field. Dioscorides and Galen put much emphasis on personal inspection of the plants in different seasons and in different locations in order to match the botanical and lexical taxonomy. Reproduced by permission of the Dean and Chapter of Exeter Cathedral

or minerals) and on complex medicines, or mixtures of several ingredients in medical recipes. As we have seen (p. 235), some plants might be classed as both foods and drugs. Juniper is an example (discussed at *Simple Medicines* 6 = 11.836–7 K), as is cedar (*Simple Medicines* 7 = 12.16–17 K).

In writing these treatises, Galen faced a number of organizational problems, in additional to technical consideration. *On Simple Medicines* and *On the Powers of Foods* are catalogues of long lists of items, which Galen has drawn from many years of research and many case studies and experiments. How are they to be ordered coherently? Order is partly determined by readership. A lay audience might benefit from an alphabetical order, which Galen uses for some but not all the books of *On Simple Medicines*. Expert doctors might be happy to work by medical categories. So *On the Powers of Foods* is ordered according to the most common and most efficacious foods (most nourishing first – wheat in book 1 and pork in book 3). Similarly, *On the Thinning Diet* begins with the most efficacious for thinning thick humours, the onion, and concludes with the least, cheese and honey. Galen also writes in a vivid and rhetorical way, with much variation, from bald lists in *Simples*, anecdotes and evidence in *On the Powers of Foods*, vituperative rhetoric in parts of *On Natural Faculties*, and dazzling rhetorical performances in *On Prognosis*.

Galen organized his vast output with considerable care, and discusses the organizing principles and production difficulties of his books in *On My Own Books* and *On the Order of My Own Books*. He has a system of cross-reference between books, and thus in *On the Powers of Foods*, for example, sometimes refers his reader to *On Simple Medicines* – for the discussion of certain properties of the liver, for example. By comparing these two treatises in particular, we can detect further organizing principles at work. Galen puts a large number of cereals and pulses into *On the Powers of Foods*, certainly more than the Hippocratic author mentioned in *Regimen* II. He also mentions more marginal plants. But he does not mention many of the vast number of fish. He is attempting to be comprehensive, not in the sense of mentioning everything possible, but in covering all relevant categories. How does he set about this task? There is an instructive passage at 2.51. Galen here discusses celeries and the related alexanders (*hipposelinoi*), water parsnips (*sia*) and Cretan alexanders (*smyrnia*). His entry covers a range of aspects:

1. Medical properties: these plants are all diuretic, and in women promote menstruation.
2. Terminology: in Rome, *smyrnion* (Cretan alexander) is known as *olisathron*.
3. Classification: these plants are possibly not nutritious foods (*trophai*), for they are all *opsa*, like onions, garlic, leeks, wild leeks and all sharp plants.
4. Usage as food: celeries are most used because they are pleasant and good for the stomach; alexanders and water-parsnips less; much Cretan alexander is sold in Rome.

5. Seasonality: Cretan alexanders are eaten as stalks in spring, as leaf only in winter.
6. Flavour: Cretan alexanders are sharper, more heating and more aromatic than celery.
7. Cooking: Cretan alexander can be eaten raw, or cooked with oil and *garum* or wine and vinegar. Vinegar and *garum* dressing is also possible with optional oil (also for celery). Alexanders and water-parsnips are eaten boiled. Salads may be made up from celery or Cretan alexander in combination with lettuce (a blander plant with cool juice): the combination is tastier and more beneficial. Rocket, leeks or basil can also be added in the same way.

All these categories have been recurring matters of interest in this book: Galen's discussion of flavourings (*opsa*) particularly so. *Opsa*, as we have seen elsewhere, are the tasty supplements to cereals, the tasty plants, fish and meat which in modern terminology provide additional proteins, vitamins and minerals to the cereal base of the diet. What Galen here means by *opsa* is similar: tasty foods which make a smaller calorific contribution to the diet but have more taste and impact. He lists other examples as hyssop, oregano, fennel and coriander. Of these, only fennel gets its own entry in *On the Powers of Foods*. The others are listed in *Simples*, as drugs. In other words, they modify the humoural system; they do not simply sustain and build the body, which foods strictly do. There is not, however, a strict dividing line between foods and drugs since many items, such as onions and garlic, may be classified as both.

Galen is not unaware of conventional definitions of *opsa* as tasty supplements which might have luxurious connotations if overdone. For he goes on to say that cookery books that discuss such flavours as rue, hyssop, oregano, fennel and coriander are of common interest to cooks and doctors, but these two groups have different goals and aims. 'We doctors aim at utility, not pleasure.' Galen returns us squarely to Plato's prescription in *Gorgias*. A concession is, however, made. Unpleasantness (*aedia*) in food can often bring about a failure to digest properly, so it is better for food to be moderately pleasant. This concession made, he goes on to say that cooks use bad flavourings to produce pleasurable tastes and so bad digestion ensues.

In this instructive chapter, Galen practically gives us recipes for salads and cooked dishes based on celery and similar plants. The distinctions he makes also play out more widely in the treatise. One of the most favoured flavourings of the Greco-Roman palate, silphium, is not included in its own right in *On the Powers of Foods*. Nor is pepper, cumin or coriander. These are all listed in *Simples* as drugs, or modifiers which change the body. Basil and fennel do squeeze into the food treatise, but only just. Basil is an *opson* which is falsely said to generate scorpions, but otherwise produces bad juice, is bad for the stomach and is indigestible. Fennel is described entirely in social terms, with no medical comment: 'Sometimes it grows of its own accord like dill, but they also sow it in gardens and use it very often for flavouring like dill. They also use fennel as an *opson* (a tasty dish). People near us [in Asia Minor] store it rather like pyrethrum and terebinth, so that it is useful the whole year round, like onions and turnips and such things. They serve some with vinegar alone, some with vinegar and brine.' (1.56)

This social element, which takes in where foods are bought and sold, what class of people eats them and what the local terms for the item might be are strong features of Galen's treatments of foods. His social range is much wider than that shown by Athenaeus and other 'literary' and less technical authors, as we shall see in the next chapter. He mentions the poor cereals and beans that peasants eat because these help to define the boundaries of the human diet. At the other end of the social spectrum, he is wary of the rich foods prepared by cooks for the elites of Rome and other cities. But he admits some shared interest between doctors and cooks. This wariness probably accounts for the small number of fish that he lists in book three of *On the Powers of Foods*. If he were providing a fully comprehensive nutritional encyclopaedia, he could have included hundreds of fish names. Instead, he mentions fewer than other authors. It is hard not to think that this is explained by the association of fish with the rich man's table, subject matter more suitable for the cookery book than the medical treatise. Fish after all did not lack medical properties, as many other authors pointed out. The suspicion is strengthened by Galen's mention of river pollution linked with cook shops among other urban industries and by a professed inability to understand why the liver of a red mullet might be prized by Roman gourmets. And also by the lack of interest in small fish that were available to all at very low cost. For all his technical abilities, Galen has fallen prey to the cultural assumptions of his times about cooks, fish and luxury. But this is not a criticism. Of course his intellectual world is shaped by the cultural forces of the Roman Empire and the social and cultural beliefs it shared widely. It is part of his greatness that he held Plato in as much regard as Hippocrates and saw technical prowess as part of a philosophical enterprise.

The intellectual range of Galen is astonishing. He addresses medical, botanical, environmental and social considerations, as we have seen. But he went on, too, to interest himself in philosophy, commentaries, literary texts and the history of libraries. He provided lists of his own books and how to order them, and comments on contemporary life, many of them in anecdotal form, that bring much richness to the contemporary scene. He also resembles his near-contemporary Athenaeus in offering a review of a millennium of Greek culture, as expressed in both technical and literary texts. For this reason he offers the perfect introduction to our final, literary chapter. He also proves what the Hippocratic writers demonstrated at the beginning of this chapter, that medical writers were at the heart of ancient thinking about food and not set apart in a technical enclave.

9
Introduction

Food in literature is generally a device to throw light on a character or situation rather than an indicator of eating trends. There are still points to be gathered, though, provided the filter of the author's personal view is taken into consideration. Our entire knowledge of the gastronome Archestratus, for instance, is gathered from disparaging allusions to his work in the post-prandial ramblings of Athenaeus.

In Victorian times Charles Dickens would use mealtimes to display the gusto or diffidence of those dining as indicators of personality and perhaps social station. He radiates a generally benevolent outlook on eating that sees the genial and well-intentioned Mr Pickwick tucking in fairly regularly to tables laden with good things, in contrast to the unused and uneaten wedding banquet of the jilted Miss Haversham in *Great Expectations*. Most famously, Ebeneezer Scrooge's conversion from miser to philanthropist is signalled by his sending out for a large turkey to celebrate Christmas dinner with the Cratchit family.

This may well indicate that Charles Dickens was a man who enjoyed his food as much as it indicates anything about the food and availabilities of the time. The images conjured up, however, of hearty and generous portions and a good time being had by all remain emblematic of what British people think of as good in food and dining.

Cookery books are another matter. It is deeply unlikely until recently that the cook could read and still less likely that he could have afforded to buy a book. The books on food and cookery that have survived from the period – most would have been lost in the fire at the library in Alexandria – are aimed at those at the eating end of the proceedings rather than those at the cooking end. Cooking is a manual skill passed on either from mother to daughter in the home or from master to apprentice in the workplace. Until recent times, those cooking grand meals, either for wealthy or noble families or from last century in hotels and restaurants, would have been unlikely ever to eat the meals they cooked. They were working class servants preparing meals for wealthy families. Early cookery books such as La Varenne's *Le Cuisinier françois* in 1651 were aimed at those directing the cooks and had minimal explanations of the ingredients, no cooking methods and rarely even any information as to the proportions in which the ingredients were to be used.

That cookery books should be aimed at those dining is neither a new concept nor an old one. If Archestratus' work was written to be read aloud to those dining then it was not significantly different in spirit to many – perhaps even most – cookery books published today.

A cookery book comes in one of two styles. It may be a manual to be used in a kitchen with careful instructions on the preparation and ratios of each ingredient. This sort of book will have diagrams or step-by-step preparation photographs and be kept in or near the kitchen. Alternatively, it will be what is known as aspirational and be designed for reading, its purpose to conjure up the smells and setting of dishes. These books will have photographs of gnarled country folk picking vegetables against a backdrop of the sun setting over Tuscan hillsides. The recipes may or may not work and in any case may be dependent on ingredients unobtainable out of the area. Restaurant chefs' cookery books work on a similar basis, with the book and its pictures acting as souvenir of a great meal but with recipes that may well call for a brigade of cooks working in concert or advanced craft skills that cannot reasonably be expected from the keen amateur.

There is nothing superior with either type of book. The manual is the more recent, though, taking over from the oral and practical cooking traditions. The aspirational book, however, has plenty in common with food writing throughout the centuries and aims to inspire and amuse the diner rather than the cook.

Food in Literature

> Many such persons, Athenaeus says, attended the dinner given by Larensis, bringing, like contributions to a picnic, their literary works rolled up like covers for the couches. (Epitome of Athenaeus *Deipnosophistae* 1.4b)

Many literary passages have been quoted throughout this book. Indeed, links have often been made between texts that might be described as 'literary' and those that are 'technical' or 'philosophical/scientific'. In many ways these are misleading categories, for the poems of Homer, Greece's earliest and pre-literary epics, were used in later centuries not just as repositories of literary truth but also as a foundation for the educational order, including scientific and technical advice. We shall see later, for example, how Athenaeus of Naucratis showed in the third century AD that Homer offered the best model for sympotic conduct. Conversely, we saw in the last chapter that Galen, who might at first sight appear to be only a technical author of medical texts, in fact considered himself an all-round philosopher who could instruct also in all aspects of thought, language and culture.

The aim of this chapter, therefore, is fourfold. First, briefly, to highlight certain features of literary texts that link closely with the social, religious and scientific features identified in earlier chapters. Second, to identify the main aspects of literature's engagement with food and eating. Third, to show the engagement with food of certain literary genres, such as epic, satire and tragedy. Finally, this chapter will draw the themes of the book together with a review of our much-discussed authors from

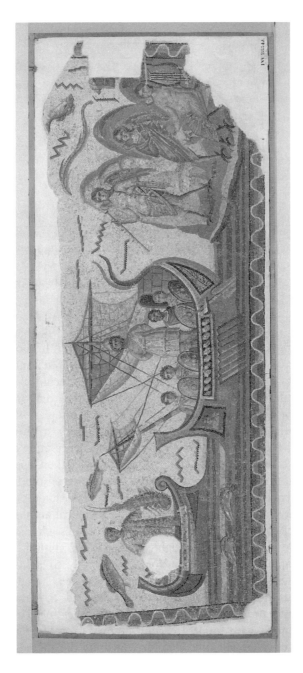

FIGURE 9.1   Ulysses and the Sirens, from *The Odyssey* by Homer (mosaic), (3rd century AD) Musee du Bardo, Tunis, Tunisia. This mosaic from Dougga in Tunisia reflects the wealth of provincial life for some in North Africa. The image was placed at a well, hence the suitability of the marine subject. The scene represents Odysseus tied to the mast to resist the alluring song of the Sirens, who are represented as young women. The subject reflects the enduring importance of Homer in the literature and art of the later Roman Empire. In this version, Odysseus is tempted not only by the Sirens, but also by a giant lobster that a fisherman holds aloft in his boat. Photo: www.bridgeman.co.uk

the Greco-Roman period, Athenaeus and Galen, who will help to achieve a synthesis between 'literary', 'scientific' and cultural traditions.

Three examples will illustrate the serious engagement of literature with earlier subjects of this book. In book 17 of the *Odyssey*, Telemachus continues to be troubled by the suitors of his mother Penelope. One of the most outspoken of them, Antinous, attacks Eumaeus the swineherd for bringing another beggar (in fact, Odysseus in disguise) to the table (375–9, trans. Shewring):

> Infamous swineherd, why have you brought this man to town? Have we not vagrants enough besides, loathsome beggars, scavengers of our banquets? Are you not content to have men gathering here already to devour your master's sustenance (*bioton*)? Must you invite this fellow too?

There are various ethical complexities in the hypocritical speech of Antinous, not least his own gluttony and lack of reciprocity, which Telemachus points out in line 404. For the moment I underline the economic and religious element: Eumaeus the swineherd raises pigs in the countryside for his master's table in town. He runs the rural unit of production for the point of consumption in the palace. Furthermore, in this economy, the wealth of Odysseus is measured to a significant extent in animals owned. As regards the feeding of beggars, there is a religious injunction from Zeus to reinforce social practice.

The catalogue of wrongs in Juvenal's Rome includes the consumption of imported fish (*Satire* 5):

> my lord will have his mullet, imported from Corsica or from the rocks below Taormina: home waters have been fished out to fill such ravening maws . . .

Juvenal slots this example into a complex ethical agenda which is explored below. But his example also reflects Rome as the central point of exchange in a large empire, where goods from throughout the known world are made available.

The third example comes from the *Life of Luxury* of Archestratus of Gela. The author of this poem from the fourth century BC focuses much attention on parody, the ethics of eating fish and other 'literary' matters. But there is also an interest in terminology. In fragment 13 Olson & Sens, the reader is advised,

> don't leave aside the fat gilt-head from Ephesus, which local people call '*ioniscus*'.

The interest in local variants in terminology in order to identify fish and other taxonomically challenging species is characteristic of 'scientific' authors such as Aristotle and Galen, but it is also found in 'literary' authors of hexameters such as Archestratus.

The Major Literary Themes on Eating and Drinking

Many relevant themes are well-known literary features. I begin with urban corruption and rural simplicity. Aristophanes' comic hero in *Acharnians*, Dicaeopolis, longs for his home village where people barter for food and fuel, in contrast with the portrait of Athens in other plays, where the market traders cheat the buyers of fish and other foods. Five hundred years later, Juvenal's urban dweller is the victim of fraud and deception, while on Juvenal's rural farm chaste servants serve simple food. This literary topos cuts across the advantages that a city might bring. We shall see examples of inconsistency between the topos and the impact of foods imported from abroad – into urban markets predominately. For with rustic simplicity lines up also nostalgia for purer times in the past and dislike for trade. Trade, a feature of the movement of foods that was discussed above, is more ambivalently treated in literature than its importance would appear to warrant. There is a tension between local production and imported goods, which is economically complicated, but in literature often more clearly resolved in favour of local agriculture. The fourth theme is the exploitation of feasting and communal eating to bring a satisfactory conclusion. This is most strikingly seen in comedy. The next theme is the impulse of pleasure and desire, which might lead to that fatal lack of control that was explored in Chapter 7. A further theme already mentioned in Chapter 1 follows a developmental model from primitive beginnings to present sophistication/excess. An alternative model is the decline from a golden age to 'now'. (Compare Pliny on gardens and vegetables in Chapter 4.) By this route the Roman Empire might be portrayed either as the most advanced or the most corrupt of human societies.

Food and Genre

Certain literary genres particularly focused on food. Gowers (1993) is an influential study of food in the lesser genres in Latin literature, in particular of satire, comedy and epigram. Here food contributes to a world that self-consciously lacks the grand themes of the tragic or epic worlds. That is not to deny, however, that in Homeric and other epics, food is central to exchanges both between mortals and between mortals and gods. I discuss both Homer and tragedy below. But it is to say that while subjects relating to food (trade and agriculture, social gatherings, festivals and sacrifice) might be found in many genres of literature from history to love poetry, a high food content is likely in those self-consciously low genres discussed by Gowers (1993). Thus Archestratus describes fish and cooking in a parody of epic verse; pseudo-Hesiod parodies the austere archaic poetry of Hesiod to describe fish (a portion is quoted at the beginning of Chapter 5); and scurrilous Hellenistic stories of courtesans by the poet Machon have a high food content.

I noted in a previous chapter, on Hippolochus' description of the wedding meal of Caranus (Chapter 2, p. 50), that literary narrators often adopt an ironic tone, in order to cut through the excessive richness of endless words on the courses of a banquet. This feature is evident, for example, in Archestratus, in Petronius, and in Athenaeus.

Many of the food-rich genres are 'low'. Some are what Mikhail Bakhtin (1968) has characterized as 'popular-festive'. Greek and Roman comedy is a particularly good example, which uses the language of the street and of the body to assault the social pretentions of the rich and powerful (see Gowers 1993, Wilkins 2000, ch. 1). There is a stress on body size, appetite, on the throat and the belly, the digestive organs, farting and excretion. Gluttons demand the sensation of hot food passing down the throat, to be consumed as quickly as possible.

Galen can help us to see why many moralizing texts, including the literary ones here and philosophical ones in Chapter 7, were concerned about the dangers of desire and appetite. The liver, as we saw in the review of Galen's physiology in Chapter 8, located both bodily and spiritual desire in the same place. This was a powerful combination that needed always to be kept under control, particularly when linked to social aspects of desire. There was the wish to compete with other members of the elite, or with other courts. There were the temptations of luxurious foreign ways, in Persia or Greece or Macedonia, according to period. There were the temptations of empire, which brought all the goods of the whole known world to the markets of Athens, and on a much larger scale to Rome. Because these commercial inducements to desire were so strong, moralizing texts came to value the simplicity of country ways, of the past and of ritual ways, whether religious or ancestral (not selling the ancestral home for parties and ephemeral foods and wines). This book has tried to identify other important aspects of food; but in this chapter I will shortly explore those literary texts that focus on food and excess.

The major genres of sympotic poetry and the prose *Symposium* were addressed in Chapter 6. There are many descriptions of banquets in ancient texts, but it is the symposium – the later part of the meal – that is particularly linked with other cultural activities such as poetry, games of various kinds, philosophy, comedy and intellectual pursuits.

Much poetry from the archaic period onwards was written for sympotic performance and on sympotic themes. Elegy is probably the most important, and the major poems of Theognis and Xenophanes were discussed above. They set out the function of food, drink and myth within an ethical framework, which lies behind much sympotic poetry of this period. I have argued in Wilkins (2000) that the dramatic genre of comedy is a form of sympotic poetry. I discuss comedy below, since its use of a popular performance space renders its social and political role somewhat (but not totally) different from poetry composed for private occasions.

In prose, Plato's *Symposium* was extremely influential in form over many centuries. Its philosophical importance apart, this work reflects on a group of friends gathered together and what they should agree to do on this occasion, which combines a meal followed by a drinking session. The food is usually less important (except in Lucian and Athenaeus), and if the main aims are philosophical, as is usually the case, drinking is kept at a low level also. I have noted above some of the occasions on which Plutarch sets sympotic debates in his *Sympotica (Table-Talk)*. Plato sets a wonderful model for the genre, however, in maintaining the balance between discussion of aesthetics and ontology, and drinking activity. Most of the symposiasts had drunk too much the previous night, as they had been celebrating a victory of the tragic poet Agathon, but Alcibiades enters late and drunk and injects a strong Dionysiac spirit into the evening. At the end, Socrates triumphs in all activities, having pronounced the most advanced philosophy (a version of Plato's Theory of Forms), having been compared with a Silenus, or acolyte of Dionysus, and having also drunk everyone else under the table and walked home in the early morning.

While some themes remain constant from 'Classical Greece' to the Roman imperial period, others also develop and become more prominent. This is particularly true of books which give a wide cultural survey of aspects of food and dining, with an encyclopaedic range. These include certain books of Pliny's *Natural History*, Plutarch's *Table-Talk*, and the *Deipnosophistae* of Athenaeus. These books can draw on literary predecessors, technical works from the botanists, doctors and agricultural authors, and also collections of linguistic and literary types. Food had been an appropriate criterion for literary criticism from an early period. So Aristophanes has his lead character in *Frogs*, Dionysus, criticize the plays of Euripides for their domestic flavour (how to organize the shopping and the kitchen and good health), and Plato's Socrates notes the absence of fish in the verses of Homer.

It is worth remembering also that technical literature was 'factual' in a sense, but was also subject to strong cultural determinants, as we have seen frequently in Cato and Pliny. Pro-Roman sentiment is usually tempered by liberal reading of Greek authors, as Columella notes. He aims to 'endow Agriculture at last with Roman citizenship (for it has belonged thus far to writers of the Greek race)' (*On Agriculture* 1.1.12–13).

Food in Homer I

Our enquiry into food in literature must start with that best of travel poetry, Homer's *Odyssey*. Odysseus and his comrades are blown off course and the journey takes years. They meet strange people, and part of their strangeness is to be found in their eating habits. First they go to Ismarus, the city of the Cicones in Thrace, and sack it. The Cicones eat standard Greek food, but a priest of Apollo has an especially strong wine which is twenty times the strength of ordinary wine. Then they sail to North Africa and meet the lotus-eaters, who give them the honey-sweet lotus fruit to eat. It is a wonderful food, but it makes the eater lose his identity and his desire to go home. The companions of Odysseus have to be forced to leave this paradise after eating this fruit.

Then they come to the island of the giant Cyclopes, a different sort of paradise, where there are 'soft moist meadows where vines might flourish and never cease. Its soil would make for easy ploughing; they might reap tall harvests there in season, for beneath the surface the loam is rich. Moreover there is a good harbour there.' All the features a Greek would like about the place – good agriculture, good port facilities – the Cyclopes have no interest in. Rather, they are cannibalistic shepherds who eat the companions of Odysseus raw for supper after bashing their heads on the floor and tearing them limb from limb. The next place they sail to is the island of King Aeolus whose six daughters are married to his six sons. They spend all their days feasting: 'through the daytime the hall is rich with savoury smells and murmurous with the sound of music', says Homer. Another sort of paradise – especially after the hellish Cyclops – but with irregular marriage arrangements and levels of feasting impossible to achieve in a rocky, mountainous country like Greece. Then they come to Telepylus, the lofty town of the Laestrygonians. These are more man-eating giants who spear men like fish. Then they come to the island of Aeaea, where Circe lives. She is a 'goddess with braided hair, with human speech and with strange powers'. The most notable power for our purposes is the ability to turn men into pigs. This is a confusion of categories. Human beings normally sacrifice pigs and eat them. Odysseus then goes down to the Underworld. The dead need special food – blood – because they have lost their human strength. Then they meet the Sirens, who, like the lotus-eaters, stop a man getting home. 'They sit in a meadow; men's corpses lie heaped up all around them, mouldering upon the bones as the skin decays.' Then comes Scylla, who sits on a cliff yelping horribly. She grabs and devours six of Odysseus' companions 'who shrieked and held out their hands to me in their extreme of agony'. Then Odysseus gets to the island of Ogygia where Calypso lives, another 'goddess of braided hair and of strange powers and of human speech'. She offers to make Odysseus immortal so that they can eat the same food, ambrosia, and she won't have to prepare different meals for them both, mortal food for him, ambrosia for her.

Odysseus eventually forces himself to leave this wonderful partner, turning down her offer of ambrosia and immortality, and sails on to the Phaeacians. They are rather like Aeolus. They live close to the gods and have limitless agricultural supplies, in a slightly different kind of paradise. It is the Phaeacians who ship Odysseus back to his home in Ithaca and to his mortal wife, Penelope, to whom he is delighted to return after his various divine girlfriends. He returns to his own culture, where people eat grain, drink wine mixed with water, use the oil of the olive tree and sacrifice agricultural animals in the approved Greek model.

There are various indicators that distinguish one culture from another. One is agricultural products and how they are processed and eaten. Another is the relationship that is established between the human and the animal world. We return to an incident in Odyssey book 12 that I omitted just now. Odysseus and his companions, after for the most part escaping from the man-eating Scylla, arrive at the 'lovely island of the sun-god'. Although warned by Circe not to eat the cattle of the sun god, the companions of Odysseus try to sacrifice them while he is asleep. They are not able to sacrifice in the normal way (the Promethean way set out in Chapter 1) because, says Homer, they have no barley grains to sprinkle on the animals' heads, no wine to pour a libation to the god. They had somehow joined the Cyclops, the Laestrygonian giants and Circe in mixing up the relationship between human beings, the masters of sacrifice, and agricultural animals, the creatures which are sacrificed. (See further p. 32 and Vidal-Naquet 1981.)

Food in Homer II

The archaic Greeks sought to come to terms with the Minoan and Mycenaean periods in the earliest literature that has survived from antiquity, the *Iliad* and *Odyssey*. Food plays a prominent role in both. These epic poems present a complex mixture of Mycenaean and later elements, since they were composed in a long and evolving oral tradition. There are numerous important features for the history of food in the Homeric poems, in addition to the travels of Odysseus.

Reciprocity: gods and humans

In the *Iliad*, nearly all exchanges at the human level and between heroes and gods are marked by the slaughter and consumption of cattle. Meals are described only briefly, but the preparation of the animal and other ritual activity are described in considerable detail. The acceptance of food or sacrifice by a human or god marks an exchange that is working; the refusal to share a table or accept a sacrifice marks an (often disastrous) rupture in relations. The consumption of food in the *Odyssey*, too, is built on this reciprocal pattern at the human level and in dealings between humans and gods. The suitors of Penelope in particular fail to reciprocate meals. In addition to other defects, they do wrong by eating the wealth of Odysseus, expressed in terms of cattle and pigs, without a reciprocal exchange of wealth by offering hospitality to Telemachus and the household of Odysseus.

The human and the natural world

In one notable passage in *The Odyssey*, the role of the king is defined in relation to the production of food: 'a virtuous king fears the gods and rules a strong well-peopled kingdom. He upholds justice, and under him the dark soil yields wheat and barley; trees are weighed down with fruit, sheep never fail to bear young and the sea abounds in fish – all this because of his righteous rule, so that thanks to him his people prosper' (19.109–114, trans. Shewring). The disguised Odysseus is here comparing the reputation of such a king with that of Penelope. The king is seen to uphold not just the agricultural but also the wider natural order, with plants, animals and fish flourishing within a kingdom that in addition honours the gods and has a flourishing and resilient population.

Human need

This large context into which food is placed is found too in the remark of Odysseus to Eumaeus (17.286–9). 'A man cannot put away the cravings of the accursed belly, which brings so much trouble into life and makes us rig ships to cross the seas and harry our enemies' (trans. Shewring). Human beings are not god-like creatures. They are always in need of sustenance and in that sense are governed by their stomachs (a theme that is taken up in Vernant's discussion of the myth of Prometheus which I reviewed in Chapter 1). That need cannot always be met (there were endemic food shortages in the ancient world), and, as Odysseus expresses it, and as Plato later expresses it (see Chapter 7), failure in the supply of food leads to warlike expeditions in ships. According to some accounts, failures in supplies of food prompted some ancient communities to establish colonies overseas. Food shortages in ancient cities were frequently a source of instability.

Food shortages in Homer are experienced by Odysseus and his crew on their voyage and also by the beggars at the palaces of the rich. In Ithaca, the suitors of Penelope show no more respect to beggars – in particular to Odysseus disguised as a beggar – than they do to the estate of Odysseus. Beggars are allowed to solicit food, and act under the protection of Zeus, but some suitors show no respect and hypocritically object to the giving away of food to a beggar even though they contribute nothing themselves. All conditions of men, women and gods are thus considered in the *Odyssey*. More so than the *Iliad*, this poem considers the swineherd and the production of animals, the beggar and those of no account at the feast and the battle for food between what some Britons term the deserving and the undeserving poor. Homer sets out this battle in the words exchanged between the disguised Odysseus and the beggar Irus. These food producers and people who have no automatic right to an equal share of the feast figure strikingly in the *Odyssey*. They have appeared frequently in this book, first of all as part of 'those who do not belong to the elite' – that is, some 90–95 per cent of the population. They have appeared too as that part of the population so beloved of literature, the parasite of the Greek banquet and the client of the Roman banquet, which I considered in Chapter 2 (pp. 73–4).

Medicine and special foods

In the *Iliad*, Book 11, wounded and weary warriors are given a fortifying potion, or *kykeon*, of wine, cheese and barley meal, with honey and an onion. Concern is also expressed in the later books of the *Iliad*, that Achilles, mad for revenge for the death of Patroclus, will not consider the needs of the soldiers for sustenance before a day's fighting. Achilles' own refusal to eat reflects his deranged mental state. Drugs too are mentioned in Helen's soothing drug that is added to wine, and in the special root of *moly*, which Odysseus is given to counter the magic of Circe.

Greek and non-Greek

I reviewed above the strange foods that Odysseus and his comrades encounter during their wanderings over the ocean: almost none match their own staples of cereal, wine, olive oil, and their own distinctive form of animal sacrifice. This alimentary career marks a path veering this way and that between divine and bestial food, as we shall see.

Detailed descriptions

Certain operations are described in detail many times in Homer. This is true, in particular, of the slaughter of animals and the preparation of meat for consumption. All that is on offer at mealtimes is often summarized as 'foods of all kinds' (which does not suggest the limited diet interpreted by some later sources) and description often extends to items of furniture and tableware, in particular to drinking cups.

Meals

The *Iliad* and *Odyssey* provide models of commensality which both reflect early Greek society and influenced later thought. We shall see below the critique and application of Homeric models in later periods. The Homeric poems use mealtimes as the focus for exchange at both the human and divine levels. Mealtimes take place on daily and special occasions in the *Odyssey* (a wedding in book four; the daily meals of the suitors in later books) and in the *Iliad* they intersperse the scenes of battle. Meals generally follow a description of sacrifice, and are often followed by a session of drink and music in which wine mixed with water is enjoyed. This is an early version of the symposium, in which garlands, the mixing of wine with water and the singing of songs and poetry take place, but the participants sit and do not recline.

The refusal of the gods to accept a sacrifice, or of a human being to participate in a meal, marks a major breach in the social and religious order. *Iliad*, books 9 and 24, illustrate meals working well at difficult moments. Eating takes place within the aristocratic networking system known as *xenia*, within which strangers are welcomed with a bath and food before they are asked to identify themselves. If they are known to their hosts, then food is offered reciprocally for earlier meals or anticipated meetings in the future.

The poet is interested in describing the details of sacrifice and cooking. Less space is given to the eating of food and the description of the meal. The foods most commonly found are beef and bread, but 'all kinds of food' are often served. We shall see much interest in later centuries in what the diners were served.

We might say in summary that the earliest literature of Greece used foods and codes of eating to express identity; to reveal correct and incorrect conduct and success or otherwise in exchanges between gods and mortals and among mortals themselves; and to establish social hierarchy.

The Reception of Food in Homer

The Homeric epics cast a long shadow over later literature. Athenaeus provides a particularly striking example. He picks up the comments on the absence of fish in Homer made by Plato and some fourth-century comic poets. His diners discuss Homeric practice at some length, initially in Book One of the *Deipnosophistae*, which unfortunately survives only in a summarized form, known as the Epitome. There appears to have been a scholarly debate over the degree of luxury that was allowed into epic by Homer, whose main aim is said to have been to promote a life of simple eating and ethical probity. Extraordinary claims are made on the significance of fish and vegetables. At 1.24e–f a diner says,

> The heroes had vegetables [*lachana*] also served to them at meals. That they are acquainted with the growing of vegetables is clear from the words, 'beside the farthest line of trimly planted garden beds.' Moreover they ate onions too, though they are full of unhealthy juices.

Because this is the summarized part of Athenaeus, we do not know the identity of this diner-speaker, or if it is the same person who says shortly afterwards (1.25d),

> But the poet is silent about the eating of vegetables, fish, and birds because that is a mark of greed, and also because it would be unseemly for the heroes to spend time in preparing them for the table.

It is likely, however, that these words are a short version of a debate over the role of food in Homer which the speakers derived from scholarly sources perhaps dating back to the fourth century BC. They reflected also the preoccupations of their own time in the second century AD. Now, Homer was the touchstone for literary, ethical and technical issues. Even vegetables could be referred to in the hallowed text: are they ruled to be *opsa* (and not *sitos*); or are they of too low a status to be considered? Do vegetable plants count, or only vegetables prepared for the table?

Similarly, later, in Book Five, Homer is taken as the approved model for the symposium, against the models of the philosophers Plato and Epicurus, even though reclining at table had not yet been introduced. Again, the suppression of excess is taken to be Homer's chief aim. In these passages Athenaeus both preserves some of the ancient debate on Homer in the Hellenistic libraries, and also takes the poems as a model for his own times. The Deipnosophistae are dining at the home of the apparently wealthy Roman magistrate Larensis, and are reflecting on correct procedures, and levels of magnificence that are allowed. They are clearly not following the prescription for simplicity that they claim Homer was following. The comments on the symposium in Book

Five also precede the elaborate descriptions of public feasting by the Hellenistic kings. The Homeric readings could then be taken as an ironic comment on later dining, and on the Deipnosophistae themselves, because of the great extravagance their own food declares (especially the fish in Book Six, 224b–d).

Whether or not an ironic reading is the best, Athenaeus provides striking evidence for the reading of Homer in later centuries. For the interest in Homer at mealtimes we might compare Plato's adaptation of Menelaus as the best man at the feast in the *Symposium*. Plato also hypothesizes a homosexual relationship between Patroclus and Achilles in the *Symposium*. Later interest in Homer includes the arrival of the entertainers known as Homeristae at the dinner of Trimalchio in Petronius; and the mosaic of Ulysses and the Sirens, illustrated on p. 248. Tracing Homer through these wide spaces of time and culture to the cultural synthesis offered by Athenaeus allows us to see how a text at the heart of the Greco-Roman cultural and educational system was used and reused to reflect contemporary concerns. This is discussed profitably in Davidson (1997).

The readings of Homer that the Deipnosophistae discuss among themselves are revealing. Some of them are precious or perverse readings. Some of them make claims that it is difficult to prove. Homer has a catch-all phrase of 'all kinds of good things' (*Odyssey* 4.55, 7.176) that are often served at mealtimes. Whether or not these included fish and fruit is quite unclear. But it is the case that Homer follows certain procedures. There is less discussion of eating than there is of the preparation of food, especially of meat, and than there is of drinking afterwards. Homer thus appears to set the tone that follows in much sympotic literature, that the occasion of the *deipnon*-symposium is often referred to, but that the sympotic part where there is poetry and singing is the part that is highlighted, at least as far as literature is concerned.

Galen himself, often an exception to this generalization, sometimes reflects the world view of the urban elite. He reflects in *On Uneven Bad Temperament*, for example, [43 Grant] that an idle style of life might lead to uneven bad temperament, adding, 'long ago, so it seems, no one suffered like this, because to live with such ease and abundance was unheard of . . .'. Galen has taken us into the model of development favoured by Hesiod, Cato and Juvenal, namely that powerful people in particular work less than they did in strict republican times. Wealth has brought *otium* or *schole*, a life of leisure, and with it increased bad health.

Greek and Roman Comedy and Tragedy

Another prominent genre can be found over several centuries on the comic stage, where food is celebrated in popular festive forms. This is true of comedy in the Greek city states (fifth to third centuries BC) and in its Roman version presented by Plautus and Terence (third to second centuries BC). One striking feature of the comic discussion is the invention of early paradises where there is no shortage of food and it is plentifully available in utopian form, begging that it be eaten (see p. 60). The fifth-century poet Pherecrates provides an example, from his *Miners* (fragment 113.3–9):

> Rivers full of porridge and black broth flowed babbling through the channels, spoons and all, and lumps of cheese-cakes too. Hence the morsel could slip easily and oilily of its own accord down the throats of the dead. Blood-puddings there were, and hot slices of sausage lay scattered by the river banks just like shells.

This is the literature of scarcity, to be contrasted with the literature of excess produced by the rich who looked in horror at the excesses of some, often allegedly the young, among their privileged peers (see Chapter 7, Davidson 1997, Wilkins 2000).

The comic versions of these utopias are particularly important, given their presentation to a wide public, which is not likely to have been the case for the texts of Plato or Thucydides, for example.

Comedy provides a valuable counter to the special, privileged world of the archaic symposium. There, in the poetry of Theognis, Pindar and others, ideals of aristocratic excellence were extolled, and exclusive gatherings of peers among the elites of city states promoted. This picture of the symposium has encouraged the idea that it remained an institution exclusively of the elite in the city states of the fifth and fourth centuries. To some extent this is true. The rich had more frequent and grander symposia. But they were not exclusive to the elite, as I argue in Chapter 6.

Comedy's value for this study lies in its civic forum. Its audience was enormous, in Athens and Syracuse some 15,000 citizens and others. There is much debate about the composition of the audience, but not about its size, or the stunning ability of comic verse to combine high literary expression with the colloquial language of the street. Like its sister form, tragedy, comedy was put on in civic festivals which expressed the mythologies, ideology and concerns of the whole community. This audience drawn from all classes is almost unique in ancient literary production. In addition to an unusually large and varied audience, the comic poets also wrote within striking literary and religious rules. Thus the tragic poets, with notable exceptions, removed many of the details of the table from their plays, and chose to represent them in a supplementary fourth play to round off the trilogy, that is, a burlesque or satyr play. The comic poets by contrast incorporated food and eating to an exaggerated degree. These estimates are made in comparison with, for example, Homeric epic, which does not strip out references to eating as does tragedy.

Where Homeric epic portrays the sacrificing of animals frequently in the *Iliad* and scenes of eating on many occasions in the *Odyssey*, tragedy plays down such occasions. Feasting tends to be mentioned as an activity that was once enjoyed (see Wilkins 2003) – but is no longer. Feasting within the tragedies often takes on disastrous significance, which is linked to the dislocation in the relations between gods and humans that is marked by corrupt sacrifice. These rituals do not go according to plan, and are frequently assimilated with murder. This feature is brought out powerfully in myths of cannibalism and of ritualistic murder which are regularly found in tragic myth. The first is illustrated by Aeschylus in his *Agamemnon*, in which the captured Trojan priestess Cassandra describes a dark vision in which she sees the murder of the children of Thyestes (1219–1222): 'children killed as if at the hands of their kinsmen. They clearly have their hands full of meat – their very own flesh – and their vital organs with their intestines – oh groan with pity – which their father had tasted.' In this vision, the children's flesh is divided into the three categories followed for the division of the animal in sacrifice, meat, vital organs and entrails (see Vernant 1989 and Chapter 1).

A more extensive connection between sacrifice and murder and the dismemberment of the human body by analogy with the sacrificial butchery of an animal is made in Euripides' version of *Electra*. This analogy has been explored by Durand (1989). Aegisthus, the wicked stepfather, is sacrificing a bull and invites passing strangers (who are in fact his estranged stepson Orestes and his friend Pylades) to join in a sacrificial feast to the nymphs. In an extended speech (774–858), the messenger shows Aegisthus cutting the throat of a heifer, which Orestes is invited to dismember. He reveals the white flesh, skins the animal, and opens up the area under the rib cage. The liver is found (in so many ways a significant vital organ) but it has no lobes, while the spleen also is physically unpropitious. Orestes proposes that they set about feasting on the organs that must be tasted in sacrifice, but while Aegisthus is bending forward to separate the parts of the liver, Orestes strikes him in the discs of the backbone and breaks his back. The whole body of Aegisthus collapses, and he spins round, breathing his last, 'dying badly in unnatural death'. Euripides runs sacrificial procedure and murder so closely together that while Aegisthus is engaged in the first he is struck down as if he were a bull to be stunned. There are many ambiguities in this speech, which uses the fusion of animal and human death to raise dark questions about the death of the tyrant and the role of the wronged Orestes. The passage is disturbing by design. The ritual, while alluding to the feast in which the participants were expected to take pleasure, constantly returns the audience to details that are not right. This includes the animal's body, the human plane, and by implication the divine order presiding over this religious occasion. Tasting the meat is twice referred to. The pleasure of eating is, as always, close to the sacrificial act. We should compare this passage with the two passages of Menander quoted in Chapter 3 on the balance between piety and pleasure at the sacrificial table.

That is not to say that tragedy excludes food altogether. Euripides describes a magnificent feast at Delphi in his *Ion*, in which the people of Delphi are invited to an al fresco meal in tents whose fabrics illustrate the stars in the heavens and miraculous beasts. They put on garlands and eat a delightful feast (which is not described in detail) to their heart's content and move on to the symposium. Gold cups and perfume are supplied and drinking begins – leading to the attempted poisoning of the young Athenian hero Ion. The poisoning of the drinking cup brings the scene close to the life at court of Alexander and the Hellenistic and other kings who lived in fear of poisons and other attacks on their lives.

If tragedy presents food as severely compromised through the disruption of the sacrificial order, comedy, for all its eager embrace of eating and the pleasures of the body, does not view food in a bland light. There is comic censure of gluttons, of powerful people who guzzle down more than their share; and there is concern over sacrifices that tend too much towards pleasure. But tragedy and comedy were put on at the same festivals of Dionysus in Athens. This fertility god was apparently honoured by different forms of hymns before drama was invented, and once drama took shape, different aspects of the god

FIGURE 9.2   The Exeter vase, a vessel for wine or water, which may have been designed for sympotic purposes, carries an image of Electra and Orestes at the tomb of Agamemnon. Agamemnon's name is inscribed on the tomb, and the characters are identified by name where necessary. If this is sympotic ware, then the drinkers had before their gaze a key scene from the *Electra* of Euripides, or of another poet. The drama had moved from the stage to the sympotic space. Courtesy of the Department of Classics and Ancient History, University of Exeter

were celebrated in the different genres. Tragedy portrayed a disturbing Dionysus who broke up the established order and introduced the natural world into human affairs: the most extreme version of this is to be found in the *Bacchae* of Euripides which shows the tyrant Pentheus helpless with his civic and military power beside the androgynous god who could not be confined to the normal categories of Greek or foreign, male or female, mad or sane, natural or cultured. Dionysiac myth does not appear explicitly in many plays, but the attack on order and fixed civic categories by psychologically fearsome forces is seen in nearly every play. There is little fearsome to be seen in comedy, which presents a disordered world put right by comic forces who temporarily subvert the power structure, reinforce the solidarity of the chorus and citizenry, and affirm the strong human desires for communality in feasting and sexual union. *Acharnians* is a comedy notable for its praise of Dionysus and enactment on stage of a number of his civic festivals. That is not to say that the play lacks disturbing elements, for the comic hero achieves a Dionysiac paradise at the end of the play in an apparently anti-communitarian spirit that refuses to share his special peace treaty with anyone.

Comedy is invaluable for this book because of its 'popular-festive' nature, which I discuss in Wilkins (2000). Two illustrations must suffice. In *Ecclesiazusae* (*The Assembly-Women*), which Aristophanes wrote in 392 BC, the women of Athens take over the city. This is an example of comic utopia, with the union of all citizens into one sexual unit, and the amalgamation of all property into one community. As with other comic utopias, there are disturbing suggestions that the communal sharing of wealth and sexuality will not work. Here are the proposals for dinners (675–97):

BLEPYRUS: And where are we going to have our dinner?

PRAXAGORA: I shall have all the lawcourts and stoas converted into dining rooms for men.

BL: And the speaker's platform. What use will you have for that?

PR: I'll stand the mixing bowls and water jugs there. And the little children can sing epic poetry about the men who fought bravely in war. And if someone has proved a coward, he'll be shamed into not dining.

BL: By Apollo, that's nice. To what use will you turn the machines for allocating lots?

PR: I'll put them in the agora. I'll stand near the statue of Harmodius and allocate everyone by lot. So on getting his lot everyone can go away in the knowledge of the letter against which he will dine. And there'll be an announcement for those in the beta category to follow in order to dine in the Royal Stoa. And the thetas to the next stoa, and the kappas to the barley-sellers' stoa.

BL: To bend over?

PR: No, to dine there.

BL: And the man whose letter is not drawn to allocate a dinner place – such people will be driven away?

PR: That won't happen among you. We will provide everything for all unstintingly. The result will be that everyone will come out drunk with his garland and carrying his torch and the women in the side streets will fall upon the men from the dinners saying, 'Come here to us. Here's a pretty young girl.'

The machinery of democracy is being put to sympotic use. Two points are worth noting. First, there was much dining and drinking for public officials in the democratic city, as well as provision for reviewing the food supply every month. So the comic proposal is an extension of what was built into the system, an extension into the comic paradise such that no one would go hungry. Second, the women wait for the men outside the dining halls. This proto-communist system does not go so far in sexual politics as to have men and women dining together.

The second comic passage is from the *Wealth* of Aristophanes. This mythical parable shows the blind god of wealth restored to sight, with astounding consequences. Once the god can see, mortals no longer have need of the gods because the good have wealth enough. Priests and gods thus face starvation, as they do in Aristophanes' earlier play of 414 BC, *Birds*. It is the cure for blindness, however, that I wish to concentrate upon. This takes the form of an incubation, and recalls religious practice already discussed in Chapters 3 and 8. The narrator is Carion the slave.

Wealth is bathed in the sea, and then settled down in the precinct. Cakes (*popana*) and incense are offered (661–2), and they lie down on rustic couches (*stibades*). Among the other patients is an old woman with a pot of *athare* (wheat porridge), on which the slave has designs. But his food-gathering plans are less advanced than those of the priest who snatches sacrificial cakes (*phthoes* and *popana*) and dried figs from the altar. The slave fears the god will come round the shrine garlanded and catch him stealing the porridge. The old woman too is suspicious. The slave hisses like a sacred snake to frighten her and grabs the porridge. The old woman farts with fear; the slave, full of porridge, farts also. The god's attendants hold their noses, but the god does not care, because he is an excrement eater. The god passes by the patients with a pestle and mortar and medicine chest. He treats a blind politician with garlic, fig juice, sea onion and vinegar, which causes great pain to this much-hated figure. Wealth, meanwhile, is cured by the sacred snakes. Once restored to the city, he ensures that the ordinary people do not go hungry (762–3), and brings a widespread sense of well-being to all good people.

This is a standard comic formula for the triumph of ordinary people over the powerful (gods as well as human beings), which I discussed in Wilkins (2000). What is unusual (and therefore very valuable: see Edelstein & Edelstein 1945) is the detailed account of incubation. The comedy 'explains' how offerings to gods are collected and perhaps consumed by priests: where else would they go? The god too is presented in material and very comic form. Because the testing of faeces and urine is standard medical practice for diagnosis, the god is impervious to farts that dismay his assistants. The cure is snake-based. The punishment 'cure' of vinegar etc. for the politician (even if it were not a punishment) does not seem to belong to divine incubation but to the alternative therapy of the doctor.

As I stressed in Wilkins (2000), comedy provides material detail for ancient eating that often far excels any other source.

Comedy's identity as a popular genre did not preclude its value for the elite. It could be incorporated into other literary productions of a later period. It attested to a pure form of Attic diction, and also to many aspects of Athenian culture in the 'classical' period. For these reasons, comedy appears in the works of Plutarch (who, however, dislikes its vulgarity), of Athenaeus (who likes the verbal dexterity and details of real meals), and of Galen. The last draws on comedy both for evidence about food terms and for stylistic reasons. He also wrote a number of books on the language of the poets of 'Old' Comedy, Eupolis, Cratinus and Aristophanes.

There is a discussion of comedy in Plutarch's *Table-Talk* (7.8 = 711B–713F). Old Comedy is too rough. It needs a grammarian to interpret it for each person, like a wine pourer behind each guest. Much better is song, which offers staple fare in the form of words, and has music as an *opson*. This is an interesting assimilation of cultural forms (comedy and songs) by metaphor into sympotic forms.

Comedy in the later Greek period in which Plutarch, Galen and Athenaeus were writing came to take on a function beyond that of playful or satirical comment that was so important at its original performance in theatres. It could be used at symposia and in learned discussion, as Plutarch shows. It can also be used, as we have seen, to attest the right terminology in Classical Greek. Comedy, like Homer, helps later authors to establish the classical terms of reference. This is one reason why Athenaeus draws on comedy so extensively. It offers myriad references to food, and also establishes the technical vocabulary. Use of comic verse thus adds scholarly depth as well as wit and a satirical tone that is particularly suitable at the symposium. Comic verse had a further function: it was clear and memorable. This point is made most clearly in a geographical text of the second century BC, the *Periodos Ges* (*Journey round the Earth*) of Pseudo-Scymnus. This curious work is in comic iambic verse, because, declares the author

(3–4), it expresses each point succinctly and clearly and (33–44) comic verse is memorable and its concise nature provides precision and persuasiveness, along with a certain charm. This scholarly use of comic verse is seen also in the work of Apollodorus of Athens, who is frequently cited in Athenaeus. It is seen too in verse prescriptions which Galen cites as examples of doctor's recipes, which are less likely to allow errors in transcription because of the safeguards provided by the rhythm of the verse.

Athenaeus' extensive use of comedy, therefore, has a playful, 'sympotic', explanation; it has a content-driven explanation because food and feasting were intrinsic to comedy; and it has a scholarly rationale also.

Roman Satire

The satires of Horace, Juvenal, Petronius and others are rich in allusions to food, as Gowers (1993) and others have shown. The term satire itself may derive from the image of a laden plate or table. I have noted above themes of nostalgia and rural purity which are strong in satire. Also strong are gluttony, hierarchical patterns of dining (Juvenal *Satire* 5, quoted on p. 57) and a sense of the rich pickings on offer for the Roman elite. In *Satires* 2.4 and 2.8, Horace presents first Catius, who has been listening to the wrong kind of philosophy. He has been advised to go to excessive length (in the poem's terms at least) to find the finest ingredients. Many choice ingredients attached to particular places are recommended, in a form similar to Archestratus' *The Life of Luxury*. In 2.8, the host, Nasidienus, abuses the tolerance of his guests with his obnoxious wealth.

Petronius' Trimalchio is the *pièce de résistance*, for, while echoing Plato's *Symposium* (Dupont 1977), his meal includes rich and poor guests, a profusion of food, consideration of entertainments and food shortages in the wider community, and all kinds of small touches which it is difficult for a modern reader to judge precisely. Is Petronius the 'arbiter of elegance' described by Tacitus at the court of Nero? Is Trimalchio a parody of Nero? Trimalchio takes a large interest in his bowel movements. Is this vulgarity because of the subject matter, or because he discusses the matter to excess? We have seen in Chapter 6 that themes of death and the symposium are often to be found together. Is Trimalchio morbid, or just a little more interested in his death than average? Or is it just the size of his tomb that is a problem? Trimalchio has many meat courses, predominately pork. And he serves little fish. Does this indicate his servile origins? Or is this good Roman fare?

In another nice touch, discussed by Conte (1996: 172), Trimalchio follows the principles of self-sufficiency and buys food only from his own estates. In moralizing texts it is laudable to avoid the temptations of the market. But it turns out that Trimalchio's estates extend over most of southern Italy, and into Africa. And he is able to grow Indian mushrooms and citrons. Thus he avoids the market but has access to all the riches of Empire.

Trimalchio is a gross figure, but many dishes and activities at his meal are exaggerated forms of aspects of meals and symposia which we have seen elsewhere in this book. The moralizing role of the satirist seems to be clear. But the historian of food is left with many more puzzles and ambiguities.

Satire reflects great riches, on the tables of the rich; in its range of foods, and in its vocabulary and ironic tone. I have shown in Wilkins (2004) that while some satirical rhetoric is absurd and overblown, other examples are reflected in much more sober authors such as Galen. Pliny, also, in his encyclopaedic format, echoes some of the abuses at table against which the satirists fulminate. We saw on p. 199 Pliny's views on contemporary misuse of wild boars at table. Juvenal reflects similarly in his first Satire: 'what a grossly ravening maw that man must have who dines off whole roast boar – a beast ordained for convivial feasting!'

The Revealing Anecdote

Athenaeus is one of many authors who have endless stories to tell of a man who . . . , a woman who . . . These anecdotes usually reveal a particular character trait, often gluttony or a related failing. Eating and social engagements provide fertile ground for such revelations. Athenaeus quotes the Stoic philosopher Chrysippus, for example, on the gourmand (*opsophagos*) Philoxenus (1.5d–e):

> I remember a certain gourmand, who was so far lost to all feelings of shame before his companions, no matter what happened, that in the public baths he accustomed his hand to heat by plunging it into hot

water, and gargled his throat with hot water that he might not shrink from hot food. For they used to say that he had actually won the cooks over to serving the dishes very hot, his object being to eat up everything alone, since nobody else was able to follow his example.

This is the exemplary anecdote, used by the philosopher or ethical teacher to illustrate the dangers of excess or socially deviant conduct. The man who takes too much pleasure in his food is in danger of committing the ultimate social crime, eating alone.

This example belongs to the pattern of thought explored in Chapter 7. Many genres of literature used such anecdotes. Authors who assemble and quote bodies of varied material, such as Athenaeus, Aulus Gellius and Aelian, are a particularly striking case. It is to such authors that we owe our knowledge of authors such as Machon, whose *Chreiae* is a series of anecdotes about gluttons and courtesans. Machon was also a writer of comedies, a genre which shared an interest in such subject matter. The most pertinent series of anecdotes concern a harp player called Stratonicus (*Deipnosophistae* 8.348e–349f: see Gilula 2000). His profession brought him to a number of symposia; his witty remarks made him worth remembering; and his professional travels round the Mediterranean brought variety to the anecdotes. In Pella (Macedonia) he insulted a rival musician and got drunk; in Abdera he made jokes about shellfish; in Pontus he went to the royal court; in Corinth a woman farted at a drinking session. In addition to their ethical and entertainment value, these anecdotes provide social vignettes that may have value as evidence and also demonstrate, like the poem of Archestratus, an interest in place. In this case variation in place brings out regional features, some of them well known (the prostitutes of Corinth, for example), others less conventional (Pella brings out conditions of the spleen). While Machon's anecdotes of Stratonicus give a topographical slant to clever remarks, his salacious anecdotes about courtesans are mainly based in Athens but give rein to female wit at the *deipnon* and symposium (*Deipnosophistae* 13.578b–583d).

Anecdotes of eating and drinking are frequently included by the ancient biographers in order to bring out features of the character of their subject. Two striking examples are provided by Suetonius, *Augustus* and Plutarch, *Cato the Elder*. Suetonius makes striking comments about the emperor in a summary of dining habits at the end of *Augustus*. Augustus had less pretentious dining furniture than many a private individual. He gave very formal dinners, with strict regard to hierarchy. He was often not present for the beginnings or ends of such occasions. He had between three and six courses; he was a good host in leading guests to relax. Though formal, these meals included entertainment by musicians, actors and circus entertainers. He played jokes on people at meals on festive occasions, including the Saturnalia. In private, he ate frugally, preferring, 'the food of the common people, especially the coarser sort of bread, small fishes, fresh hand-pressed cheese, and green figs of the second crop' (trans. Graves). In private, he ate informally, a few grapes with bread in his litter; or a few mouthfuls of bread at the baths after a day eating nothing.

The character sketch is graphic: this is very successful biographical writing. The evidence is gleaned from memoirs and the letters of Augustus, which may lend veracity to the account. But the principal interest for the present study lies in the implied assumptions of the author. Thus, the emperor is expected to have lavish furniture, like other monarchs. Regard to hierarchy fits other evidence for Roman meals and is expected. As regards the host's absence for part of the meal – does that indicate a bad host, to contrast with his putting guests at ease with a good social manner? Is it normal procedure? Trimalchio certainly absents himself from his guests. Is a head of state expected to have too little time to spare for long formal meals day after day? So is there thus a blend of great formality – on the level of social hierarchy – and of an element of informality – the meal did not revolve continually around the emperor? A Roman reader in the first century AD was clearly better placed to answer such questions than we are. Finally, Augustus the frugal eater. Suetonius gives us a helpful comment on the diet of the common people (compare Chapters 2, 4 and 5). He also implies that Augustus felt at home with such a diet, which contrasted with the formal meals of up to six courses, and kept him in contact with the ideology of Republican simplicity, which he sought to promote in much propaganda and legislation. The revelation of the private and informal eating of the ruler is a strength in the biographer's painting of the true nature of his subject. It is also a recurrent feature in biographical writing to show the ruler's interest in activities linked with the common people, simply because of the vast gulf between the ordinary person and the court. Thus Nero was not the only emperor who liked to go out disguised at night and spend time in bars – before moving on to stabbings and robbery (Suetonius *Nero* 26).

Plutarch uses comment on the organization of food in a more integral fashion in his *Cato the Elder*. Cato is the great icon of the Republic in his own and later ages, as we saw on pp. 199–203. Plutarch tells us

(4) 'his powers of expression merely set a standard for young men, which many of them were already striving their utmost to attain. But a man who observed the ancestral custom of working his own land, who was content with a cold breakfast, a frugal dinner, the simplest clothing, and a humble cottage to live in, and who actually thought it more admirable to renounce luxuries than to acquire them – such a person was conspicuous by his rarity.' For Plutarch details of daily life in this biography are as important as the great speeches of Cato in giving a likeness of the man. Cato has unusual habits, drinking only water and not complaining about food cooked by his batman while on campaign (1), working and eating with his slaves (3), drinking the same quality wine, as a praetor and consul, as his slaves (4). His wife is unusual too: she sometimes breastfeeds the slave children to seal their commitment to the family unit (20). Even for Plutarch, who admires the stand against luxury, Cato is a fearsome figure. He sold old slaves, like worn-out beasts of burden, in a spirit that betrayed not only meanness (*mikrologia*) but also harshness and a failure to recognize the bond between man and man (5). Plutarch, negotiating between the second century BC, his own period (the second century AD) and his philosophical beliefs, creates an impressive account: in a sense the reader is as surprised as Valerius Flaccus, a wealthy neighbour of Cato, to discover that when invited to dinner, Cato proved a gentle and charming guest, in need only of a little support and nourishment in civilized values (3). (On Plutarch's use of anecdote in general, see Duff 1999.)

Much use of the anecdote draws on ethical norms, which the author assumes the reader might share. The reminder that gluttony is a bad thing is made vivid and colourful if a small incident or *bon mot* can be inserted. A different use of anecdote seems to characterize the work of Galen that we have used extensively in this book, *On the Powers of Foods*. Elsewhere Galen uses anecdotes to give case studies, rather as expanded versions of the cases in the Hippocratic *Epidemics*. In his polemical works also, he uses anecdotes to reveal his excellence in diagnosis and treatment in comparison with his rivals (*On Prognosis*). But we have encountered many examples of encounters with peasants or reports that they had to eat their pigs and then the acorns reserved for pig food. These anecdotes extend his range and give him a strong claim to authority. He has been to Alexandria and Rome, and gives examples from these big centres. He has tested out a very wide geographical range. And added to this a wide social range, with the evidence for general principles proved from cases in his own home province of Mysia. The cases help to show the importance of preparation (is this wheat bread or boiled wheat flour?), and the importance of the characteristics of the individual patient.

Athenaeus *The Deipnosophistae*

This book concludes with a work that scarcely belongs to a genre, Athenaeus' *Deipnosophistae*. It is a curious work that is difficult to approach, and yet is widely quoted in all books on ancient food. A brief account is needed of its purpose and strengths.

The material is organized to follow the order of the meal. The overall structure is a *Symposium*, in the Platonic tradition, but the structure sometimes seems quite chaotic, now a chat over dinner, now a list of items (sometimes in alphabetical order, sometimes not). Many readers have found it very difficult to follow, not least because there is extended quotation from texts, which are not fully integrated into the conversation. Thus for many, Athenaeus is a repository of quotations, a large number of which have been lifted out and used in this book.

First we should establish that Athenaeus and his fellow Deipnosophistae are bringing Greek culture to Rome (see the epigraph at the head of this chapter). In return for a series of meals from the host, Larensis, the diners, some of whom are Roman, some Greek, quote relevant literary and technical works relevant to that stage in the meal. In this sense Athenaeus is a typical Greek author of his age.

He is also an encyclopaedic author, like Pliny and in a sense Galen. His work is the closest to *Larousse gastronomique* or the *Oxford Companion to Food* that the ancient world produced. If he did not use alphabetization consistently, neither did Galen, for example, in his handbook on drugs, *On Simples*.

Athenaeus gives his speakers rhetorical characteristics. There are the hungry Cynic philosophers, and the pedantic Ulpian. The mass of material is leavened by witty exchanges, which derive from comedy and popular philosophical debate. The debates allow contrasting views to be offered. Thus it is important on the one hand that Athenaeus quote *The Life of Luxury* of Archestratus of Gela. This poem mentions many fish from many places (of central importance for Athenaeus' seventh book). The poem is also mentioned early in the *Deipnosophistae*. It in a sense is a seminal work for Athenaeus' project. But at the same time Archestratus recommends greed and luxury, which conflict with the professed moral code of Athenaeus and Larensis. Thus Archestratus is often introduced with sarcastic comment, linking him with the supposed hedonist Epicurus or contrasting him with the austere Hesiod, and even by quoting him through the hostile Stoic philosopher Chrysippus.

If Athenaeus is ambiguous about Archestratus, both promoting him and denigrating him, what is his relationship with the great patron who supplies all the meals, Larensis? The tables of Larensis are notable for their magnificence (6.224b). He seems to have achieved the success of the Hellenistic kings celebrated in book 5, of Caranus, Antiochus and the Ptolemies that we discussed in Chapter 2. But elsewhere in the work (especially in book 12), luxury and magnificence precede a fall. Athenaeus seems to share some of the ambiguities of Roman satire. Here is Rome, at the centre of a world empire, who can draw all things in to her markets and to her tables. Many citizens benefit. Aelius Aristeides praises the power of Rome (26.11–13), just as Hermippus the comic poet praised Athens at the time of Pericles.

Hermippus writes (fragment 63):

> Tell me now, ye Muses . . . all the blessings . . . which [Dionysus] hath brought hither to men in his black ship. From Cyrene silphium-stalks and ox hides, from the Hellespont mackerel and all kinds of salt-dried fish, from Thessaly, again, the pudding and ribs of beef . . . The Syracusans supply hogs and cheese . . . from Syria frankincense.'

Many more sympotic delights follow. (See Wilkins 2000.)

These are great blessings. But they are also a cause for concern, leading to wealth and rich meals for the few, and all too often for the ignoble few such as Trimalchio or Nasidienus. In Athenaeus, there is no overt criticism of the great host Larensis, but there is much ethical content, not least in the rich anecdotal material which safely satirizes absurd eaters from the distant past.

While there is this ethical strand in Athenaeus, there is also a strong desire to collect a wide range of relevant data on whatever might be at issue, the fig, for example, or the wine-flicking game of *cottabos*. Athenaeus and his fellows draw their literary material from a wide range of works, from literature (Homer or comedy, for example), from history, from technical authors – botanists, doctors – and from a wide range of special studies: detailed accounts of cities in Asia Minor, for example, surveys of cults, of fish, of garlands. The *Deipnosophistae* attests in a way only the *Oxford Classical Dictionary* or Pauly Wissowa (1894) can do the sheer richness and diversity of ancient literature and technical writing. All of this Athenaeus and his fellow diners bring to the dinner table. It is all material suitable for the symposium. Thus diners reflect on what they are doing, and partly because they are in Rome and not in Greece, there is a merger between the *deipnon* part of the meal and the symposium. Athenaeus has created an encyclopaedia for the table. Like all encyclopaedias it raises awkward questions about organizational principles and boundaries drawn between relevant and unwanted material. The editorial tone is light, in comparison with the satirists. So in place of Trimalchio we have a host who resembles a Hellenistic king. Romans can afford to do this, since they are at the centre of the known world, and, as Athenaeus says, draw all things to Rome. See pages 49–51 and 209: Rome is the new Egypt, the wealthiest place on earth. But the Romans still need to understand their Greco-Roman past. And they still need to know about the riches of the Greek East. They are thus offered an encyclopaedic review of the Mediterranean world. It is an encyclopaedia of food and drink, and it is written in 15 books or papyrus rolls, which can be brought out and recited by Athenaeus one by one as the meal proceeds. Athenaeus' friend Timocrates to whom the book is addressed can thus see the richness of Greek culinary and literary culture as offered by the Deipnosophistae, course by course. Athenaeus, Timocrates, Larensis and the others, together with us, the readers of the *Deipnosophistae*, can thus marvel at what Greece and Rome share. We can also reflect uneasily on the magnificent tables of Rome, which are so much at odds with the simple life that the Deipnosophistae appear to believe that Homer, apparently the 'model' for symposia, promoted in his epics (see especially p. 260 above).

It is often a relief to find so much reference to Homer in Athenaeus, since many of the authors quoted are not in the ancient canon, or even household names. Athenaeus sometimes seems to go out of his way to quote authors like Archestratus and Matro, rather than Aristophanes and Thucydides. It is important to recognize however, that Athenaeus takes the canon as read. His readers know their Herodotus and Polybius, their Sophocles and Plutarch. Athenaeus sees his task as drawing out every possible reference to food and drink in these canonical authors; to add all such references from authors lost in the recesses of libraries; and to give shape to all this material by setting Homer as the model for all that is positive, and Plato as the negative pole. A light comic tone is maintained in the dialogue between the Deipnosophistae, and at points key Roman values are stressed (tradition at the end of Book Six; marriage at the beginning of Book Thirteen). There is no real sense in the book that Larensis is seriously at risk from all his wealth and luxury. In the words of Guiseppe Zecchini, Athenaeus seems to think that Larensis is somehow inoculated against such dangers.

For any serious student of food in Greek and Roman cultures, no better compendia of evidence will be found than the works of Galen and Athenaeus. Likewise these two, together with Plutarch and Pliny, give an unrivalled overview of the defining features and overall synthesis of Greek and Roman practice at the table.

Recipes

The references to specific food dishes available to us are tantalizingly brief. Exceptions are either for big-time over-consumption by the rich and greedy or indications of what might be provided for agricultural workers in the pages of gastronomically uninspiring tomes like Cato's *de agricultura*. Pliny's description of the manufacture of the pastry, *tracta*, shows a result much the same as phyllo or strudel pastry and there are references to this being stirred into dishes as a thickening agent. Most reconstructions, however, call for imaginative guesswork to fill in the gaps.

Cookbooks as manuals are of course relatively recent. Cooks are unlikely to have been literate and the assumptions made would be that those cooking would be familiar with the ingredients, cooking times and even proportions to be used.

Breads and doughs are the easiest to reconstruct even from the vaguest references. These mixtures simply do not work if the ratios of liquid to flour aren't correct. The relative quantities of grain or pulse to liquid needed to set any polenta like porridge or milkcake will be the same now as then.

Kandaulos

The Lydian sauces kandaulos and karyke achieved great popularity and were quoted by several sources. Athenaeus gives some detail from a recipe by Hegesippos of Tarentum which has it as 'made of boiled meat, breadcrumbs, Phrygian cheese, anise and fatty broth'. Not too appetising so far then.

However, the amount of breadcrumb used and the size of the chunks of boiled meat will determine whether the dish is sauce, soup or stew but not the overall taste and style of the dish. The word for anise also covers dill, still in common use in the area, though anise itself is native to the western Anatolian region which actually includes Lydia. If dill seeds are used then a recognizable, interesting and tasty dish results. If anise is used then a stronger, less familiar, flavour similar to liquorice is produced. Phrygian cheese was made with mare's milk and may be a touch awkward to find, so feta substitutes.

1kg breast of lamb – boned and cubed
200gr feta cheese
100gr fresh breadcrumbs – ideally from flatbread
1 tablespoon dill seeds – crushed
1 tablespoon chopped dill
1 tablespoon chopped chives

Cover the lamb cubes and dill seed with water then bring to the boil.
Lower the heat and simmer until soft.
Cut the cheese into cubes and add to the stew.
Stir in the breadcrumbs. Let these thicken the broth, then add salt and chopped herbs.

Staititae

The combination of honey and sesame was a common one and recurs in many guises, sometimes rolled in sesame and sometimes in poppy seeds. This version derives from Athenaeus volume 6: 'the soft dough is poured upon a frying pan and on it are spread honey, sesame and cheese'. Fritters like these are still made. Arab cuisine has from medieval times included a dish called Ataifi, which has a texture more like a scotch pancake and is usually dipped in syrup or cinnamon after cooking. Yeast had been well known since early Egyptian times when it was used for brewing but doesn't seem to have been in widespread or general use for pastry or bread-making.

1 tablespoon honey
120gr plain flour
200ml water
pinch salt
oil for frying

Topping

cheese
honey
toasted sesame seeds

Mix the honey, water and flour into a dough.
Heat a pan then add a little oil. Add the dough a tablespoonful at a time and cook like a pancake on both sides.
Spread with warmed cheese and honey then dredge with toasted sesame seeds.

Olive spread

This recipe is recorded by Cato and uses all the main flavourings of the time. Still fine on a piece of warm flatbread with some hummous like chickpea dip.

100gr pitted green olives
100gr pitted black olives – don't buy ready-pitted black olives which are made by colouring green ones. Separate the stone from the flesh yourself.
50ml olive oil
1 tablespoon wine vinegar
1 teaspoon each – crushed cumin seed, coriander seed then
1 tablespoon chopped mint, rue and fennel leaves

Bibliography

Allbaugh L G 1953 *Crete: A Case Study of an Underdeveloped Area* (Princeton, NJ: Princeton University Press)

Arnott W G 1996 *Alexis: The Fragments* (Cambridge: Cambridge University Press)

Astin Alan E 1978 *Cato the Censor* (Oxford: Clarendon Press)

Bakhtin M 1968 *Rabelais and his World* (Cambridge, MA: MIT Press)

Barnish S J B 1987 'Pigs, plebeians and potentes: Rome's economic hinterland c.350–600 AD', *Papers of the British School at Rome* 55: 157–85

Babbitt F C 1972 *Plutarch's Moralia IV* (London: Harvard University Press)

Baudy G 1995 'Cereal diet and the origins of man: Myths of the Eleusinia in the context of ancient Mediterranean harvest festivals' in Wilkins, Harvey & Dobson: 177–205

Beard M, North J and Price S 1998 *Religions of Rome* (Cambridge: Cambridge University Press)

Bekker-Nielsen T 2005 (ed.) *Ancient Fishing and Fish Processing in the Black Sea Region* (Aarhus: Aarhus University Press)

Berthiaume G 1982 *Les rôles du mageiros* (Leiden: E J Brill)

Bottero J 2004 *The Oldest Cuisine in the World: Cooking in Mesopotamia* (Chicago: University of Chicago Press)

Bowie A 1993 *Aristophanes: Myth, Ritual, Comedy* (Cambridge: Cambridge University Press)

Bowie E L 1986 'Early Greek elegy, symposium and public festival', *Journal of Hellenic Studies* 106: 13–35

Braun T 1995 'Barley cakes and emmer bread' in Wilkins, Harvey & Dobson: 25–37

Braund D C 1995 'Fish from the Black Sea: Classical Byzantium and the Greekness of trade' in Wilkins, Harvey & Dobson: 162–71

Braund D C and Wilkins J 2000 *Athenaeus and his World* (Exeter: Exeter University Press)

Braund S M 1996 'The solitary feast: A contradiction in terms?', *Bulletin of the Institute of Classical Studies* 41: 37–52

Briant P 1996 *Histoire de L'Empire Perse* (Paris: Fayard)

Brock A J 1916 *Galen: On the Natural Faculties* (London: Harvard University Press)

Burkert W 1979 *Structure and History in Greek Mythology and History* (Berkeley, CA: University of California Press)

Burkert W 1985 *Greek Religion* (Oxford: Blackwell; German edition *Griechische Religion*, Stuttgart: Kohlhammer, 1977)

Buxton R G 1994 *Imaginary Greece: The Contexts of Mythology* (Cambridge: Cambridge University Press)

Camporesi P 1993 *The Magic Harvest: Food, Folklore and Society* (Oxford: Polity Press; trans. of *La terra e la luna*, Milan: Il Saggiatore 1989)

Cary E 1914–27 *Cassius Dio: Historia Romana* (London: Harvard University Press)

Cassin B, Labarrière J-L, and Romeyer Dherbey G 1997 *L'Animal dans l'Antiquité* (Paris: J Vrin)

Chang K C 1977 *Food in Chinese Culture* (New Haven, CT: Yale University Press)

Claridge A 1998 *Rome* (Oxford: Oxford University Press)

Clark G 1999 *On Abstinence from Killing Animals* (London: Duckworth)

Coe S and Coe M 1996 *The True History of Chocolate* (London: Thames and Hudson)

Conrad L I, Neve M, Nutton V, Porter R and Wear A 1995 *The Western Medical Tradition 800 BC to AD 1800* (Cambridge: Cambridge University Press)

Connors C 1998 *Petronius the Poet* (Cambridge: Cambridge University Press)

Conte G B 1996 *The Hidden Author* (Berkeley, CA: University of California Press)

Corbier M 1989 'The ambiguous status of meat in ancient Rome', *Food and Foodways* 3: 223–64

Couplin F 1998 *Guide nutritionnel des plantes* (Lausanne)

Csapo E and Slater W J 1994 *The Context of Ancient Drama* (Ann Arbor)

Curtis R I 1991 *Garum and Salsamenta* (Leiden: E J Brill)

Curtis R I 2001 *Ancient Food Technology* (Leiden: E J Brill)

Curtis R I 2005: 'Sources for production and trade of Greek and Roman processed fish' in Bekker-Nielsen 2005: 31–46

Dalby A 1987 'The banquet of Philoxenus', *Petits Propos Culinaires* 26: 28–36

Dalby A 1988 'Hippolochus, the wedding feast of Caranus the Macedonian', *Petits Propos Culinaires* 29: 37–45

Dalby A 1993 'Food and sexuality in Classical Greece' in Mars & Mars: 165–90

Dalby A 1996 *Siren Feasts* (London: Routledge)

Dalby A 1998 *Cato: On Farming* (Totnes: Prospect Books)

Dalby A 2000 *Empire of Pleasures* (London: Routledge)

Dalby A 2003 *Food in the Ancient World from A to Z* (London: Routledge)

Davidson A 1972 *Mediterranean Seafood* (Harmondsworth: Penguin)

Davidson A 1999 *The Oxford Companion to Food* (Oxford: Oxford University Press)

Davidson J 1995 'Opsophagia: Revolutionary eating at Athens' in Wilkins, Harvey & Dobson: 204–13

Davidson J 1997 *Courtesans and Fishcakes* (London: HarperCollins)

Davies R 1971 'The Roman Military Diet', *Britannia* 2: 122–42

Debru A 1997 *Galen on Pharmacology* (Leiden: E J Brill)

de Lacy P 1978–84 *Galen: On the Doctrines of Hippocrates and Plato* (Berlin: Akademie)

De Selincourt A 1954 *Herodotus: The Histories* (Harmondsworth: Penguin)

Detienne M 1994 *The Gardens of Adonis* (Princeton: Princeton University Press, 1977 Hassocks; French edition Les jardins d'Adonis Paris: Gallimard 1972)

Detienne M and Vernant J-P 1989 *The Cuisine of Sacrifice Among the Greeks* (Chicago: University of Chicago Press; trans. of *La cuisine du sacrifice*, Paris: Gallimard 1979)

Deubner L 1932 *Attische Feste* (Berlin: H Keller)

Dittenberger W 1898–1901 *Sylloge Inscriptionum Graecarum* (Leipzig: Hirzelius)

Donahue J F 2005 forthcoming *The Roman Community at Table during the Principate* (Ann Arbor, MI: University of Michigan)

Douglas M 1966 *Purity and Danger* (London: Routledge and Kegan Paul)

Douglas M 1984 (ed.) *Food in the Social Order: Studies of Food and Festivities in Three American Communities* (New York: Russell Sage Foundation)

Douglas M and Nicod M 1974 'Taking the biscuit: the structure of British meals', *New Society* 30: 744–7

Duff T E 1999 *Plutarch's Lives: Exploring Virtue and Vice* (Oxford: Clarendon Press)

Dunbabin K M 1999 *Mosaics of the Greek and Roman World* (Cambridge: Cambridge University Press)

Dunbabin K M 2003 *The Roman Banquet: Images of Conviviality* (Cambridge: Cambridge University Press)

Dupont F 1977 *Le Plaisir et la Loi* (Paris: Maspero)

Durand J-L 1989 'Greek animals: Toward a topology of edible bodies' in Detienne and Vernant 1989: 87–118

Edelstein L 1967 *Ancient Medicine* (Baltimore, MD: Johns Hopkins University Press)

Edelstein E J and Edelstein L 1945 *Asclepius: Collection and Interpretation of the Testimonies* (Baltimore)

van der Eijk P 1997 'Galen's use of the concept of "qualified experience" in his dietetic and pharmacological works' in Debru: 35–57 van der Eijk P 2000 *Diocles of Carystus* (Leiden: E J Brill)

Ellis S 2000 *Roman Housing* (London: Duckworth)

Ferguson W S 1944 'The Attic Orgeones', *Harvard Theological Review* 37: 73–140

Fiddes N 1991 *Meat: A Natural Symbol* (London: Routledge)

Fisher N 1993 'Multiple personalities and Dionysiac festivals: Dicaeopolis in Aristophanes' *Acharnians*', *Greece and Rome* 40: 31–47

Fisher N 2000 'Symposiasts, fish-eaters and flatterers: Social mobility and moral concerns' in Harvey & Wilkins: 355–96

Flower B and Rosenbaum E 1958 Apicius: de re coquinaria. The Roman Cookery Book (London: George G Harrap & Co. Ltd)

Foley H 1993 *The Homeric Hymn to Demeter* (Princeton: Princeton University Press)

Forbes H and Foxhall L 1995 'Ethnoarchaeology and storage in the ancient Mediterranean: Beyond risk and survival' in Wilkins, Harvey & Dobson: 69–86

Foxhall L and Forbes H 1982 'Sitometreia', *Chiron* 12: 41–90

Fraenkel E 1960 *Elementi plautini in Plauto* (Florence: La Nuova Italia)

Frazer J G 1951 *Ovid: Fasti* (London: Harvard University Press)

Frayn J 1993 *Markets and Fairs in Roman Italy* (Oxford: Clarendon Press)

Frayn J 1995 'The Roman meat trade' in Wilkins, Harvey & Dobson: 107–14

Frost F 1999 'Sausage and meat preservation in antiquity', *Greek, Roman and Byzantine Studies* 40: 241–52

Gallant T 1984 *A Fisherman's Tale* (Ghent)

Gallant T 1991 *Risk and Survival in Ancient Greece: Reconstructing the Rural Domestic Economy* (Stanford, CA: Stanford University Press)

Garnsey P D A 1988 *Famine and Food Supply in the Graeco-Roman World* (Cambridge: Cambridge University Press)

Garnsey P 1998 *Cities, Peasants and Food in Classical Antiquity* (Cambridge: Cambridge University Press)

Garnsey P 1999 *Food and Society in Classical Antiquity* (Cambridge: Cambridge University Press)

Gaskin J 1995 *The Epicurean Philosophers* (London: Everyman, J M Dent)

Gentili B 1988 *Poetry and its Public in Ancient Greece: From Homer to the Fifth Century* (Baltimore, MD: Johns Hopkins University Press; trans. from Italian)

Gilula D 2000 'Stratonicus the witty harpist' in Braund & Wilkins 2000: 423–33

Goody J 1982 *Cooking, Cuisine and Class* (Cambridge: Cambridge University Press)

Gowers E 1993 *The Loaded Table* (Oxford: Clarendon Press)

Grant M 2000 *Galen on Food and Diet* (New York: Routledge)

Graves R 1957 *Suetonius: The Twelve Caesars* (Harmondsworth: Penguin)

Gray P 1986 *Honey from a Weed* (New York: Harper & Row)

Green P 1967 *Juvenal: The Sixteen Satires* (Harmondsworth: Penguin)

Grimm V 1996 *From Feasting to Fasting: The Evolution of a Sin. Attitudes to Food in Late Antiquity* (London: Routledge)

Gruen Erich S 1984 *The Hellenistic World and the Coming of Rome* (Berkeley, CA: University of California Press)

Gulick C B 1927–50 *Athenaeus: The Deipnosophistae* (London: Harvard University Press)

Harvey D and Wilkins J 2000 *The Rivals of Aristophanes* (London: Duckworth)

Henrichs A 1990 'Between country and city: Cultic dimensions of Dionysus in Athens and Attica' in Griffith M and Mastronarde D J (eds) *Cabinet of the Muses* (Chicago: University of Chicago Press)

Hicks R D 1925 *Diogenes Laertius: Lives of Eminent Philosophers* (London & Cambridge Mass.)

Hill S and Wilkins J 1996 'Mithaikos and other Greek cooks' in Walker H (ed.), *Cooks and Other People: Proceedings of the Oxford Symposium on Food and Cookery* 1995 (Totnes: Prospect Books) 144–48

Heltosky C 2004 *Garlic and Oil: Food and Politics in Italy* (Berg: Oxford and New York)

Hordern P and Purcell N 2000 *The Corrupting Sea* (Oxford: Blackwell)

Innes M M 1955 *Ovid: Metamorphoses* (Harmondsworth: Penguin)

Jameson M H 1988 'Sacrifice and animal husbandry in Classical Greece' in Whittaker C R (ed.) *Pastoral Economies in Classical Antiquity* (Cambridge: The Cambridge Philological Society): 87–119

Jones C 2002 *The Great Nation: France from Louis XV to Napoleon* (London: Penguin/Allen Lane)

Larousse gastronomique (2001) (New York: Clarkson Potter)

Jouanna J 1992 *Hippocrate* (Paris: Fayard; English trans. 1999, Baltimore, MD: Johns Hopkins University Press)

Jouanna J 1996 'Le vin et la médecine dans la Grèce ancienne', *Revue des Etudes Grecques* 109: 410–34

Jouanna J and Villard L 2002 *Vin et santé en Grèce ancienne (Bulletin de Correspondance hellénique Suppl. 40)* Paris

Kadletz E 1988 *Animal Sacrifice in Greek and Roman Religion* (Ann Arbor, MI: University of Michigan Press)

Karali L 2000 'La malakofaune à l'âge du Bronze et à la période géometrique' in Luce: 115–32

Kenney E J 1984 *Moretum. The ploughman's lunch, a poem ascribed to Virgil* (Bristol: Bristol Classical Press)

Keyser 1997 'Science and magic in Galen's recipes' in Debru: 175–98

Kleberg T 1957 *Hotels, Restaurants et Cabarets dans l'Antiquité romaine* (Uppsala: Almquist & Wiksell)

Lambert Gocs M 1990 *The Wines of Greece* (London: Faber & Faber)

Laurence R 1994 *Roman Pompeii: Space and Society* (London: Routledge)

Lee H D P 1971 *Plato: Timaeus and Critias* (Harmondsworth: Penguin)

Leigh M L 2004 *Comedy and the Rise of Rome* (Oxford: Oxford University Press)

Lévi-Strauss 1970 *The Raw and the Cooked: Introduction to a Science of Mythology* (London: Jonathan Cape; trans. of *Le cru et le cuit: Mythologies I* Paris: Plon 1964)

Lévi-Strauss C 1978 *The Origin of Table Manners* (London: Harper; trans of *L'Origine des Manières de Table* Paris: Librairie Plon 1968)

Lissarrague F 1990 *The Aesthetics of the Greek Banquet* (Princeton: Princeton University Press; trans of *Un flot d'images* Paris: Biro 1987)

Liversedge J 1958 'Roman kitchens and cooking utensils' in Flower & Rosenbaum: 29–37

Longo O and Scarpi P 1989 *Homo Edens* (Verona: Diapress)

Luce J-M 2000 (ed.) *Paysage et alimentation dans le monde grec* (Toulouse: Presses Universitaires du Mirail)

Lutz C E 1947 'Musonius Rufus, the Roman Socrates' *Yale Classical Studies* 10: 3–147

McGee H 2004 *Food and Cooking: An Encyclopaedia of Kitchen Science, History and Culture* (London: Hodder)

MacMullen R 1981 *Paganism in the Roman Empire* (New Haven, CT: Yale University Press)

Mair A W 1928 *Oppian, Colluthus, Tryphiodorus* (London: Harvard University Press)

Mars G and Mars V 1993 *Food, Culture and History* (London: London Food Seminar)

Mason S 1995 'Acornutopia? Determining the role of acorns in past human subsistence' in Wilkins, Harvey & Dobson: 12–24

Maybe R 1972 *Food for Free* (London: Collins)

McGovern P E 2003 *Ancient Wine: The Search for the Origins of Viniculture* (Princeton, NJ: Princeton University Press)

McKeown J 1987 *Ovid: Amores* (Liverpool: Francis Cairns)

Mikalson J D 1975 *The Sacred and Civil Calendar of the Athenian Year* (Princeton, NJ: Princeton University Press)

Miller J I 1969 *The Spice Trade of the Roman Empire* (Oxford: Oxford University Press)

Miller S 1978 *The Prytaneion: its Form and Architecture* (Berkeley, CA: University of California Press)

Minar E L, Sandbach F H, Helmbold W C 1936–86 *Plutarch: Moralia* vol 8 (London: Harvard University Press)

Mitchell S 1993 *Anatolia I* (Oxford: Oxford University Press)

Murray O 1990 (ed.) *Sympotica* (Oxford: Clarendon Press)

Nutton V 2004 *Ancient Medicine* (London: Routledge)

Olson S D and Sens A 1999 *Matro of Pitane and the Tradition of Epic Parody in the Fourth Century* BC (Atlanta, GA: Scholar's Press)

Olson S D and Sens A 2000 *Archestratos of Gela* (Oxford: Oxford University Press)

Panayotakis C 1995 *Theatrum Arbitri: Theatrical Elements in the Satyrica of Petronius* (Leiden: E J Brill)

Parke H W 1977 *The Festivals of the Athenians* (London: Thames & Hudson)

Parker R 1983 *Miasma* (Oxford: Clarendon Press)

Parker R 1987 'Festivals of the Attic Demes', Acta Universitatis Upsaliensis, *Boreas* 15: 137–47

Parker R 1996 *Athenian Religion: A History* (Oxford: Oxford University Press)

Paton W R 1922–7 *Polybius: The Histories* (London: Harvard University Press)

Pitman V 1998 *An Investigation into the Sources of Holistic Medicine in the Hippocratic Corpus: a Comparative Approach Using the Caraka Samhita of Ayurveda* (unpublished MPhil thesis, Exeter)

Pocock G and Richards C D 1999 *Human Physiology: The Basis of Medicine* (Oxford: Oxford University Press)

Porter R 2002 *Blood and Guts: A Short History of Medicine* (London: Penguin)

Powell O 2003 *Galen: On the Properties of Foodstuffs* (Cambridge: Cambridge University Press)

Purcell N 1985 'Wine and wealth in ancient Italy' *Journal of Roman Studies* 75: 1–19

Purcell N 1995 'Eating fish: The paradoxes of seafood' in Wilkins, Harvey & Dobson: 132–49

Rackham H 1935 *Pliny: Natural History* (London: Harvard University Press)

Radice B 1963 *The Letters of the Younger Pliny* (Harmondsworth: Penguin)

Rathje A 1990 'The adoption of the Homeric banquet in central Italy in the orientalizing period' in Murray: 279–88

Relihan J C 1993 *Ancient Menippean Satire* (Baltimore, MD: Johns Hopkins University press)

Renfrew J 1973 *Palaeoethnobotany* (New York: Columbia University Press)

Rice D G and Stambaugh J E 1979 *Sources for the Study of Greek Religion* (Atlanta, GA: Scholar's Press)

Rickman G 1971 *Roman Granaries and Store Buildings* (Cambridge: Cambridge University Press)

Robertson N 1993 *Legends and Festivals: the Formation of Greek Cities in the Light of Public Ritual* (Toronto: University of Toronto Press)

Robinson J 1994 (ed.) *The Oxford Companion to Wine* (Oxford: Oxford University Press)

Romeri L 2002 *Philosophes entre mots et mets* (Grenoble: Millon)

Rosivach V J 1994 *The System of Public Sacrifice in Fourth Century Athens* (Atlanta, GA: Scholar's Press)

Sallares R 1991 *The Ecology of the Ancient Greek World* (London: Duckworth)

Sancisi-Weerdenburg H 1995 'Persian food: Stereotypes and political identity' in Wilkins, Harvey & Dobson: 286–302

Scheid J 1998 *La religion des Romains* (Paris: Armand Colin/Masson)

Scheid J 2001 *Religion et piété à Rome* (Paris: La Decouverte)

Schmitt-Pantel P 1992 *La Cité au Banquet* (Paris: Armand Colin Cursus)

Seaford R 1994 *Reciprocity and Ritual* (Oxford: Clarendon Press)

Shaw B 1982/3 'Eaters of flesh, drinkers of milk: The ancient Mediterranean ideology of the pastoral nomad', *Ancient Society* XIII–XIV: 5–31

Shewring W 1980 *Homer: The Odyssey* (Oxford: Oxford University Press)

Singer P N 1997 *Galen: Selected Works* (Oxford: Oxford University Press)

Slater W J 1976 'Symposium at sea', *Harvard Studies in Classical Philology* 80: 161–70

Slater W J 1991 *Dining in a Classical Context* (Ann Arbor, MI: University of Michigan Press)

Sorabji R 1993 *Animal Minds and Human Morals: The Origins of the Western Debate* (London: Duckworth)

Spang R 2000 *The Invention of the Restaurant* (Cambridge, MA: Harvard University Press)

Sparkes B 1962 'The Greek kitchen', *Journal of Hellenic Studies* 82: 121–37

Strong R 2003 *Feast: A History of Grand Eating* (London: Pimlico)

Svoboda R 1992 *Ayurveda: Life, Health and Longevity* (London: Penguin)

Tchernia A 1986 *Le Vin de l' Italie Romaine: Essai d' Histoire Economique d'après les Amphores* (Rome: Collection de l'école Française de Rome)

Thompson D A W 1947 *A Glossary of Greek Fishes* (London: Oxford University Press)

Thompson H A and Wycherley R E 1972 *The Agora of Athens (The Athenian Agora* XIV) (Princeton, NJ: Princeton University Press)

Tieleman T 2003 *Chrysippus' On Affections* (Leiden: E J Brill)

Tzedakis Y and Martlew H (eds) 2002 *Minoans and Mycenaeans: Flavours of their Time* (Athens: Hellenic Minsitry of Culture)

Vellacott P 1967 *Theophrastus: The Characters Menander: Plays and Fragments* (Penguin: Harmondsworth)

Vernant J-P 1989 'At man's table: Hesiod's foundation myth of sacrifice' in Detienne & Vernant: 21–86

Veyne P 1990 *Bread and Circuses: Historical Sociology and Political Pluralism* (Harmondsworth: Penguin; trans. of *Le pain et le cirque: sociologie historique d'un pluralisme politique* Paris: Editions du Soleil 1976)

Vickers M and Gill D 1994 *Artful Crafts: Ancient Greek Silverware and Pottery* (Oxford: Clarendon Press)

Vickers M Impey O and Allen J 1987 *From Silver to Ceramic: The Potter's Debt to Metalwork in the Greco-Roman, Chinese and Islamic Worlds* (Oxford: Ashmolean Museum Publications)

Vidal-Naquet P 1981 'Land and sacrifice in the *Odyssey*: A study of religious and mythical meaning' in Gordon R *Myth, Religion and Society* (Cambridge: Cambridge University Press)

Visser M 1986 *Much Depends on Dinner* (Toronto: McClelland & Stewart)

Visser M 1992 *The Rituals of Dinner* (London: Penguin)

West M L 1974 *Studies in Greek Elegy and Iambus* (Berlin/New York: De Gruyter)

Wilkins J 1993 'Social status and fish in Greece and Rome' in Mars G and Mars V (eds), *Food, Culture and History* (London): 191–203

Wilkins J 2000 *The Boastful Chef: The Discourse of Food in Ancient Greek Comedy* (Oxford: Oxford University Press)

Wilkins J 2000a 'Food preparation in ancient Greece: The literary evidence' in Hurcombe L and Donald M (eds) *Gender and Material Culture* (London: Macmillan)

Wilkins J 2000b 'Edible choruses' in Harvey and Wilkins: 341–54

Wilkins J 2001 'Manger, chercher, se promener à la campagne: Les méthodes de recherche d'Athénée et de Galien au IIème siècle de notre ère', *Cahiers Glotz* XII: 213–28

Wilkins J 2003 'Banquets sur la scène comique et tragique' in C Orphanos and J-C Carrière (eds) *Symposium: Banquet et Représentations en Grèce et à Rome* Pallas 61: 167–74

Wilkins J 2004 'Land and sea: Italy and the Mediterranean in the Roman discourse of dining', *American Journal of Philology* 124: 359–75

Wilkins J 2005 'Fish as a source of food in antiquity' in Bekker-Nielsen: 21–30

Wilkins J 2005a 'Hygieia at dinner and at the symposium' in King H (ed) *Health in Antiquity* (London: Routledge)

Wilkins J Harvey D and Dobson M 1995 *Food in Antiquity* (Exeter: Exeter University Press)

Wilkins J and Hill S 'The flavours of ancient Greece' in *Spicing Up The Palate, Studies of Flavourings Ancient and Modern*, Proceedings of the Oxford Symposium on Food and Cookery 1992, (ed.) H Walker (London: Prospect Books, 1993) 275–9

Wilkins J and Hill S 1994 *Archestratus: The Life of Luxury* (Totnes: Prospect)

Wills J 1998 *The Food Bible* (London: Quadrille)

Wills W L 1985 *Idol Meat in Corinth* (Chico, CA: Scholar's Press)

Wissowa G 1894 *Paulys Real Encyclopädie der classischen Altertumswissenschaft* (Stuttgart)

Zecchini G 1989 *La cultura Storica di Ateneo* (Milan)

Zubaida S and Tapper R (eds) 1994 *A Taste of Thyme: Culinary Cultures of the Middle East* (London: I B Tauris)

Index